UNDERSTANDING MATHEMATICS
IN THE LOWER PRIMARY YEARS

UNDERSTANDING MATHEMATICS IN THE LOWER PRIMARY YEARS

revised and expanded edition

Derek Haylock and Anne Cockburn

P·C·P

Paul Chapman
Publishing Ltd

Paul Chapman Publishing Ltd
A SAGE Publications Company
6 Bonhill Street
London EC2A 4PU

British Library Cataloguing in Publication Data

Haylock, Derek W.
Understanding mathematics in the lower primary years. –
Rev. ed.
1. Mathematics – Study and teaching (Elementary)
I. Title II. Cockburn, Anne III. Understanding early years
mathematics
372. 7'044

ISBN 1 85396 352 6

Typeset by Dorwyn Ltd, Rowlands Castle, Hants
Printed and bound in Great Britain by Athenæum Press Ltd,
Gateshead, Tyne & Wear

C D E F G H 9 8

Contents

Acknowledgements

Many people helped to create this book. In particular we would like to express our appreciation to those teachers who attended our in-service course at the University of East Anglia prior to the writing of the first version of the book. We are particularly grateful for their willingness to discuss openly their own queries and confusions about the mathematics they have to teach in their classrooms. So, to the two Marys, Enid, Averil, Diana, Cathy, Laura, Lesley, June, Maxine, Suzanne and Amanda: thank you. Our acknowledgements also go to the many teachers, pupils, colleagues and students who over the years have helped us to formulate our ideas and those who have shared their ideas and comments as we have worked on this new version. Special thanks also go to Derek Haylock's daughter, Catherine Bates, a local first-school teacher, for allowing him access to her class. Finally, we express our appreciation to the University of East Anglia who provided the study leave for Derek that made possible the completion of *Understanding Mathematics in the Lower Primary Years*.

Introduction

Understanding Mathematics in the Lower Primary Years is about teaching and learning mathematics in the age-range of approximately 4 to 8 years. It is written for those who teach or who are preparing to teach mathematics in infant, first or primary schools and who wish to have a clearer understanding of the mathematical ideas behind the material they deal with in the classroom. We hope that the book will prove to be useful and relevant to colleagues involved in elementary or primary education in whatever country they teach.

This book started life as *Understanding Early Years Mathematics*. Since we wrote that book in 1989 there have been some significant changes in primary teaching. First, the phrase 'early years' has been taken over by the nursery (3–5s) sector, making the original title of our book somewhat misleading. Most significantly, for those of us who work in England and Wales, has been the introduction of the National Curriculum in all its various versions. Consequently, we have had a number of requests from colleagues to revise and update the original book. This we have now done, and, in the process, we have also changed the title to something more appropriate. The new book is about twice as long as the original and now covers comprehensively all areas of the England and Wales National Curriculum for mathematics. We have revised all the original material in the light of this and added three further chapters – Chapter 5 on number patterns and calculations, Chapter 8 on data-handling, and Chapter 9 on thinking mathematically.

For many people mathematics is a subject which generates a feeling of unease and insecurity. Those of us who sometimes have to admit that we are in some sense 'mathematicians' get used to responses like:

- You must be very clever if you teach maths!
- I never really understood maths at school. I just learnt to do the tricks.
- Oh no, not maths! I'm hopeless at maths.

What is it about mathematics that makes it seem so difficult? Why does this subject cause so much anxiety and unease? Need we be afraid of it? If you were hopeless at mathematics at school is there any chance that you will ever understand it, or even enjoy it?

This book is not written just for those people who can solve sixty mathematical problems in sixty seconds while standing on their heads doing the ironing. Rather, it is intended for those who feel inadequate when a mathematically gifted 6-year-old poses an awkward question; for those who have sometimes wondered exactly what are the meanings of mathematical symbols like the equals sign, but never dared admit it; for those who worry that some of the language they use when they are teaching mathematics to young children might not be absolutely correct.

We do not claim to have all the answers, but we hope that this book might help to remove some of the mysteries. We hope that we can demonstrate that understanding of mathematics need not be the sole prerogative of those who call themselves mathematicians. It is not a book of superficial tips for teachers, and we guarantee that you will not be able to canter through it. For it is a book which should make you pause for thought and reassess your own understanding of basic mathematical ideas. It might even make you a better teacher of mathematics to young children, by increasing your confidence and dispelling some of the fears and anxieties which you might have about this area of the curriculum.

Our interest in writing this book arose from our concern about the long-term effects on pupils' confidence in mathematics resulting from their teachers' own mathematical misconceptions and limited understanding of the subject. Frequently – through no fault of their own – even the most conscientious and able primary-school teachers do not consciously articulate these limitations. This is no doubt simply because they and their teachers before them were taught mathematics by drill, as a set of rules and recipes. Understanding as a goal may have played little part in their mathematics education.

For example, we have found that very few teachers have other than a limited understanding of something as basic as subtraction. The subtraction symbol is invariably associated with the words 'take away', which is but one of at least five different structures of situations associated with this operation. As we discuss in Chapter 3 of this book, other structures – such as comparison and inverse-of-addition – have much more significance in the long term. Unless young children have experience of these structures built into their understanding of the subtraction concept it seems likely that they will face difficulties later when they encounter a statement like '$3 - (-4) = 7$'. After all, how can you take something away from 3 and end up with more than you started with? It is our view that teachers of mathematics to young children need to get such mathematical ideas sorted out and clarified in their own minds.

To explore the nature of infant and primary teachers' mathematical understanding we originally invited twelve teachers of 4–8-year-olds to the University of East Anglia in Norwich over a six-week period to discuss their own mathematical needs in the light of their experience of teaching the subject to young children. Numerous queries and doubts about mathematical ideas that turn up in school mathematics activities were articulated. Gradually, some significant holes in mathematical knowledge were exposed – and, we believe, plugged – as we talked together about the nature of understanding of such basic mathematical ideas as number, place value, equality, addition, subtraction, multiplication, division, measurement, and space and shape. The satisfaction expressed by the teachers with whom we worked as previously fuzzy ideas began to fall into place led us to use the material from these discussions as the basis for the first book. Since then we have been able to draw on other conversations with teachers and student-teachers to guide the writing of the additional sections in the new book.

The first few years of schooling are vital for laying a foundation for understanding. There are big ideas in the mathematics taught in the lower primary years that will recur throughout a child's learning of mathematics. Often, lower-primary teachers are not aware of the significance of what they are talking about with children. This book sets out to help them to be more able to recognise some of these big ideas in mathematics. The first chapter introduces, for example: the idea that understanding involves building up networks of connections, particularly those between language, symbols, concrete experience and pictures; the special role of symbols in mathematics as the means whereby we represent and manipulate these networks of connections; the way in which one symbol has to be connected to a range of different situations, pictures and language; and the fundamental concepts of transformation and equivalence. These ideas are themes that run right through the book. The big idea of 'comparison' is introduced in the discussion on subtraction in Chapter 3 and then recurs as a major component of understanding measurement in Chapter 6. The central importance of pattern in number and its relationship to visual and spatial imagery are major themes explored in Chapter 5. This chapter also makes explicit some of the most fundamental principles that apply to the four basic number-operations. We hope that the discussion in Chapter 9 about the nature of mathematical thinking – and how this can begin to be developed through problem-solving and investigating in the lower primary years – provides an appropriate conclusion to a book in which we set out to encourage teachers of young children to think more mathematically themselves.

Questions and observations raised by the teachers with whom we worked (and, occasionally, by other teachers) are used throughout as illustrative material, as well as examples of children's mathematical thinking.

Although the book focuses on the understanding of mathematical ideas rather than on how to teach mathematics, pedagogical implications are considered where appropriate. Each chapter concludes with some suggestions for activities with children, designed to enhance understanding of the ideas discussed in the chapter.

At the time of writing, practitioners in England and Wales are being subjected to repeated criticisms of the standards being achieved by some pupils in mathematics in primary schools. Whatever the rights or wrongs of these criticisms, all primary teachers want their pupils to achieve the highest possible standards in mathematics and to move on from their classes with as much confidence and competence in this core subject as possible. To achieve this, we believe that teachers should recognise that they themselves should have a thorough understanding of the basic mathematical ideas that underpin the mathematics that is taught and learnt in the first few years of schooling. This book aims to develop that understanding.

Derek Haylock and Anne Cockburn
School of Education and Professional Development
UEA Norwich NR4 7TJ

1

Mathematical Symbols

I thought 6-year-old Gemma had a good understanding of the equals sign. She had no problem with sums like 2 + 3 = □ and 8 + □ = 9. Then I asked her how she did 2 + □ = 6. She replied, 'I said to myself, two, three, four, five, six, and so the answer is four. Sometimes I do them the other way round, but it doesn't make any difference.' She pointed to 1 + □ = 10. 'For this one I did ten and one and that's eleven.'

This book is about *understanding*. It has arisen from an attempt to help teachers to understand some of the mathematical ideas which children handle in the early years of schooling. It is based on our experience that many teachers and students are helped enormously in their teaching of mathematics by a shift in their perception of the subject away from the learning of a collection of recipes and rules towards the development of understanding of mathematical concepts and principles.

For many children, like Gemma in the example above, doing mathematics appears to be a matter of moving symbols around and writing them on pieces of paper, using an apparently arbitrary collection of rules. Of course, mathematics does involve the manipulation of symbols. But the learning of recipes for answering various types of questions is not the basis of understanding in mathematics. In this chapter we explore the relationship between mathematical symbols and the other components of children's experience of mathematics, and suggest a framework for discussing understanding in mathematics. By way of example in this chapter we discuss understanding of *place-value notation* and understanding of the *equals sign*. But we begin our discussion with one teacher's description of an example of some children engaged in a mathematical activity designed to develop what we would recognise as some aspects of understanding of the idea of division.

UNDERSTANDING: MAKING CONNECTIONS

Concrete materials, symbols, language and pictures

Below is a description provided by one of the infant teachers in our group of some children working on activities aimed at developing *understanding* of

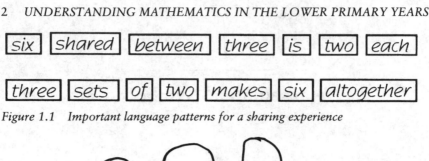

Figure 1.1   Important language patterns for a sharing experience

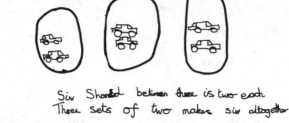

Figure 1.2   Division language linked with a picture . . .

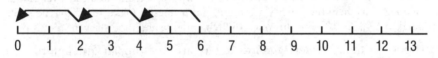

Figure 1.3   . . . and with a number line

division. This illustrates some significant components of the model we will use to discuss understanding of number and number operations:

> Three 7-year-olds in my class were exploring the early ideas of division. On their table they had a box of toy cars, paper and pencil, a collection of cards with various words written on them (*shared, between, is, each, sets, of, makes, altogether, two, three, six, nine, twelve*) and a calculator. Their first task was to share six cars between the three of them. They discussed the result. Then they selected various cards to make up sentences (see Figure 1.1) to describe what they had discovered.
>
> The children drew pictures of their sharing (see Figure 1.2) and copied their two sentences underneath.
>
> One of the children then picked up the calculator and interpreted the first sentence by pressing the keys '6 ÷ 3 = '. She seemed delighted to see appear in the display a symbol representing the two cars which they each had. She then interpreted their second sentence by pressing '× 2 = ' and, as she expected, got back to the six she started with. She demonstrated this to the other children who then insisted on doing it themselves. When they next recorded their calculations as '6 ÷ 3 = 2' and '2 × 3 = 6', the symbols were a record of the keys pressed on the calculator and the resulting display. Later on I will get them to include with their drawings, their sentences, and their recording in symbols, a number line picture like this (see Figure 1.3).

When children are engaged in mathematical activity, as in this example, they are involved in manipulating some or all of the following: concrete materials, symbols, language and pictures. They manipulate *concrete materials* – moving blocks, various sets of objects and toys, rods, counters, fingers, coins, and so forth. They manipulate *symbols* – making marks on pieces of paper, arranging them in the prescribed fashion, copying exercises from the workcard, numbering the questions, drawing lines here and there, crossing out some symbols, carrying one, filling in boxes, underlining the answer, and so on, or pressing buttons on their calculator. They manipulate *language* – reading workcards, making sentences incorporating specific mathematical words, processing the teacher's instructions, interpreting word problems, saying out loud the words that go with their recording. And finally, they manipulate *pictures* – drawing number lines, set diagrams, arrow pictures, graphs, and so on.

A model for understanding: making connections

A simple model which enables us to talk about understanding in mathematics is to view the growth of understanding as the building up of (cognitive) connections. More specifically, when we encounter some new experience there is a sense in which we understand it if we can connect it to previous experiences, or, better, to a network of previously connected experiences. The more strongly connected the experience the more we understand it. Learning without making connections is what we would call learning by rote. The teacher's role in developing understanding is, then, to help the child to build up connections between new experiences and previous learning.

We find it very helpful to think of understanding the concepts of number and number-operations (i.e. number, place value, addition, subtraction, multiplication, division, equals, number patterns, and so on) as involving the building up of a network of cognitive connections between the four types of experience of mathematics that we have identified above: concrete experiences, symbols, language and pictures. Any one of the arrows in Figure 1.4 represents a possible connection between experiences that might form part of the understanding of a mathematical concept.

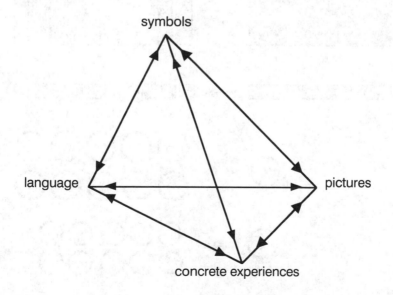

Figure 1.4   Some significant connections in understanding mathematics

In the example described above of children engaged in some simple division activities, we see them developing understanding in this sense. They are connecting their manipulation of their toy cars with the language patterns of '. . . shared between . . . is . . . each', and '. . . sets of . . . makes . . . altogether'. They are connecting their concrete experience with a picture of three sets of two things. The language of their sentences is connected with the symbols on the keys and display of the calculator. And then, later, they will be learning to interpret these symbols as a picture of three steps of two on a number line.

Another example: understanding place-value notation

The connections framework outlined above is, of course, only a model designed to enable us to discuss and recognise some aspects of understanding in mathematics. As an example of its use we will consider understanding of the important concept of place value.

This is the basis of our Hindu-Arabic number system which enables us to represent all numbers by using just ten digits. The value that each digit represents is determined by its place (going from right to left), the first place representing ones, the second tens, the next hundreds, and so on, with increasing powers of ten. Thus the digit 9 in 900 represents a value ten times greater than

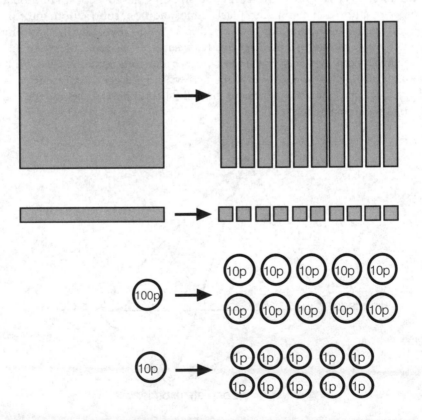

Figure 1.5 'One of these is ten of those'

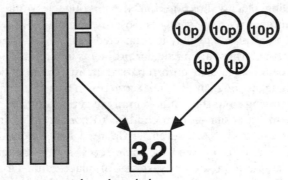

Figure 1.6   Connecting materials and symbols

it does in the number 90. Most teachers would agree that a proper understanding of place value is an essential basis for progress in arithmetic.

What is involved in understanding this concept? What connections between symbols, language, concrete experiences and pictures might be established as part of this understanding? First, the child will experience the principle of exchange in a variety of concrete situations, learning to connect the manipulation of materials with the language pattern 'one of these . . . ten of those'. This might be working with base ten materials, as shown in Figure 1.5, where a flat piece can literally be constructed from ten long pieces, or with 1p, 10p and 100p coins, in which one coin is worth ten of another sort.

Children would demonstrate understanding of this principle of exchange when they reduce a collection of base ten materials, or 1p, 10p, 100p coins, to the smallest number of pieces or coins by a process of exchange, using the appropriate language of exchange to describe what they are doing: 'one of these is ten of those', or 'one of these is worth ten of those'.

They will learn to connect collections of materials with the symbols, as shown in Figure 1.6. They might demonstrate understanding of this connection by selecting (1) appropriate base ten blocks, or (2) appropriate 1p, 10p and 100p coins, to correspond to any given two- or three-digit number written in symbols. One important component of this understanding is the use of zero as a place holder. For example, in Figure 1.7, the child will learn to connect the symbols 206 with the collection of materials shown, namely, 2 flat pieces (hundreds), no long pieces (tens) and 6 units (ones).

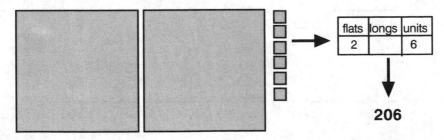

Figure 1.7   Zero as a place holder

Understanding place-value notation also involves learning to connect the language of number with the symbols. So, for example, '342' written down or appearing on a calculator display is connected with 'three hundred and forty-two', spoken. Again there are particular problems in making these connections where zero occurs. It is also unfortunate that, in common with most other European languages, English does not settle down to a systematic relationship between the language and the symbols until we get beyond the number 19. We would find it much easier to help children to connect the language and the symbols if we counted: ' . . . seven, eight, nine, ten, onety-one, onety-two, onety-three . . . ' and so on. We have come across some teachers who actually do this with children in the early stages of place-value work, as a bridge between numbers up to and numbers beyond 20. In this respect children learning about counting and place value in Japan would seem to have a distinct advantage. For example, the names of the numbers 12, 15 and 25 in Japanese (*ju-ni, ju-go, ni-ju-go*) are all built up from the words for 'ten' (*ju*), 'two' (*ni*) and 'five' (*go*) and could be translated into English as 'ten two', 'ten five' and 'two-tens five'. All the number names up to a hundred are constructed in the same logical way, making the place-value principle transparent. By contrast, we might feel sorry for the poor French child who has to learn to connect the symbols '92', for example, with a name (*quatre-vingt-douze*) that makes no reference to either the 9 tens or the 2 ones, but which could be translated as 'four-twenties-twelve'!

A further aspect of understanding of place value, connecting symbols with pictures, is shown in Figure 1.8. The child learns to connect the symbols for numbers with the important picture of the number line. This might involve, for example, locating the approximate position of a given number on a number line labelled (1) in 10s, (2) in 100s, or, vice versa, stating or writing the approximate number corresponding to a given point on a number line labelled (1) in 10s, (2) in 100s.

We can see therefore that much of what is involved in understanding place value can be identified as the building up of a network of connections between language, symbols, concrete materials and pictures. We find it helpful to regard many mathematical concepts as networks of such connections.

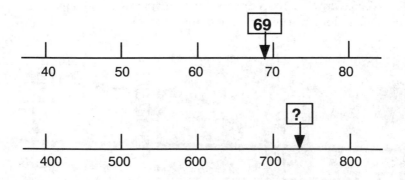

Figure 1.8   Connecting symbols with the number-line picture

WHAT ARE MATHEMATICAL SYMBOLS?

What exactly are mathematical symbols, other than marks we write on paper and learn to manipulate according to various rules? What is the function of a symbol in mathematics? What is the relationship of a mathematical symbol to our experiences of doing mathematics and handling mathematical ideas? These are some comments from some of the infant teachers in our group:

- I think of mathematical symbols as abbreviations. They're a sort of shorthand.
- They have very ambiguous meanings for me. They have different meanings depending on the situation you're using them in.
- They sometimes mean you have to do something. Perform an operation. Move some blocks around.

Mathematical symbols not just abbreviations

There is a sense in which mathematical symbols (such as 4, 28, ÷, =) are abbreviations for mathematical ideas or concepts. But it is important to note at the outset that this does not mean that a symbol in mathematics is just an abbreviation for a specific word or phrase. It is tempting to think of, say, the division sign as being essentially an abbreviation for the words 'shared be-tween'. Children often appear to view mathematical symbols in this way. One 9-year-old was using a calculator to do '28 ÷ 4', saying to himself as he pressed the buttons, 'Twenty-eight shared . . . '. At this point he turned to the teacher and asked, 'Which button's between?' It was as though each word had to have a button or a symbol to represent it. When we see children writing 41 for fourteen it is clear that they often say 'four' and write 4, then say 'teen' and write 1, again using the symbols as abbreviations for the sounds they are uttering. And so the same child will happily write 41 for forty-one a few lines later! We see a similar error when children record a number like three hundred and seventy-five as 30075 or 3075. The noughts are written down as abbreviations for the word 'hundred'.

But once we think of understanding, particularly understanding of number and number operations, as the building up of connections between concrete experiences, symbols, words and pictures, we begin to see that a mathematical symbol is not an abbreviation for just one category of concrete experiences, or just one word or phrase, or just one picture. The child has to learn to connect one symbol with a potentially confusing variety of concrete situations, pictures and language.

Hence we would suggest that a symbol in mathematics is a way of represent-ing a concept, a network of connections. The symbol then becomes a means whereby we can manipulate that concept according to precise rules. Without the symbols it would be virtually impossible for us to manipulate the concepts. The symbols of mathematics allow us both to discover and to express relationships between various concepts. For example, when we write down a statement in symbols like '2 + 4 = 6' we are expressing a relationship between the concepts of two, four and six, addition and equality, each of which, as we shall see, is itself a complex network of connections represented by the given symbol.

The teacher's suggestion above that mathematical symbols have different meanings depending on the situation in which they are being used is a very perceptive observation. One symbol might indeed represent a complex network of connections, and can therefore be applied to a variety of situations and pictures, and associated with a variety of language. This is one of the major themes in our discussion of understanding of number and number-operations in this and subsequent chapters. We explore in considerable detail how a statement in symbols such as '2 + 4 = 6' can be connected to an extensive range of different pictures, language and concrete situations. The symbols for the numbers, the symbol for the operation of addition, and the equals sign itself all have a variety of meanings depending on the situation and the manner in which they are being used. Put them altogether and the simple-looking statement '2 + 4 = 6' represents a surprisingly complex network of connections. This is at one and the same time the reason why mathematics is so powerful, and probably the reason why for many it is such a difficult subject to understand.

The equals sign

Consider, for example, the equals sign: '='. We shall see that it is precisely because a concept like 'equals' is such a complex network of ideas and experiences that we find there is not just one form of words that goes with the symbol '=' and there is a whole range of situations to which the symbol becomes attached. Some of their anxieties about the meaning of this symbol were articulated by some of the infant teachers with whom we worked:

- My 6-year-olds had problems with some questions in their maths books where they had to put in the missing numbers, like this: $6 = 2 + \square$. Most of them put in 8, of course. When I tried to explain to them how to do these sums I realised I didn't actually know what the equals sign meant myself. We would say '2 add something makes 6' if it were written the other way round, but '6 makes 2 add something' doesn't make sense.
- Is it wrong to say '4 add 2 makes 6'? Should I insist that the children say 'equals 6'?
- The word 'equals' doesn't mean anything to them. It's just a symbol, just some marks on paper that you make when you're doing sums.
- Doesn't it confuse children to say 'makes' when you're adding and then to say 'leaves' when you're taking away?
- And sometimes we just read it as 'is', like '3 add 4 is 7'.

Transformation and equivalence

To analyse the concept associated with the equals sign, we will first discuss two fundamental concepts that run right through mathematics. These are the concepts of *transformation* and *equivalence*.

Figure 1.9 represents two pieces of paper, one A4 size and the other A5 size. Perhaps we should explain that you get A1 paper by folding A0 paper in half, A2 by folding A1, and so on, and that the dimensions of the paper are cunningly chosen so that each rectangle has exactly the same proportions as the

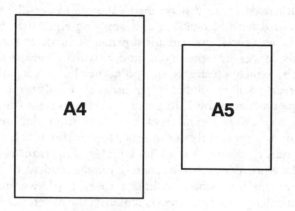

Figure 1.9 The same but different

original. (If you want to be really technical, the sides of the rectangle are in the ratio 'one to the square root of two', i.e. '1 to 1.414', approximately. And to add to the fun, A0 paper has an area of 1 m².) The upshot of all this is that the A5 rectangle is the shape produced by folding in half the A4 rectangle.

Now when we begin to make mathematical statements about the relationships between the two rectangles in Figure 1.9, we find they fall into two categories.

On the one hand, we may look at the rectangles and make observations about the ways in which they differ: one is on the left and the other is on the right, one is half the area of the other, the length of one is 1.414 times the length of the other, and so on. Statements like these are essentially using the concept of transformation. We are concerned with the changes that are observed when we move our attention from one rectangle to the other. We are hinting at what would have to be done to one rectangle to transform it to the other.

On the other hand, we may look at these rectangles and make statements about the ways in which they are the same: they are both rectangles, they are the same shape, their sides are in the same proportion. Statements like these are essentially using the concept of equivalence. We are concerned with what stays the same when we move our attention from one rectangle to the other. We are hinting at the existence of a set of shapes, called an *equivalence class*, of which these two are members. All the members of an equivalence class of shapes have some particular property or properties in common that would in certain circumstances allow us to refer to them as the same shape. (This idea of sets of shapes forming equivalence classes is discussed in detail in Chapter 7.)

More generally, when we make statements about what has changed in a situation, what is different about two things, what something has become, and so on, we are using the concept of transformation. When we concern ourselves with what is the same, with similarities rather than differences, what remains unchanged in spite of the transformation, then we are talking about equivalence. The key phrase in everyday language for describing an equivalence is simply '*is the same as*'.

Much of mathematics, not just geometrical experiences like the example above, is concerned with recognising and applying equivalences and transformations. Often a crucial mathematical principle involves the recognition of which equivalences are preserved under which transformations. An example of this, which illustrates the point nicely, is that of equivalent fractions. The reader will recall that it is in order to transform the fraction $\frac{4}{6}$, by dividing top and bottom by 2, to produce the equivalent fraction $\frac{2}{3}$ (and to record this as '$\frac{4}{6} = \frac{2}{3}$'). This is a transformation that preserves the equivalence. But it is apparently not in order to transform $\frac{4}{6}$ by, say, adding 1 to top and bottom, because $\frac{4}{6}$ does not equal $\frac{5}{7}$. This transformation does not preserve the equivalence. Unfortunately for the student of mathematics there are other situations where adding 1 to each of two numbers does preserve an equivalence, such as when calculating the difference between two numbers (e.g. '77 – 49' can be correctly and usefully transformed into '78 – 50'). At times one feels sorry for the poor pupils trying to make sense of this subject. It must seem to be quite arbitrary as to whether a particular transformation is acceptable and warrants a red tick or is unacceptable and generates a red cross.

The equals sign representing an equivalence

Strictly speaking, then, the equals sign represents this concept of equivalence. When we write down '2 + 4 = 6' we are expressing an equivalence between '2 + 4' and '6'. We are making a statement that there is something the same about 'two added to four' and 'six'. Probably the most straightforward language to go with this statement is 'two add four is the same as six'. To emphasise the underlying equivalence in arithmetic statements using the equals sign, this phrase 'is the same as' is particularly significant. It connects very clearly with the concrete experience of doing addition and subtraction with materials such as Stern blocks, or Cuisenaire or Colour-Factor rods (see Figure 1.10). When the child makes a train with a 2-rod and a 4-rod the problem is to find another rod to match this train. Recording the experience as '2 + 4 = 6' is an expression of the equivalence: the 2-rod added to the 4-rod is in one sense the same as the 6-rod. Of course, they are only the same in that they are the same length. A train made up of a blue rod and a brown rod is very different from a red rod. But lying there side by side they represent an equivalence, and this is expressed by the symbols '2 + 4 = 6'. It is worth noting that this interpretation of the equals sign makes sense of the problem we started with: '6 = 2 + □' is read as 'six is the same as 2 add something'.

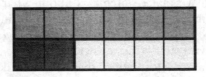

Figure 1.10 *'Two add four is the same as 6'*

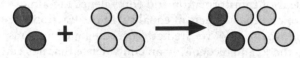

Figure 1.11 'Two add four makes six'

The equals sign representing a transformation

However, when the child puts out sets of two counters and four counters, forms their union and counts the new set to discover that there is now a set of six counters, it is a bit obscure to suggest that this is an experience of 'two add four is the same as six'. The child has actually transformed the two sets of two and four counters into a set of six (see Figure 1.11). The child's attention therefore is focused on the transformation that has taken place. This being so, it seems perfectly natural and surely appropriate to use the language 'two and four makes six' to describe the transformation the child has effected. One teacher said that she regarded the symbols as instructions to do something – in other words, to apply some sort of transformation. There is plenty of evidence that this is how children most frequently interpret the equals sign.

It is presumably to emphasise this transformation aspect that some mathematics schemes use an arrow rather than an equals sign to record activities of this sort, for example writing '2 + 4 → 6'. However, we are taking the view that in practice the equals sign represents both the equivalence and the transformation aspects of the relationship between '2 + 4' and '6'. Thus we would not want to suggest that it is wrong or in some way mathematically incorrect to associate 'makes', 'leaves', 'is', and so on, with the equals sign, and insist on the one form of words 'is the same as' or even 'equals'. Rather, we would advocate a combination of experiences emphasising the notions of both equivalence and transformation. As we have already argued, mathematical symbols are not just abbreviations for particular words or phrases. We have to recognise that the statement '2 + 4 = 6' is actually at one and the same time a representation in symbols of the transformation that has been applied to 2 and 4, and the equivalence that has emerged between '2 + 4' and '6'.

One symbol, two meanings

It could be, therefore, that the child's attention might on some occasions be directed to the transformation of two and four into six, particularly when using counters, fingers, sets of toys, pencils, sweets, and so on. And on other occasions, particularly when using some structural apparatus or when making steps on a number line, the attention might be directed to the equivalence of 'two added to four' and 'six'. On both occasions the child might record their activity as '2 + 4 = 6'. But this might be accompanied in the first case by the words 'two add four makes six', and in the second case by the words 'two add four is the same as six'. The use of different language appropriate to the situation is inevitable and perfectly acceptable, demonstrating that the child is gaining experience of both the transformation and the equivalence built into the relationship between '2 + 4' and '6'.

These two ideas of transformation and equivalence are almost always present whenever we make statements of equality. In the fractions example above, when we write down '$4/6 = 2/3$' we are both recording a transformation that has been applied to the $4/6$ and recognising an equivalence that has emerged. There is a sense in which $4/6$ is not the same as $2/3$. Using one meaning of the fraction notation, four slices of a cake cut into six equal parts is different from two slices of a cake cut into three equal parts. But there is something very significantly the same about these two situations – they produce the same amount of cake – which prompts us to recognise an equivalence and to record it with the equals sign. This is just the same with '$2 + 4 = 6$'. Two piles of cubes, one containing two and the other containing four, look quite different from a pile of six cubes, yet there is a sameness about the two situations that warrants the use of the equals sign.

So, what does the equals sign mean? Strictly we should concede that it means 'is equivalent to', or 'is the same as', in whatever sense is determined by the context. And we should say that perhaps this is an aspect of the meaning of the symbol that is underplayed by teachers. It would be no bad thing for children's mathematical development for the phrase 'is the same as' to occur more frequently in their talk and in the talk of their teachers. But as with all mathematical symbols we have to learn to connect the equals sign with a complex variety of situations, operations and language, sometimes focusing on the transformation and sometimes on the equivalence. Understanding mathematics right from the earliest years involves us in learning to attach the same symbol to a potentially bewildering variety of situations and language. This is even true of the first mathematical symbols we encounter, those used to represent numbers. And this will be the subject of our next chapter.

SOME ACTIVITIES WITH CHILDREN

At the end of each chapter we provide a few examples of activities that teachers might use with children to develop the mathematical ideas explored in the text. The activities are all aimed at developing what we might recognise as understanding. They are not intended to cover comprehensively the material in the chapter, but we hope that they may provide teachers with some indication of ways in which the ideas we have outlined in the preceding pages might influence their practice. We have deliberately not specified ages for the children. Many of these activities can be used with a wide age-range, either as they are given here or by appropriate modification.

Activity 1.1: connections (add and subtract)
Objective To develop connections between symbols, concrete experiences, language and pictures, using the concepts of addition and subtraction.

Materials A box of counters (or toys, or pennies); paper and pencil; strips of card with words associated with addition and subtraction written on them (such as: take away, add, leaves, makes); cards with numbers from 1 to 20 written on them; a calculator; a duplicated sheet of number lines marked from 0 to 20.

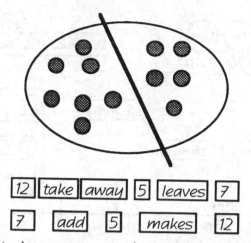

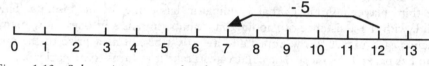

Figure 1.12   Connecting language patterns with a picture of subtraction

Figure 1.13   Subtraction connected with the number line

Method   Develop an activity, for a small group of children, using subtraction and addition, similar to that using division and multiplication outlined at the beginning of this chapter. The children can be provided with a prompt sheet that says: counters, sentences, picture, calculator, number line. The children should start with two of the numbered cards, e.g. 12 and 5. It is explained to them that this means they put out 12 counters, move 5 to one side, and count how many are left. They then have to connect this with the appropriate language, e.g. they use the cards provided to make up two sentences: '12 take away 5 leaves 7' and '7 add 5 makes 12'. They then have to draw a picture on their paper to show what they have done and write the sentences underneath, as shown in Figure 1.12.

To make the connection with symbols they then have to press the keys on the calculator that correspond to their actions with the counters: '12 − 5 = 7' and '7 + 5 = 12'. Finally they must represent the relationship on a number line, as shown in Figure 1.13. The teacher should discuss with the children how their number-line diagram shows both '12 − 5' and '7 + 5'.

Activity 1.2: bundling in tens
Objective   To provide topic-based, practical experience of the place-value principle of bundling into tens.

Materials   A Paddington Bear, pretend (or real) biscuits, packing material, and a three-minute timer with a buzzer.

Method   This could be an activity for three children, as part of an ongoing project on the Paddington Bear theme. Two children package biscuits into rolls

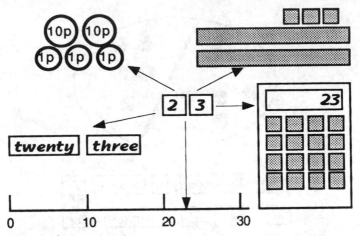

Figure 1.14 Making connections

of ten at a time, while the third sets the timer going. When the buzzer sounds the third player announces that Paddington has come for his biscuits. This child, with the assistance of Paddington, counts (in tens and ones) how many biscuits each player has wrapped and awards a biscuit as a prize to the one who has packed the most. The children can take it in turns to be packers.

Activity 1.3: connections (place value)
Objective To develop understanding of place value by making connections between symbols, concrete experiences, language and pictures.
   Materials A pack of cards with numerals 0 to 9 written on them, and strips of card with the words: one, two, three, . . . nine, and twenty, thirty, forty, . . . ninety; 10p and 1p coins; base-ten materials such as Dienes blocks (units and longs); a calculator; a number line marked from 0 to 99 (such as a metre rule marked in centimetres); a movable pointer for indicating numbers on the number line.
   Method A small group of children turn over two of the numeral-cards, e.g. 2 and 3. They arrange them side by side to make a 2-digit numeral, e.g. 23. They then have to make all the possible representations of this with the materials provided, as illustrated in Figure 1.14. (Because the 'teens' do not fit the same language pattern as the subsequent numbers they are excluded from this activity – teachers should arrange the cards, therefore, so that 1 is not used in the tens position for this activity.)

Activity 1.4: say, press, check, write
Objective To practise adding or subtracting 1, 10, 100, as part of the understanding of place value.
   Materials Pencil and paper, a calculator with a constant addition and subtraction facility (most have this).
   Method Children work in pairs. The teacher writes on the top of their sheet of paper one of the following instructions: Add 1, Add 10, Add 100, Subtract 1, Subtract 10, Subtract 100. Underneath this the teacher writes a line

of five starting numbers. For example, with 'Add 10' the children might have the starting numbers 23, 49, 30, 16 and 4.

For each starting number the children have to produce a column of numbers by continually adding 10 (or whatever the instruction is), e.g. 23, 33, 43, and so on, until they reach the bottom of the page. This is done by a process of 'say, press, check, write'. The starting number is entered on the calculator, followed by the instruction (e.g. 23 + 10). One child *says* what the next number will be, the other then *presses* the equals key and *checks* that the first child is correct. Then the first child *writes* the result. They can take it in turns to be the first child. Note that, if the calculator has a constant addition facility, all that is required after entering 23 + 10 is continually to press the equals key to get each number in the sequence.

The same process applies with any instruction (+1, +10, +100, −1, −10, −100) and any starting numbers. Teachers should not be cautious about letting children investigate subtraction examples where their calculator takes them into negative answers.

Activity 1.5: missing numbers
Objective   To help children understand missing number sums and the meaning of the equals sign.

Materials   Some Stern blocks, or equivalent materials where the numbers from 1 to 10 are represented by coloured rods or sticks of coloured cubes joined together.

Method   First investigate how the children handle a collection of missing number sums, where the box for the missing number might be in any one of six positions. For example, using the sum 3 + 5 = 8, they could look at: 3 + 5 = □, 3 + □ = 8, □ + 5 = 8, □ = 3 + 5, 8 = □ + 5 and 8 = 3 + □. Which type of questions do they find easiest? most difficult? Talk with the children about how they interpret the questions and discover what language they use for the equals sign. Explore the suggestions that children might be helped to make more sense of these questions (1) by using the phrase 'is the same as' to go with the equals sign, and (2) by connecting the symbols in these questions with corresponding manipulations of coloured number-rods.

SUMMARY OF KEY IDEAS IN CHAPTER 1

1. A simple model for talking about understanding is that to understand something is to connect it with previous learning or other experiences.
2. Mathematical activity involves the manipulation of concrete materials, symbols, language and pictures.
3. Connections between these four types of experience constitute important components of mathematical understanding.
4. A mathematical concept can be thought of as a network of connections between symbols, language, concrete experiences and pictures.
5. A mathematical symbol is a way of representing a mathematical concept that enables us to manipulate it and to discover and express relationships with other concepts.
6. Understanding the concept of place value includes being able to move between the language and symbols used for numbers, concrete experiences with base-ten materials and coins, and the number-line picture.

7. The concepts of equivalence and transformation refer respectively to statements of similarity and statements of difference or change.
8. The equals sign strictly means 'is the same as' or 'is equivalent to'. But often in practice it represents both an instruction to apply a transformation – in which case language such as 'makes' and 'leaves' is appropriate – and the equivalence that emerges.
9. One mathematical symbol, such as the equals sign, can be connected with a wide variety of different concrete situations, language and pictures.

SUGGESTIONS FOR FURTHER READING

At the end of each chapter we include a short list of references that might be of interest to readers who wish to consider specific aspects in more detail. In addition, at the end of the book, we provide a brief biography of texts that we have found particularly useful and informative.

Ashlock, R. B. (1987) Use of informal language when introducing concepts, *Focus on Learning Mathematics*, 9, pp. 31–6. (Ashlock discusses how to avoid some of the confusions that can arise when young children are introduced to formal mathematical language.)

Bove, S. (1995) Place value: a vertical perspective, *Teaching Children Mathematics*, May, pp. 542–6. (Bove argues that, by using a vertical rather than a horizontal number line, children gain a clearer understanding of the relationship between place value and number size.)

Dickson, L., Brown, M. and Gibson, O. (1984) *Children Learning Mathematics*, Cassell, London. (Look especially at section 4 on mathematical language, words and symbols. This is a useful survey of research findings.)

Donaldson, M. (1978) *Children's Minds*, Fontana, London. (A classic account of the way children interpret and respond to mathematical situations.)

Haylock, D. (1995) *Mathematics Explained for Primary Teachers*, Paul Chapman Publishing, London. (Chapter 2 provides a detailed explanation of place value.)

Hiebert, J. (1988) A theory of developing competence with written mathematical symbols, *Educational Studies in Mathematics*, 19, pp. 333–55. (Hiebert presents a theory of how competence with written mathematical symbols develops and how the sequencing of the content of instructional activities may be used to reduce the possibility of pupils' mathematical behaviour becoming overly mechanical and inflexible.)

Hughes, M. (1986) *Children and Number: Difficulties in Learning Mathematics*, Blackwell, Oxford. (In Chapter 7 of this fascinating book Hughes describes some of the difficulties children experience when they first encounter written symbolism in mathematics.)

Shoecraft, P. (1989) 'Equals' means 'is the same as', *Arithmetic Teacher*, April, pp. 36–40. (Shoecraft discusses strategies to encourage children to think of the equals sign as a relational symbol rather than an operator.)

Williams, H. (1996) Beginning 'beginnings', *Mathematics Teaching*, 156, pp. 8–13. (A lively discussion of some of the experiences of young children as they begin to encounter mathematics.)

2

Number

A 7-year-old child was asked to write a story to go with the symbols '5 – 3' (child's spelling retained!):

> Once upon a time there lived a nubere and he was called 5 and he was very lonly. Won day he saw a nubere 3 and he was lonly to saw he went up to him and sad well you be my frinde. Yes he sad becase I have no frinde to play with. Saw five and three were good frinds and they were happy and the nexed day they went four a pikenik and had a good time. They had cakes and drink and sandwich and biskites and they came home and got into bed with a hot water botel.

WHAT IS A NUMBER?

What is three?

This child's delightfully amusing interpretation of numbers as characters in a story with lives of their own might cause us to pause and ask ourselves what numbers mean to us. What, for example, is three? Close your eyes and bring to the forefront of your mind an image of the number three. Describe the image in your mind.

- I can see three dots arranged in a triangle.
- A set of three fruits, an apple, an orange and a banana.
- Three dots in a line.
- A triangle, a shape with three sides.
- The symbol 3.
- Someone holding up three fingers.

This question has been asked to hundreds of teachers and student-teachers and almost invariably the responses are similar to those above, falling into two categories: either the image described is a set of three things, dots, sides of a triangle, fingers, sweets, vague unspecified objects or splodges, and so on; or, less frequently, the picture imagined is just the symbol 3.

Clearly the symbol is not the number. As discussed in Chapter 1, the symbol allows us to represent the concept of three and to manipulate it and to relate it

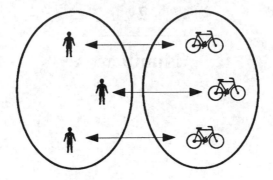

Figure 2.1   One-to-one matching

to other numbers. But the actual symbol that we use is fairly arbitrary. Other cultures use other symbols and other words, but the same network of connections that constitutes the concept of three lies behind them. If occasionally we want to distinguish the symbol from the number it represents then we can refer to the *numeral* 3. Numerals are the marks we make on paper, such as 3, 26, 819, when we record and manipulate numbers. Incidentally, in our discussion of place value in Chapter 1 we have already used the word *digit* to refer to the 8, the 1 and the 9 in the numeral 819.

The image of three that clearly dominates the thinking of most adults is the idea that three is a set of three things. When the infant teacher needs to explain to a child a problem involving the number 3 the most likely thing to appear on the desk will be a set of three counters, three blocks, or, if nothing else comes readily to hand, three fingers. Not surprisingly, therefore, children's stories about number usually interpret numbers in this way – as sets of things: 3 children, 3 teddies, 3 sweets, and so on. It could be suggested then that 'three' is what all these sets of three things have in common. Three is seen as a concept abstracted from many examples of sets of three things. One-to-one matching of objects in one set of three with objects in another set of three, as illustrated in Figure 2.1, is designed to concentrate the child's perception on what is the same about the two sets.

Again we see the notions of transformation and equivalence in operation. For example, when a child matches a set of three cups, one to one, onto a set of three saucers, the operation of matching shifts the focus away from the differences between the cups and the saucers in favour of what is the same about them, namely their threeness. The following conversation with some of our infant teachers raises an important point:

D. Here's an interesting question: is three an adjective or a noun?
C. It must be an adjective, because you talk about three things. Three apples, three bananas and so on. It describes the set.
E. I think it can be both.
D. To convince me that it can be a noun you need to give me a sentence beginning with the words 'Three is . . . '
C. Three is a number.

E. Three is less than five.
A. Three is a factor of twelve.
D. Three is a prime number.

When three changes from an adjective to a noun like this it is no longer attached to the sets of three things, it has a life of its own. We can talk about 'three' as though it exists independently of the sets to which we might connect it. It could be suggested that a key stage in the development of the concept of number is this transition from number as an adjective to number as a noun.

The cardinal and ordinal aspects of number

In fact, this view of the way in which number concepts develop is very simplistic and makes little allowance for the complex network of connections between concrete experience, language, pictures and the symbol 3, which constitute the concept of three. So far we have only talked about connecting the symbol with concrete situations consisting of sets of three things. This is only one aspect of a number, referred to as the *cardinal* aspect. But to what else, apart from sets of things, can we attach the symbol 3?

- What about the 3 on a clock face – that's not denoting a set of three things, is it?
- I live at number 3, but I don't live in a set of three houses!
- Or page 3 in a newspaper?
- It's like the number 3 bus. It's just a label that helps us identify one bus from another.

The 3 on a number 3 bus is indeed just a label, a number used, in what is sometimes called the *nominal* aspect, just to label items and to distinguish them from one another. When used like this the symbol is hardly operating as a number at all. Behind the other responses above, however, is another very important category of images of the number 3. This is called the *ordinal* aspect of number: numbers used not just to label things but also to *put them in order*. Room number 3, house number 3, the 3 on the clock face, page 3 in a book – these are labelled 3 because in some ordering system they come between 2 and 4. When the timetable for the number 3 bus is printed after the timetable for the number 2 bus and before that for the number 4, then the 3 is now being used not just in a nominal sense but in the ordinal sense. Notice that there is no 'threeness' in the cardinal sense about this use of the number 3. Page 3 is not a set of three pages, it doesn't necessarily contain a photograph of a set of three people or a set of three objects, nor does it contain just three words or three sentences. It's labelled 3 simply because it is located between page 2 and page 4.

We want to emphasise that this ordinal aspect is not an obscure or secondary aspect of the concept of number in spite of the fact that almost none of us brings to mind an ordinal image when asked to think of three. This ordinal aspect of the number is as central and important as the cardinal aspect, and one we use all the time in our everyday lives whether it be finding our page in a book, locating a room in a strange building, looking up a date in a calendar, or deciding whether it's our turn to get padded up ready for the next wicket to fall.

Counting

It is, of course, in counting that the cardinal and ordinal aspects come together. What is involved in counting? First of all the child learns a pattern of noises, memorised by repetition in all sorts of situations both in and out of school: 'One, two, three, four . . . ' and so on. This set of sounds is probably just as meaningless as many traditional nursery rhymes, serving merely to demonstrate the young child's amazing capacity for sequential learning. Then the child has to learn to co-ordinate the utterance of these noises with the physical movements of a finger and the eye along a line of objects, matching one noise to one object. (The two-syllable word 'seven' sometimes poses a particularly difficult problem of co-ordination.) As each number is spoken it is being used in an ordinal sense, to label the objects and to order them – number one, number two, number three, and so on. But then the child has somehow to discover that the ordinal number of the last object is the cardinal number of the set. What a stunning and powerful discovery this is! One 4-year-old was counting objects in her head and suddenly announced with great excitement, 'Three is three, isn't it!' More counting, then, 'Four is four! And five is five!' It was as though she was counting to three and then realising that when you got to three you actually had a set of three things, and similarly with four and five.

A network of connections for understanding number

The importance of the ordinal aspect means therefore that a very significant part of understanding number is the connection between the symbols and the picture of number incorporated in a number line, one example of which is shown in Figure 2.2. Possibly even more effective for developing number concepts is a similar line arranged vertically, so that the numbers get larger as you go up and smaller as you go down. Either of these lines is a picture of number that emphasises particularly the ordinal aspect. Another example incorporating this ordinal aspect would be a number strip – a line of squares numbered in order – as occurs in many board games. The number three is one point on the number line, or one square on the number strip, not a set of three points or a set of three squares, and its main property is that it lies between two and four.

It appears, therefore, that the answer to the question 'What is three?' is far from straightforward. The concept of a number like three appears to involve a network of connections between the symbol 3, the word 'three', concrete situations of sets of things, using the cardinal aspect, and pictures of number involving the ordinal aspect, such as number lines. Hence it seems that at a very early age the child encounters one enormous difficulty that runs right

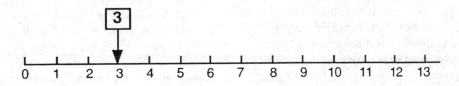

Figure 2.2   The number line emphasises the ordinal aspect of number

through mathematics: that one symbol is used to represent vastly different situations. Not just different in the way in which a set of three sweets is different from a set of three plates, but as different as the questions, 'How many pages have you read today?' and 'What page are you on?' Both questions might elicit a response of 'three', but with two completely different meanings.

Of course, the different meanings of the symbol are not totally unrelated and arbitrary, as, for example, two different meanings of some words might be, such as 'well' (in good health) and 'well' (of water). But the connections are by no means at a simple level of perception and the teacher has a major task to help the child to make the connections and to build them into a coherent network.

Nor are the cardinal and ordinal aspects of number the whole story. Consider the use of number in the following sentence, overheard when a teacher was talking to a group of children: 'There are three children in class four who are five.' This demonstrates the way in which we expect even young children to connect number symbols and words to very different situations. In the space of ten simple words the teacher has used numbers in three widely differing ways. The three children constitute a cardinal 3 and class four is an ordinal 4. The five (years old) is an example of number used in a measuring context. The different ways in which numbers are used in measurement will be discussed in Chapter 6 of this book.

Laying the foundations for understanding number

It is important for teachers of young children to lay foundations of experience and networks of connections on to which future experiences of number can be built. In this respect the cardinal aspect of number is a very limited view of what numbers are. It is not difficult, for example, to extend your understanding of numbers to make connections with negative numbers if the ordinal aspect and the associated picture of the number line are a strong part of your concept of number. All that is required is to extend the number line the other side of zero and to use appropriate labels for the new points. In a local department store the buttons in the lift are labelled 3, 2, 1 and 0 for the 3rd, 2nd, 1st and ground floors. How mathematically pleasing to note that the button for the basement is labelled −1! This is a straightforward and obvious extension of ordinal number.

We would argue, therefore, that young children should do as much of their number work moving up and down number lines, or similar manifestations of the ordinal aspect, as they do manipulating sets of counters and blocks, so that they connect the symbol 3 and the word 'three' just as much with the idea of a label for a point or a position as with sets of things. We cannot stress too strongly that *numbers are not just about sets of things*.

We have talked about mathematical concepts as networks of connections between concrete situations, symbols, language and pictures, and highlighted the problem that understanding the concept involves one symbol being connected to a wide range of often very different situations. We have seen that even the basic and seemingly elementary concept of number has this problem built into it, with the same numeral being applied to very different experiences. The discussion about the possible overemphasis on the cardinal aspect at the expense of the ordinal aspect raises another point of general applicability and great significance to infant-teachers. There is a danger that we might continually reinforce just one particular connection in the network of connections constituting a mathematical concept at the expense of equally important or even ultimately more significant connections. If this one connection dominates the child's thinking about the concept, it may be difficult later to build on new experiences that do not readily connect with this part of the network. For example, if the idea that numbers are sets of things is continually reinforced in the early years and is the dominant connection, it is not surprising that negative numbers appear very mysterious when they are met later on. You can't think of −3 as a set of things! And if you cannot make connections with previous learning then no understanding but only rote learning can occur.

Learning with understanding progresses most smoothly by what Piaget called a process of *assimilation* of new ideas into existing networks of connections. When material does not connect readily to the existing network, understanding can be achieved only by a restructuring of that network in order to accommodate the new experiences. Many pupils clearly fail to achieve these restructurings, particularly in mathematics, and continue with their limited and inadequate networks of connections. It is because of this that we are emphasising the importance of infant-teachers providing experiences of number early on, particularly activities with the number line, that will provide a basis for later learning with understanding when pupils encounter numbers other than those used for counting.

Understanding zero

Close your eyes and think of zero. Describe the image in your mind.

- It's very hard to think of nothing!
- I can see a set with nothing in it, like a circle with nothing inside.
- I thought of putting out three chocolates then eating them!

Is zero a number? Many people feel that it isn't really a proper number, not like one, two or three. It's just nothing. In fact it's not uncommon for the word 'nothing' to be attached quite freely to the symbol 0.

A group of student-teachers were given a table showing the numbers of children in a class with birthdays in each month and asked which month had the smallest number of birthdays. Some of them had great difficulty in accepting that the month without any birthdays had the smallest number, because they did not think of zero as a number. This fixation on the idea that zero is nothing is, of course, part of the overemphasis on the cardinal aspect of number. If you have a set of 0 objects in your hand then, of course, you have nothing in your hand. But is zero nothing more than nothing? We have already seen that the cardinal view of a number is very limited. Once we consider the ordinal aspect, zero is then not just as good a number as any other but becomes a very significant and important number. It is the point before one on the number line, and sometimes the starting point; it is the ground floor in the department store; it is midnight on my digital watch. A temperature of zero degrees is certainly not an absence of temperature!

So understanding the concept of zero involves connecting the symbol and the language, not just with 'nothing' and empty sets but also with ordinal pictures of number where zero is very definitely something.

- The problem is that we sometimes call it zero, we sometimes call it nought and sometimes nothing. Other numbers like one have only one name.
- When children do take away sums and get nothing left they tend to say 'nothing', but when they count backwards they always say 'zero' at the end, like a countdown for a spaceship.
- Counting backwards is very clearly an ordinal aspect of number, isn't it?
- Do books have a page number zero?

Does this book have one? How could you label the pages that come before page 1?

A note on negative numbers

We would like to suggest at this point that if greater emphasis is given to the ordinal aspect then negative numbers become very much easier to understand than fractions and decimals. There is, therefore, a good case for introducing them to children before any formal work on fractions or decimals, using appropriate contexts such as number lines, temperatures, page numbers in a book and going up and down in lifts. One teacher reported her experience of using a number line with 5-year-olds:

> I put a vertical number line on the wall with zero and numbers written above it, up to about 10. We did some counting forwards and backwards. Start at 3 and count forward two; where do you get to? That sort of thing. I had marked some points below zero, but not labelled them. I then asked them to start at 1 and count back three. They did this quite happily and one of the girls amazed me by saying that the point we had arrived at was minus two! I don't know where she got this idea from, but the others picked it up immediately and handled the idea with no difficulty. One of the children pointed out that there was the same pattern of numbers above zero as below zero.

Other teachers have found that young children can link this kind of number-line experience of negative numbers with their experience of repeatedly subtracting one on a calculator and slipping quite naturally and confidently below zero in the answers displayed.

A MATHEMATICAL ANALYSIS OF NUMBER

In this section we will outline the development of number from a mathematical point of view. Although this introduces some fairly abstract mathematical material, the infant-teachers we have worked with were unanimous that the analysis was both comprehensible and helpful to them in their own understanding of what they are doing in teaching number to young children. It is also important for those laying the foundations of number to know what later

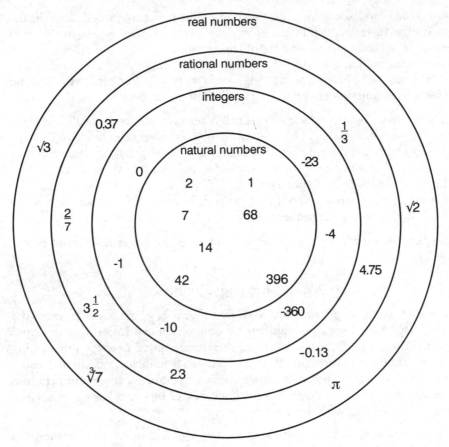

Figure 2.3   A mathematical development of number

ideas will have to be built on to those foundations, so that they do not limit children's experiences of number to only those that are appropriate to the numbers we use for counting.

Moving outwards from the centre of Figure 2.3, we will see that this development of number begins with the positive whole numbers, the numbers we use for counting, called the *natural numbers*, then proceeds to expand the set of numbers to what are called *integers*, then *rational numbers*, and finally *real numbers*. Notice that each of these sets includes the previous sets.

Unstable truths, changing properties and new possibilities

In the course of the following analysis we will consider each set of numbers in turn. Although the material here is directed at developing the teacher's own understanding of what numbers are, at each stage some pedagogical implications will become apparent. One important theme is that as we move from one set to the next larger set certain mathematical properties change. In fact some things that are true become no longer true, some things that are false become true and some things that were not possible become possible.

It is important for teachers of young children to be aware of this phenomenon. For example, many children from their early experiences of multiplying with whole numbers (such as '2 × 3' or '5 × 2') get the idea that multiplication makes things bigger. This would appear to be true in most cases they encounter – three sets of two objects make a set of six, 5 multiplied by 2 becomes 10, and so on. Perhaps their teachers even encourage them in this notion? But this is a false assertion when you come to multiplying by other sorts of numbers. For example, if you multiply 5 by 0.4 the answer (2) is smaller than the 5 you started with. The problem for us – as teachers – is that these ideas picked up through early experiences of number are very persistent and resistant to change. One 15-year-old girl, tackling a complicated algebraic equation, had correctly simplified it to '10 x = 5'. Having demonstrated impressive mathematical skills in attaining this point, she then turned to her teacher and announced that this was stupid because you couldn't multiply 10 by something and get an answer less than 10! The idea that multiplication makes things bigger – which presumably she had picked up when she was about 7 years of age – had persisted through all those years of mathematical experience.

Similar notions are that subtraction makes things smaller and that you cannot subtract a larger number from a smaller number. Many young children these days merrily pressing buttons on calculators are finding for themselves that the second of these assertions is clearly not true! If you haven't done this yourself try entering '2 – 6 =' on a simple calculator and see what happens.

The natural numbers

The set of *natural numbers* consists of those numbers that we use for counting: 1, 2, 3, 4, 5, 6, 7, 8, 9, 10, 11, . . . going on for ever. We have discussed earlier in this chapter how these numbers have both cardinal and ordinal aspects. The basic properties of these numbers are that there is a starting number (one), then for each number there is a next number. This nextness property is an important idea that children find fascinating, particularly with big numbers. They like the idea that no matter how big a number you write down there's always another one following it! 'What's the next number after forty-six? After fifty-nine? After one hundred and seventeen? After two thousand and ninety-nine?' (All those who said three thousand, like one of the authors, think again!)

The basic operation that can be performed on this set of natural numbers is addition. Any two numbers can be combined using this operation of addition to produce a number, called the sum of the two natural numbers, which is still in the set of natural numbers. So the natural number 2 added to the natural number 4 produces the natural number 6. Mathematicians say that the set is *closed* under addition. In other words, the addition of two natural number always produces a natural number.

Integers

The *inverse* of addition is the operation known as subtraction. We call it the inverse of addition because, for example, '6 – 2' is defined mathematically as meaning what must be added to 2 to give 6. But the set of natural numbers is not closed under this new operation of subtraction. For example, we cannot find a natural number that is equivalent to '2 – 6'. However, this becomes possible when we extend the set of numbers to include negative numbers and zero. The new set produced by this extension, called the *integers*, consists of all whole numbers, positive, negative and zero: . . . –4, –3, –2, –1, 0, 1, 2, 3, 4, . . . going on for ever in both directions. Note that the set of integers includes the set of natural numbers.

Now that we take 'number' to mean a member of this set of integers we find that subtraction – which was not previously always possible – becomes always possible. We can always subtract one number from another, for example, '2 – 6 = –4'. But other things have changed as well. For a start we've lost the idea of a first number, since now our set of numbers goes on for ever to the left of zero as well as to the right. So we could no longer say that there's nothing less than 1, or even that there's nothing less than zero. But much more significantly we should note that we have lost the cardinal aspect of number. We can no longer think of numbers as sets of things. We could not demonstrate '2 – 6', for example, by putting out sets of counters and manipulating them in some way. We could, of course, demonstrate it very simply with a number line, as one of our teachers showed with her 5-year-olds in the example quoted earlier in this chapter. This idea that numbers are sets of things, which, as we have seen, so dominates our thinking about number, really doesn't survive for very long in this mathematical development of the concept of number.

The next operation that appears in this development is multiplication. The set of integers is closed under multiplication. In other words, if you multiply one integer by another the result, called the product of the two integers, is an integer, every time. So, for example, the product of 6 and 2 is 12, the product of 6 and –2 (think of 6 steps of –2 on the number line) is –12. (The explanation of why mathematicians choose to define the product of –2 and –3 to be +6 is abstract, formal, and beyond the scope of this book!)

Rational numbers

The inverse of multiplication is the operation known as division. As with the relationship between subtraction and addition, we call this the inverse because, for example, '6 ÷ 2' is defined mathematically as meaning what must be multiplied by 2 to give 6. Now we find that the set of integers is not closed under this new operation of division. We cannot find integers that are equivalent to '2 ÷ 6' or '13 ÷ 5', for example. This then becomes possible by extending the set of numbers to include fractions (and decimals, of course, since decimals, like 0.37 and 4.3, are just fractions, such as $37/100$ and $43/10$, written in a particular way). The new set produced by this extension is called the set of *rational numbers*. It consists of all those numbers that are the *ratio* (hence the word rational) of two integers. For example, 2.3 is a rational number because it is the ratio of 23 to 10, i.e. it is equivalent to $23/10$, or '23 ÷ 10' (this is also written sometimes as 23:10). Similarly, 3½ is a rational number because it is equivalent to $7/2$; –0.13 is a rational number because it is equivalent to $-13/100$; and so on. Note that our set of rational numbers includes the set of integers, which itself included the set of natural numbers. So, for example, the integer –3 is also a rational number because it can be expressed as the ratio –³⁄₁, and the natural number 6 is also a rational number because it can be expressed as ratio ⁶⁄₁.

We now mean by 'number' a member of the set of all whole numbers, positive, negative or zero, and fractions or decimals. We are now able to label points on the number line between the integers. And we now are always able to divide one number by another. In other words, the set of rational numbers is closed under division (with one exception – division by zero is not permissible). We have moved on from the stage where the only ways we can deal with '13 ÷ 5' are by saying '5 doesn't go into 13', or by giving the result as '2 remainder 3'. We are now able to state an equivalence between '13 ÷ 5' and the rational number 2.6.

So something that was not always possible is now possible. Other things have changed as well. Suddenly we have lost the nextness property. What is the next number after 2.8? Is it 2.9? How about 2.81? or 2.801? Clearly, there is no next number. An associated gain is that it is now always possible to insert a number between two given numbers. When 'number' meant integer we could not always do this. There was no number between 6 and 7, for example. But now that 'number' means rational number, this is always possible. And you can go on and on doing this for ever. This is quite mind-boggling and requires a complete reorganisation of our thinking about what numbers are. For any two numbers, it appears that you can go on and on for ever putting more and more numbers in between them.

Young children find some difficulty with the concept of 'between' when applied to numbers, which is not surprising if the cardinal aspect is dominant in their thinking. 'Between' is a spatial concept. Young children handle it quite successfully in spatial contexts, such as following an instruction to sit between two individuals. Using this spatial notion of the concept of 'between', children can play simple games that involve finding numbers between two given numbers on a number line. This is another case where the number line, which is a spatial image of number, helps to develop an important concept.

Real numbers

There is yet another extension to the set of numbers, to what mathematicians call the set of *real numbers*. There are numbers that are not rational (i.e. not exact fractions or decimals) but which nevertheless represent real points on the number line, or real lengths. For example, the length of the diagonal of a square of side one unit is actually equal to the square root of 2 (this is written in symbols as $\sqrt{2}$). This is a real number, representing a real length, coming on the number line somewhere between 1.4 and 1.5 or, to be more precise, somewhere between 1.41 and 1.42 or, to be even more precise, somewhere between 1.414213 and 1.414214. But we cannot write down the value of this number exactly in our base-ten, place-value number system. (This means we could not write down a decimal number that, when multiplied by itself, gives the exact answer 2.) All we can say is that it lies between two particular rational numbers. Think of it like this: you can take the bit of the number line between 1

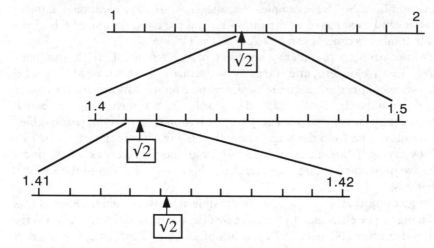

Figure 2.4   Locating the square root of 2

and 2 and divide it up into ten equal parts – when you have done this √2 will lie between two of the subdivisions, as shown in Figure 2.4. You can then divide this section into ten equal parts and √2 will again lie between two of them. And you can go on and on doing this for ever and ever, dividing the line into ten equal parts, becoming smaller and smaller, and none of your subdivisions will ever land exactly on √2!

Now √2 is not a freak. There are millions of numbers like this, in fact an infinite number of them – the square root of 3, the cube root of 7, and so on – all real numbers in the sense that they represent real points on the number line and real lengths. And yet if they are not rational numbers, if they cannot be expressed exactly as a fraction or a decimal, then we cannot actually write them down exactly in our number system! This is quite a dramatic loss, but what we have gained is a continuum of numbers, a complete number line in which every point is associated with a number.

The significance of this mathematical analysis

The reader may possibly have found some of the ideas in this last section difficult to understand. In other words, it may have been difficult to connect them with his or her existing network of ideas about what numbers are. But we hope that this experience might enable us all to appreciate what it is like for children as their experiences of number are gradually broadened, what it is like to have to come to terms with things that were true becoming false, the false becoming true, the impossible becoming possible and even, in our last step, the possible becoming impossible.

Finally, we would emphasise that this analysis reinforces the view that, even when young children are only at the stage of handling natural numbers, it is important that their activities with number are not limited to those that are relevant only to natural numbers. When other sorts of numbers are encountered later on they will then have some framework of experiences on which to build. In this chapter we have for this reason made much play, for example, on the importance of number-line experiences. In the next two chapters the analysis of number operations, particularly that of subtraction, will provide further illustrations of this important principle.

SOME ACTIVITIES WITH CHILDREN

Below are some examples of activities that might be used with children in the lower primary years to develop their understanding of both cardinal and ordinal number. The emphasis is on understanding. Clearly, activities like these need to be supplemented by others that focus more directly on counting-skills.

Activity 2.1: between
Objective   To develop the concept of 'between' in the context of numbers.
   Materials   A large number line drawn on card, using whatever range of numbers is appropriate for the children concerned; plastic token coins as prizes; a pack of cards with numerals 0 to 9 written on them; two red and three blue cardboard flags.
   Method   This is a game for a small group of children. One child, who is confident in using the number line, acts as umpire. The pack of cards is split into two halves, one to generate tens and the other to generate ones. Two cards are turned over by the umpire and a red flag placed at the corresponding point on the number line (e.g. if 2 and 3 are turned over, a flag is placed at 23). Two more cards are turned over and the other red flag positioned accordingly – such as the flag placed at 80 in Figure 2.5. Players then take it in turn to turn over three pairs of cards. Each pair generates a two-digit number. For each number the child must position a blue flag on the number line. If this is done correctly a penny is awarded by the umpire as a prize. If the blue flag lies between the red flags then an extra penny is awarded.
   In the example shown in Figure 2.5 the child has correctly positioned flags for 45, 12 and 06, and thus wins 4 pennies.

Activity 2.2: I have, who has? (cardinal numbers)
Objective   To develop recognition of cardinal numbers.
   Materials   Prepare a pack of ten cards, with sets of dots on one side and numerals on the other as shown in Figure 2.6. Note that these are arranged so

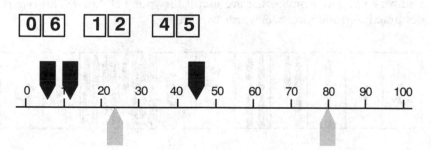

Figure 2.5   The between game (Activity 2.1)

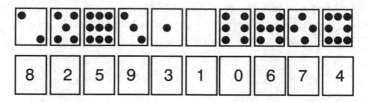

Figure 2.6 Cards for Activity 2.2

that the number of dots on one card corresponds to the numeral on the next, in a continuous cycle.

Method Three children play this version of the game. The cards are shuffled and dealt, the remaining card being placed dots-upwards in the centre of the table. The child who has the card with the numeral corresponding to the number of dots displayed places it beside the card in the centre. When all players have agreed that this is correct the card is turned over to reveal the next number to be sought. The first player to dispose of all his or her cards is the winner. As they play the children should say something along the lines of 'Who has three?' 'I have three . . . Who has five?' and so on.

Activity 2.3: green bottles
Objective To develop the connections between the cardinal and ordinal aspects of number.

Materials Three number strips labelled from 0 to 10; a pack of twenty-two cards, two each depicting ten green bottles, nine green bottles, eight green bottles, . . . one green bottle, blank.

Method This is a game for three children, each of whom has a number strip to work on. The cards are shuffled. One at a time each player turns over a card and places it on the ordinal number corresponding to the cardinal number of the set of green bottles shown. A player who at any stage turns over a number already covered on his or her strip can exchange it for any card he or she wishes from an opponent's number strip. The first player to get three consecutive numbers covered, as, for example, shown in Figure 2.7, wins the round. (The game can be linked to the song 'Ten green bottles' which is one of a number of counting-songs that are useful for young children. This one provides practice in counting backwards from ten.)

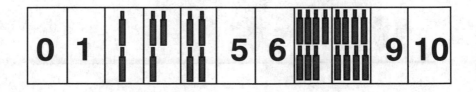

Figure 2.7 Relating cardinal and ordinal numbers in Activity 2.3

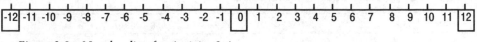

Figure 2.8   Number line for Activity 2.4

Activity 2.4: positive and negative
Objective   To extend children's experience of ordinal number into negative integers.

Materials   Prepare two dice (write on plain wooden or plastic cubes) – one with three faces labelled '+' and three labelled '–', the other numbered from 1 to 6; also required is a number line as shown in Figure 2.8, labelled from –12 to +12, and a coloured counter (or a small toy) for each player.

Method   This is a game for two to four children. To begin with, all their counters are placed on zero. In turn each player throws the two dice and makes the corresponding move on the number line with his or her counter. For example, if the dice show '–' and '3' the child moves their counter 3 steps to the left; if they show '+' and '3' the child moves the counter 3 steps to the right. Every time a player reaches (or passes) +12 or –12 he or she scores a point and returns to zero.

Activity 2.5: number displays
Objective   To connect together the language, symbols, concrete experiences and pictures of natural numbers.

Materials   Anything appropriate that the children can find at school or at home!

Method   Make a class display of each natural number from 1 to 10, to which children can add examples from time to time as they come across them. Small groups of children can be given particular responsibility for one display and be encouraged always to be on the lookout for examples of their special number.

For example, the display for 'four' might contain pictures of four people cut from a magazine, pictures of other sets of four things, such as four legs on a table or four legs on an animal, some examples of the written word 'four' cut from newspapers, foreign words for 'four', Roman numeral IV, a birthday card for a 4-year-old, a house number 4, a square, a photograph of a footballer with 4 on his shirt, a number line with 4 highlighted, page 4 from an old book, a clock showing 4 o'clock, a 4 o'clock programme cut from the TV schedules, facts about 4 such as '4 = 3 + 1', '4 = 7 – 3', and so on.

Activity 2.6: trial and improvement
Objective   To give young children an introduction to the idea of getting closer and closer to a solution, using a calculator, and to reinforce the idea of 'between'. (This is an important mathematical process that later provides valuable experience of irrational numbers.)

Materials   A calculator.

Method   The children are given a story along the following lines – 'I thought of a number. I put my number on a calculator, added 5 and multiplied

Table 2.1 Guesses for the number in Activity 2.6

Guess	Answer	High or low
5	50	too low
10	150	too low
20	500	too high
12	204	too low
15	300	got it!

by my number. The answer was 300. What was my number?' Clearly, the actual calculation used can be made easier or harder, as appropriate for the children. The calculator-key sequence for the above example can be recorded for them like this: □, + 5, × □, = . (This assumes that the calculator used is a basic calculator that ignores 'precedence of operators', e.g. it does not give precedence to multiplication over addition, but simply does the operations in the order they are entered.) They then try this procedure on the calculator with various numbers until they find the one that works. They should keep a record of the numbers they try and the answers obtained, as shown, for example, in Table 2.1, as they get closer and closer to the correct number. Having found one number that gives an answer too low (e.g. 10) and another too high (e.g. 20), their attention should be directed towards trying a number between these two (e.g. 12) as their next guess.

Later, when they have experience of using decimals on a calculator, this can extend to activities with irrational numbers, such as finding the square root of 10 (i.e. finding a number that multiplied by itself gives 10).

SUMMARY OF KEY IDEAS IN CHAPTER 2

1. The concept of a number involves a network of connections between the number symbol, the number name, pictures (such as the number line) and concrete situations (such as sets of counters).
2. There is a potential danger in continually reinforcing just one particular connection in the network of connections constituting a mathematical concept (such as numbers as sets of things) at the expense of equally important connections (such as numbers as points on a number line), particularly if the connection emphasised is of limited long-term significance.
3. The idea of a number as representing a set of things (e.g. three ducks, five fingers, ten counters) is called the cardinal aspect of number.
4. Sometimes numbers are used purely as labels (e.g. a number 3 bus). This is called the nominal aspect of number.
5. The idea of number as a label for putting things in order (e.g. page 3, room 9, floor −1) is called the ordinal aspect of number.
6. Counting brings together the cardinal and ordinal aspects of number.
7. The ordinal aspect of number, particularly in the form of the number-line picture, is the one on to which we can more readily build extensions to our understanding of number, such as negative numbers.
8. Zero does not represent just an empty set (i.e. nothing), but also has, for example, important ordinal meanings, such as a significant point on the number line, the ground floor in a building, or freezing point in a temperature scale.
9. The set of natural numbers consists of those numbers used for counting: 1, 2, 3, 4, 5, . . . going on for ever.

10. The set of integers comprises all whole numbers, positive, negative or zero: . . . –4, –3, –2, –1, 0, 1, 2, 3, 4, . . . going on for ever in both directions. The set of integers includes the set of natural numbers.

11. The set of rational numbers consists of all numbers that can be expressed as the ratio of two integers (i.e. all the integers themselves plus all types of fractions, including decimal fractions).

12. A real number is any number representing a point on a number line. The set of real numbers includes the rationals. It also includes irrational numbers like $\sqrt{2}$ that cannot be written down exactly in our number system, but that nevertheless represent real points or real lengths.

13. Although we cannot write down the exact value of an irrational number in our number system we can specify two rational numbers between which it lies (e.g. $\sqrt{2}$ lies somewhere between 1.414213 and 1.414214).

14. As the concept of a number develops – through the sets of naturals, integers, rationals, reals – the properties of number change. For example, the cardinality of number is lost in moving from naturals to integers, and the nextness property is lost in moving from integers to rationals.

15. It is important that young children's early experiences of number should not be limited to those that are relevant only to natural numbers (i.e. numbers as sets of things) but should also include an equal emphasis on activities based on the ordinal aspect (such as number lines).

SUGGESTIONS FOR FURTHER READING

Brown, M. (1986) Outdoor negatives, *Mathematics Teaching*, 114, pp. 14–15. (Brown describes how easily two young children picked up the concept of negative numbers and considers the implications for teaching.)

Dickson, L., Brown, M. and Gibson, O. (1984) *Children Learning Mathematics*, Cassell, London. (Section 3 is a review of research findings related to children's understanding of number that relates to the material in this chapter and the next two.)

Gelman, R. and Gallistel, C. R. (1978) *The Child's Understanding of Number*, Harvard University Press, Cambridge, Mass. and London. (This book is an excellent account of two psychologists' work on young children's acquisition and understanding of number concepts. It is intended for all those interested in cognitive development in general and those interested in the foundations of mathematical thought in particular.)

Haylock, D. (1995) *Mathematics Explained for Primary Teachers*, Paul Chapman Publishing, London. (Chapter 15 explains what primary-school teachers need to know about positive and negative integers.)

Hopkins, C., Gifford, S. and Pepperell, S. (eds) (1996) *Mathematics in the Primary School: a Sense of Progression*, David Fulton Publishers, London. (The second section of this book is devoted to number and gives practical suggestions for how pupils may be encouraged to develop a real feel for the subject.)

Nunes, T. and Bryant, P. (1996) *Children Doing Mathematics*, Blackwell, Oxford. (Chapters 1–3 of this review of research into children's understanding of mathematics provides some fascinating insights into the early stages of number, counting and the place-value system.)

Schwartz, S. (1995) En-chanting, fascinating, useful number, *Teaching Children Mathematics*, April, pp. 486–91. (Some discussion and practical examples to encourage young children to learn to count effectively.)

Skemp, R. R. (1986) *The Psychology of Learning Mathematics*, Penguin Books, Harmondsworth. (In part B of this very readable book, Skemp explores the meaning of number.)

Thompson, I. (1995) 'Pre-number activities' and the early years number curriculum, *Mathematics in School*, 24, no. 1, pp. 37–9. (An interesting account of some experiences that contribute to the concept of number in young children.)

Williams, E. and Shuard, H. (4th edition, 1994) *Primary Mathematics Today*, Longman, Harlow, Essex. (Chapters 3 and 5 provide clear step-by-step accounts of how to introduce number to young children.)

3

Add and Subtract

In this chapter and the next we will analyse the concepts of the four operations of addition, subtraction, multiplication and division. We are not concerned here with how to do calculations but, rather, with the network of connections that needs to be established for an understanding of what these operations are all about.

WHAT IS ADDITION?

Mark was trying to calculate the number of drinks we would have to provide so that each player in the football tournament could have three drinks during the day. Suddenly he announced a surprising discovery: 'You can use adding for this. I reckon that's why we learn it, so we can use it for things!'

To what sorts of situations can addition be connected? What stories might go with the symbols '12 + 3', for example? Here are some examples written by the infant-teachers in our group when asked this question:

- I've got 12 red pens and 3 blue pens. How many altogether?
- There are 12 girls and 3 boys. How many children?
- John had 12 conkers, his sister only had 3. How many conkers did they have altogether?

The aggregation structure: union of two sets

Responses like these, clearly interpreting the numbers in the cardinal sense, as sets of things, share a common *structure*. We will refer to this as the *aggregation* structure of addition. 'Aggregation' is a rather pretentious term meaning simply 'bringing together'. In each of the stories given above, two distinct sets of objects, with no members in common, are brought together to form what is called the *union of the two sets*, and the cardinal number of this new set is computed (see Figure 3.1).

Aggregation is an important structure that has to be linked with addition. It forms part of the network of connections that constitutes the concept of addition. Although it is usually experienced by children first through forming the

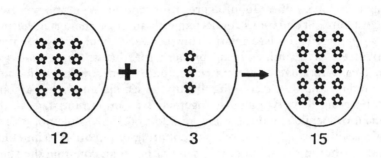

Figure 3.1   Addition: union of two sets

union of two sets, it extends quite easily to include situations where things other than sets are aggregated: putting two rods end to end to form a train; combining two prices to find the total cost; combining two weights, two quantities of liquid, and so on, to find out how much altogether.

The augmentation structure: counting-on and increasing

There are, however, situations that share a different structure, but that also have to be connected with addition. These are those situations that incorporate the ideas of *counting-on* or *increasing*. For example: start at 12 and count on 3; start with 12 and increase this by 3. We will refer to this structure as the *augmentation* structure of addition. 'Augmentation', meaning 'increasing', is another impressive-looking term for a simple idea. This idea often relates most strongly to the ordinal aspect of the numbers and is experienced most clearly in making moves on a number line (see Figure 3.2).

There are plenty of other situations in the contexts of money and various measurements that have essentially this same augmentation structure and that are to be connected with addition. For example, children have to learn to connect situations like these, using the idea of 'increasing', with the addition '12 + 3':

- The chocolate bar was 12p last week, but now the price has increased by 3p.
- The plant was 12 cm tall; then it grew another 3 cm.
- The jar contained 12 cl of water; then we poured in a further 3 cl.

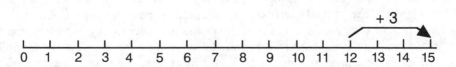

Figure 3.2   Addition: counting-on

The relationship between the two addition structures

Although we have talked about aggregation and augmentation as two different structures of situations connected with addition there is nevertheless a fairly straightforward clear relationship between them. In aggregation we have two sets or quantities being brought together to form a union or a whole. This is not hugely different perceptually from starting with one number or amount and then increasing this by the second number or amount. In fact, connecting these two models together is an important stage in the development of a child's understanding of addition. This is the point at which the child is able to apply the process of counting-on, in order to find out how many altogether in the union of two sets, rather than counting the complete set starting from 1. Counting-on using the number line is an important facilitator in this development.

Other more complex addition structures

On the whole most children find it not too difficult to connect together most of the concrete situations and pictures that go with the language and symbols of addition associated with the two structures we have considered here. We should note, however, that there are further, more complex structures of situations that are also part of the addition network but which many children find very difficult to connect with addition. These are particularly those where the language used in the problem cues the idea of subtraction. For example, '12 + 3' would be the appropriate calculation to link with each of the following word-problems, all of which contain 'subtraction' words, like 'spent', 'takes', 'less', 'difference', and yet are actually examples of various addition structures:

- John spent £3 this morning and now he has £12 left. How much did he have to begin with?
- Anne has some marbles. John takes 12 of them and Anne now has only 3 left. How many marbles did Anne have to begin with?
- Helen has £12 and this is £3 less than Anne. How much does Anne have?
- Model A costs £12 more than Model B and £3 less than Model C. What is the difference in the costs of Model B and Model C?
- John is 12 cm taller than Helen. Over the next year they both grow taller, but Helen grows 3 cm less than John grows. How much taller than Helen is John now?

We are fairly confident that most primary-school children would give the answer '9' to all these questions! However, we have given these examples only to highlight the potential problem of children responding superficially to the cues provided by random words in the problem rather than grasping its structure. Teachers should be aware that, even though the most familiar applications of addition to situations with the aggregation and augmentation structures are readily mastered by most children, there are other aspects of addition associated with more complex language structures that are far from straightforward. We realise that the reader may well feel that the logical structures of the word-problems given above are somewhat contrived and we would accept that. However, when it comes to understanding *subtraction* we find that even some of the most familiar situations to be associated with this operation are logically challenging. Subtraction is altogether a much more complex affair than addition.

WHAT IS SUBTRACTION?

Mary, a bright 7-year-old, had written down these calculations: $9 - 3 = 5$; $12 - 4 = 7$; $15 - 6 = 8$; $14 - 10 = 3$; $10 - 7 = 2$. Her teacher (T) talked to Mary (M) about what she had done:

T. Now, Mary, what sort of sums are these?
M. Takes.
T. What's this first one say then?
M. 9 take 3?
T. 9 take away 3. What's the answer for 9 take away 3?
M. [*Looking at her answer*] Five. No, that's wrong, it's 6.
T. Well, what about this one? 12 take away 4?
M. Seven?
T. [*Putting out 12 cubes*] Show me 12 take away 4.
M. [*Manipulating the cubes*] 1, 2, 3, 4. That leaves 1, 2, 3, 4, 5, 6, 7, 8. Eight.
T. How did you get 7?
M. [*Pointing to a number line at the top of the page in her textbook*] I did it on this. Look. [*She puts her finger on the 12 on the number line and counts back 4 until it rests on the 8.*] There you are, it's 7!
T. [*Pointing to Mary's finger resting on the 8*] Why isn't the answer 8?
M. Because I've taken that one away.
T. Well, show me 9 take away 3 then.
   [*Mary carries out the same procedure on the number line, until her finger rests on the 6.*]
M. It's 5. [*She looks puzzled*]
T. But why isn't it 6? You're pointing to the 6.
M. No, it must be 5, because I've taken the 6 away.
T. So what do you really think is the answer for 9 take away 3?
M. Six.

The above dialogue illustrates just how potentially difficult it is to make valid connections between some of the different structures associated with subtraction. It also highlights a significant point about language that will emerge in the subsequent analysis of this concept.

The partitioning structure: take away

First, we should ask to what sort of situations can subtraction be applied? What stories could we write to go with, say, '$12 - 3$'? These are some teachers' responses to this question:

• There are 12 birds sitting on a fence. Then 3 fly away. How many still on the fence?

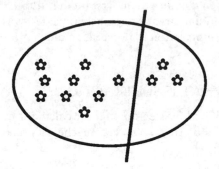

Figure 3.3   Subtraction: partitioning

- There are 12 trees in a forest and an elephant knocks over 3 of them. How many trees left standing?
- I had 12 chocolates and ate 3 of them. How many left for tomorrow?

These stories all have basically the same plot. They share what we will call the *partitioning* structure (see Figure 3.3). We find that most teachers, student-teachers and children, when asked to write a story for subtraction, produce a version of this plot. There is a set of 12 things to start with and somehow 3 of them are partitioned off, taken away, removed, eaten, destroyed, lost, blown up, stolen, given away, or mortally wounded. In each case the question posed is, essentially, *how many are left?*

All three of the stories given above use the cardinal aspect of number. Stories with similar plots can also be written with numbers used for money or measuring. These are still examples of the partitioning structure, but now the question posed is, essentially, *how much is left?*

- I had 12p and I spent 3p. How much did I have left?
- There were 12 litres of wine in my cellar. We drank 3 litres. How much wine is left in my cellar now?
- We had 12 kg of coal, but we have used 3 kg. How much coal do we have left?

Subtraction not just partitioning

As with most mathematical symbols, we find that '12 – 3' may be connected to a wide range of very different situations. Subtraction is by no means just the partitioning plot. It is not just a synonym for 'take away'. Partitioning is just one subtraction structure, and a very limited one at that.

The following stories written by children for '12 – 3' illustrate five different structures of situations connected with subtraction. They demonstrate the range of connections that have to be made to develop a fuller understanding of the concept (children's spelling retained):

1. There were 12 books on the pile. The teacher took 3 of them away. How many left?
2. If my friend is 12 and his brother is 3 how older is he?

3. There were 12 soldiers 3 were ill how many were not ill?
4. The price of a choc bar was 12p the shop thought it was deer and took 3p off.
5. Jhon was 3 and 9 year latter he was 12.

Story (1) is another example of the familiar and most frequently used *partitioning* structure, with the associated language of 'take away – how many left?' The four other structures illustrated by the other four stories are considered in turn below.

The comparison structure

Story (2), however, introduces a different but very important aspect of subtraction, what we will call the *comparison* structure. In this structure the basic plot for '12 – 3' is that the two numbers 12 and 3 are compared. A line of 12 blue cubes is compared with a line of 3 red cubes (see Figure 3.4). A price of 12p is compared with a price of 3p. A weight of 12 kg is compared with a weight of 3 kg. Notice one significant difference between this structure and that of partitioning. Both the 12 and the 3 are there right from the start. In the partitioning structure you start with the 12, and the 3 you take away is part of the 12. Here, in the comparison structure, you have the 12 and the 3 side by side and you compare them.

There are three versions of the punch-line in stories with the comparison plot. The child who produced story (2) above asked 'how older is he?' presumably meaning 'how much older?' The question could also have been 'how much younger?' or 'what is the difference in their ages?' Similarly, when comparing two sets we may ask 'how many more in A?' or 'how many less in B?' or 'what is the difference between A and B?' (Some people may prefer the word 'fewer' to 'less' in this context, but it seems to us that the distinction between 'fewer' and 'less' is disappearing from everyday English.)

'Difference' is used here in a technical mathematical sense. We do not mean, for example, that the difference between the red cubes and the blue cubes in Figure 3.4 is their colour! We should note that the difference between 3 and 12 is the same as the difference between 12 and 3, but '3 – 12' is not the same as '12 – 3'. Notice also the interpretation of 'difference between' on the number

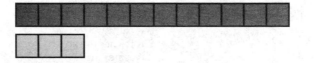

Figure 3.4   Subtraction: comparison

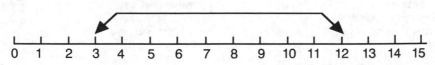
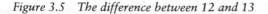

Figure 3.5   The difference between 12 and 13

line, as illustrated in Figure 3.5, where '12 – 3' is represented by the gap between 12 and 3. This is a powerful image of subtraction and one that is often used in mental calculations – many people when calculating '105 – 78' mentally, for example, would deal with it essentially by adding together the bits needed to fill the gap between 78 and 105, namely '5 + 2 + 20' (in various orders), i.e. by picturing the difference between the two numbers, possibly using a mental image of a number line.

We want to emphasise at this point how different are the actual manipulations of, say, cubes on a table, when carrying out procedures that incorporate the two structures of partitioning and comparison. In the first instance, you put out a set of 12 cubes and take 3 of them away. In the second case you put out a set of 12 cubes and a set of 3 cubes and compare them. Yet both manipulations represent the same subtraction and correspond to the same symbols, '12 – 3'. Comparing two sets or quantities to find out how many more or how many less is just as valid and important an interpretation of subtraction as taking something away from a set or quantity.

The language of comparison

The language of comparison merits some special consideration. When we make a comparison between two quantities, using subtraction, there are always two equivalent ways of stating the relationship, two sets of language available. Mathematically this is expressed by the statement:

$$A > B \text{ is equivalent to } B < A$$

In words, this reads: 'A is greater than B' is equivalent to 'B is less than A'. Hence we could either make a comparison statement using the language that

Table 3.1 Language of comparison

A is more than B	B is less than A
A is greater than B	
A is larger than B	B is smaller than A
A is bigger than B	
A is taller than B	B is shorter than A
A is longer than B	
A is higher than B	B is lower than A
A is further than B	B is nearer than A
A is wider than B	B is narrower than A
A is fatter than B	B is thinner than A
A is heavier than B	B is lighter than A
A holds more than B	B holds less than A
A costs more than B	B costs less than A
A is dearer (more expensive) than B	B is cheaper (less expensive) than A
A takes longer than B	B takes less time than A
A is later than B	B is earlier (sooner) than A
A happens after B	B happens before A
A is older than B	B is younger than A
A is faster (quicker) than B	B is slower than A
A is hotter (warmer) than B	B is colder (cooler) than A

focuses on the larger quantity, such as that in the left-hand column in Table 3.1, or we could make an equivalent statement using the language that focuses on the smaller quantity, such as that in the right-hand column.

Three stages in developing the use of this language of comparison can be identified. For example, when comparing the line of 12 blue cubes with the line of 3 red cubes shown in Figure 3.4, in the first stage the child would note simply that 'there are more blue than red' and, of course, using the equivalent statement, that 'there are less red than blue'. No actual numbers are involved in these statements. The second stage is to note that 'there are 9 more blue than red' and 'there are 9 less red than blue', actually specifying the numerical difference. The third stage is to make the generalised statements, '12 is 9 more than 3' and '3 is 9 less than 12'. It is these last observations that are connected with the subtraction '12 – 3'.

It is an interesting observation that in practice, when we make comparisons, in most situations, particularly those related to personal possession of number, money or size, we tend to use language from the left-hand column in Table 3.1 – language that makes the greater quantity the subject of the sentence. A child will complain 'It's not fair, he's got more than me', but rarely 'I've got less than him!' Inevitably the one with more becomes the focus of attention. It is significant that we seem to have more commonly used words in everyday language to express the greater aspect than we do to express the smaller one, as can be seen from Table 3.1, where 'less', 'smaller' and 'shorter' seem to have two opposites each. It is also significant that the last sentence was automatically written using the word 'more', with the longer list as the subject, when it could equally well have been written as 'we actually have less words in everyday language to express the smaller aspect'. In order to build up connections with the full range of language, teachers asking pupils to make comparisons need to make a conscious effort to use 'more' no more than they use 'less', or, to put it another way, to use 'less' no less than they use 'more'. In fact we would advocate a rule that whenever children make a comparison they should make the two equivalent statements. So if they have observed that a pencil costs 3p more than a ball-point, they should immediately be encouraged to make the equivalent observation that the ball-point costs 3p less than the pencil. If measuring leads to the discovery that Reuben is 3 cm taller than Rachel, then we also make a sentence beginning, 'Rachel is . . .'.

There is a subtle problem built into the notion of 'less than' that makes it considerably more difficult for a child to handle than 'more than'. This is illustrated by the following account of an interaction with a 7-year-old:

> I put 2 sweets in my hand and 5 in Clare's. She seemed to understand that she had more than me. I asked how many more did she have. She said she had 5 more. That seemed a reasonable response – although not the one I was looking for – since she did have 5 and she did have more. We did the obvious thing of laying our sweets out on the table and matching them, so that the 3 more in her pile could be identified. She quickly cottoned on to the idea that she had 3 more than me. We did a few more examples like this and she handled 'more than' with considerable success. I then put 2 sweets in her hand and 5 in mine. With a bit of prompting she managed to say that she had less than me. I then asked her how many less. This completely defeated her,

even when we laid out our sweets and matched them. The best she could manage was, 'I've got 2 more less than you.' I then realised what a difficult task I had set Clare. I wanted her to look at the 2 sweets in her hand and make a statement beginning with the words 'I've got 3 . . . ' (I've got 3 less than you). But she didn't have those 3, I had them!

The point to note here is that when we use subtraction in this comparison structure to make statements of the form '3 is 9 less than 12' we appear to be making a statement about the 3, since we begin with the words '3 is . . . ', but in fact the 9 is actually part of the 12, not part of the 3. If someone says that they have £9 less than you, the odd thing about the structure of the language used here is that they don't have the £9 in question. You have it! These examples underline the importance of establishing the equivalence of two statements like 'I have 9 more than you' and 'You have 9 less than me'.

There is one further point to make about the language of comparison. When children encounter the language related to the greater quantity (such as 'more than', 'longer than', 'heavier than') in a word-problem, these particular words can often signal addition rather than subtraction. For example, consider this word-problem: 'John has £58 and Helen has £37. How much more than Helen does John have?' Many primary-school children, rather than engaging with the logical structure of the problem, will simply respond to the cue given by the word 'more' by adding the numbers 58 and 37.

The complement-of-a-set structure

Story (3) has what we call the *complement-of-a-set* structure (see Figure 3.6). The basic plot for '12 – 3' in this structure is that there is a set of 12 things, 3 of which have some attribute. The question posed is how many do *not* have this attribute. The word 'not' is usually central to the punch-line of stories with this plot.

This structure is very similar to partitioning and it would seem to be not too difficult for children to learn to connect the same symbols and arithmetic processes with these two different kinds of situations.

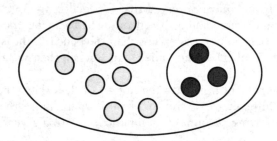

Figure 3.6 Subtraction: complement of a set

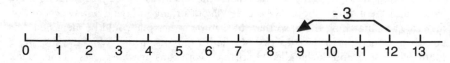

Figure 3.7 Counting back on the number line

The reduction structure: counting back

Story (4) has what we call the *reduction* structure. This subtraction structure is clearly the reverse of the augmentation addition structure. The basic plot for '12 – 3' in this case is that you start at the 12 and count back or reduce the quantity by 3. Examples of this structure might be a 12-stone person losing 3 stones of weight after dieting, or a £12 article in a store being reduced by £3. The most important picture of this subtraction structure – and therefore an important experience for children – is counting back (or down) along the number line (see Figure 3.7).

The inverse-of-addition structure

Finally, we can identify a fifth category of situations associated with subtraction, illustrated by story (5) above. We call this the *inverse-of-addition* structure. In many ways this would appear to be the most important and fundamental subtraction structure. As was seen in Chapter 2, from a mathematical point of view subtraction is actually defined as the inverse-of-addition. In this structure the plot for '12 – 3' is essentially 'What must be added to 3 to make 12?' The remarkable thing about story (5) is that it actually begins with the 3. The child who made up this story has clearly interpreted '12 – 3' as meaning that you start at the 3 and add on until you get to 12, as illustrated on the number line in Figure 3.8.

This is undoubtedly the most difficult of the five structures we are considering here for children to connect with subtraction. This is probably once again related to the fact that the language involved signals addition rather than subtraction. For example, consider these two word-problems: 'I have £37 and I want to buy a radio costing £49. How much more do I need?' and 'The radio cost £37 last week and £49 this week. By how much has the price gone up?' These are again examples where many children will pick up the wrong cues from the words 'more' and 'gone up' – words signalling addition – and respond by adding the numbers 37 and 49.

Some structural apparatus provides concrete experience of procedures which incorporate this inverse-of-addition subtraction structure very clearly.

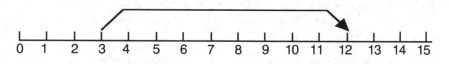

Figure 3.8   Subtraction: inverse-of-addition on the number line

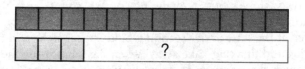

Figure 3.9   Inverse-of-addition with structural apparatus

For example, with Colour-Factor rods '12 – 3' can become a question of finding which rod has to be added to the 3-rod to make a train the same length as the 12-rod (see Figure 3.9).

Once again we want to emphasise how significantly different from other models is the manipulation of materials involved in this subtraction structure. Earlier we were putting out a set of 12 cubes and taking away 3, then we were putting out sets of 12 and 3 cubes and comparing them, and now we would be putting out 3 cubes and adding on further cubes until we have reached a total of 12. Yet all these – partitioning, comparison, inverse-of-addition, as well as complement of a set and reduction – are situations to which the subtraction symbol has to be connected. They are all part of the complex network of connections that constitute the concept of subtraction. This is a most dramatic example of the way in which one symbol is used in mathematics to represent many different and varied situations.

Overemphasis on 'take away'

When we discussed the cardinal aspect in our analysis of the concept of number in Chapter 2, we indicated that there was the potential problem of this one connection (the cardinal aspect) being emphasised too strongly in the early years of schooling at the expense of other equally important connections (such as the ordinal aspect). The same thing can be said of 'take away' in relation to subtraction. Infant-teachers may focus on the experiences of the take-away interpretation of subtraction almost to the exclusion of situations with the other structures. As we have seen, partitioning is only one subtraction structure, and a very limited one. Yet when teachers set out to demonstrate a subtraction question to children they almost invariably put out a set of objects and take some away. The comparison and inverse-of-addition structures are, in the long run, much more significant, yet too many children (and teachers) seem fixated on the partitioning structure and the associated language of 'take away'.

- I think I've just seen the light! I always used to think that the subtraction symbol (–) just meant 'take away'. But it doesn't, does it? It means lots of other things as well.
- But we always say 'take away' when we write the symbol down.
- I must admit I will find it difficult to think of it as meaning anything other than 'take away'.

Of course, subtraction is sometimes 'take away', and when this is so it is appropriate to use this language. But there are two levels of language involved here – the formal language that goes with the concept, such as 'twelve subtract three', and the language appropriate to the physical situation. This might be 'twelve take away three', but it might be 'twelve count back three', or the language of comparison, and so on. The problem that Mary encountered in the dialogue quoted at the start of this section would appear to be related to the fact that she is saying and thinking 'take away' when she is not using the partitioning structure for which the language of 'take away' is appropriate, but she is using the reduction structure and should be talking about 'counting back'.

Later in their mathematical careers, children are going to encounter calculations like '6 – (–3) = ?'. With the proper foundation of the network of connections associated with subtraction laid in the early years that has been outlined above, there is no need for subtraction with negative numbers like this to be such a mystery for them as it seems to be for many students of mathematics.

D. What do you make of this?

M. I know the answer's 9, but I don't understand why.

C. It's because two minuses make a plus.

D. Why do you smile when you say that?

C. I suppose it's because I know it's no explanation really. It's just a trick or a rule someone taught me. I've no idea what it means or why it works!

Most people feel very uneasy about a statement like '6 – (–3) = 9'. This is not surprising in view of the dominance of 'take away' in our understanding of subtraction. If you say to yourself 'six take away negative three' then you will probably imagine a pile of six objects and wonder what on earth taking away negative three of them could mean. We must assume, of course, that –3 itself has some meaning for us. Let's connect it, for example, with a temperature (or a lift button, or your bank balance, whichever is closest to your experience). Now connect the symbols '6 – (–3)' with a temperature situation, using the comparison structure, for example. Does this suddenly make sense? If the temperature inside is 6 degrees and the temperature outside is –3 degrees, then . . . ? (How much hotter is it inside? How much colder outside?) Or connect the symbols with the number line, using the inverse-of-addition structure. If you start at –3, what do you have to add to get to 6? This is not difficult mathematics, once the symbols are connected to the appropriate structures.

Other more complex subtraction structures

Finally, as we saw earlier with addition, there are a number of other variations of structures of situations that do not fall neatly into the main categories that we have outlined here but which also are connected with subtraction. Again many of these use language (such as 'earned', 'more than', 'grows') that cues addition rather than subtraction, as in these examples of word-problems, all of which should actually be connected with '12 – 3':

- John earned £3 this morning and now he has £12. How much did he have to begin with?
- Helen has £12 and this is £3 more than Anne. How much does Anne have?
- Model A costs £12 more than Model B and £3 more than Model C. How much more than Model B is Model C?
- John is 12 cm taller than Helen. Over the next year they both grow taller, but Helen grows 3 cm more than John grows. How much taller than Helen is John now?

We would predict fairly confidently that most primary-school children would give the answer '15' to all these problems. However, these are problems with somewhat contrived and complex logical structures. They are given here simply to illustrate the potential problem of children responding merely to the cues in the situation rather than grasping the structure. The main focus of our work with children must be on establishing the connections between the symbols for subtraction and the language, picture and concrete situations associated with the five main structures analysed above.

The network of connections for understanding subtraction

So, let us summarise what we see as the teacher's task in developing children's understanding of subtraction. It would appear to be a question of helping the child to build up a network of connections between the symbols and the various structures that have been outlined in the above analysis:

- partitioning,
- comparison,
- complement of a set,
- counting back/reducing,
- inverse-of-addition;

and then to operate on a range of concrete and real situations, such as:

- sets of objects,
- coins,
- prices,
- lengths,
- ages;

to experience various subtraction procedures on the picture of number in the number line; and then to connect all this with the language of subtraction, both the formal word 'subtract' and the range of language appropriate to the various actual physical situations, with a particular focus on the extensive language of comparison.

That's quite an agenda! And we have not even considered the problems of doing the sums. Perhaps we should be grateful for the emergence of inexpensive calculators, so that at times we can concentrate on building up the children's understanding, by discussing what are the appropriate operations to connect with various situations, and leave the calculator's electronic circuits to do the calculations. Certainly it is the case that knowing what calculation to do in a given situation is more important than just being able to do the calculation. Perhaps the most basic question of arithmetic is 'Which buttons do you press on the calculator to answer this problem?'

So how will understanding of subtraction be recognised? By the child demonstrating that connections between the concrete situations, symbols, language and pictures of subtraction are being established. By showing us what the symbols '12 − 3' mean in terms of a set of counters, or two sticks of cubes placed side by side, or on a number line. By being able to make up number stories using more than one subtraction structure, like the stories (1) to (5) cited above. By knowing what calculation to enter on a calculator – for a take-away situation; for finding out how many are not; for counting back or reducing; for comparing two numbers to find out how many more or how many less; and for determining what must be added to one number to give another.

SOME ACTIVITIES WITH CHILDREN

The following are some examples of activities that can be used with groups of lower-primary children to develop their understanding of addition and subtraction. The focus here is on understanding the operations and making connections, rather than on the development of skills in manipulating numbers.

Activity 3.1: stories (addition, subtraction)
Objective To help children connect the symbols for addition and subtraction with a wide range of situations and language.

Method Read the children some examples of stories for addition statements, such as '3 + 5'. For example: 'One day Henny Penny laid 3 eggs and Turkey Lurkey laid 5 eggs. How many eggs is that altogether?' Get them to make up their own stories, writing them down or even tape-recording them, for examples like '4 + 8' or '9 − 3'. Use larger numbers if appropriate. Children should share their stories with one another and discuss their validity.

Then to encourage the use of different models and contexts give specific words or phrases to be included in the story, such as 'more than', 'less than', 'increased', 'reduced', 'younger', 'older'. Alternatively, give the children the start of the story and ask them to complete it. For example, for '9 − 3': 'Mary had 9 marbles, but Tom only had . . . '

Activity 3.2: swaps (addition and subtraction)
Objective To develop connections between language, symbols, concrete experience and pictures, for the concepts of addition and subtraction.

Materials Coins, 1p and 10p; base-ten materials (longs and units); number lines; a calculator; blank paper; a collection of simple stories for addition and subtraction; cards with the following words written on them: story, number line, picture, calculator, symbols, coins, blocks.

Method A small group of children is given a starting point and a selection of cards indicating a sequence of swaps to be achieved. When they have completed all their swaps they report to the teacher on what they have done.

Figure 3.10 shows an example with a story given as the starting point, and a challenge in this case to swap this for coins, a calculator sum, then for a number-line drawing and finally for symbols. The children might respond to this challenge by putting out 8p and a further 4p to make the 12p required, enter '8 + 4 =' or even '12 − 8 =' on their calculator, draw an arrow on a number line from 8 to 12, and finally write on their piece of paper the symbols '8 + 4 = 12' or '12 − 8 = 4'. The starting point may be a story, a number-line diagram, a sum written in symbols or a picture, and the sequence of swaps varied appropriately.

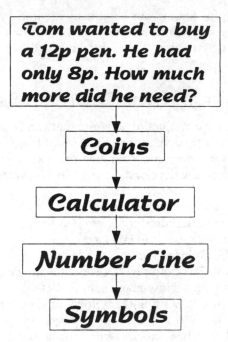

Figure 3.10   Swaps (Activity 3.2)

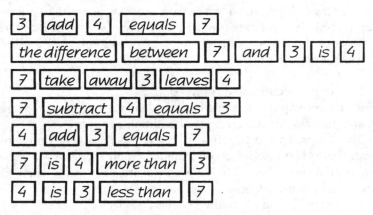

Figure 3.11   Sentences for 3, 4 and 7 (Activity 3.3)

Activity 3.3: sentences (addition and subtraction)
Objective   To develop language patterns for addition and subtraction.

Materials   Several sets of strips of card with the following words or phrases written on them: add, subtract, and, take away, more than, less than, the difference, between, makes, leaves, is, equals; several sets of cards with appropriate numerals written on them; counting materials; a number line.

Method   A small group of children is given three numbers and challenged to use the cards to make up as many different sentences as they can using these three numbers. Figure 3.11 shows some examples of what might be achieved with the numbers 3, 4 and 7. The counting materials and number line are used simply to give concrete embodiment to the children's thinking about the numbers and to check their sentences.

Activity 3.4: number-line add and subtract
Objective   To provide experience of the augmentation structure of addition and the reduction structure of subtraction through counting-on and counting-back on a number line.
Materials   Two conventional dice numbered from 1 to 6; a counter (or an appropriate small toy); a number line marked from 0 to 12; a small flag of some sort. (For a more advanced game, use dodecahedron dice with faces numbered from 1 to 12, and a number line marked from 0 to 24.)
Method   This is a simple game for a small group of players. The player going first places the flag on the number line on any number of his or her choosing. Each then plays in turn as follows. They place the counter on the zero mark, throw the first die and move the counter to this number. Throw the second die and predict which number they will finish on when they have moved this number of places. They then move and, if correct, win a point. If they finish on the number with the flag on they get a bonus point.
   A subtraction version can also be played, in which the counter starts on 12 and moves are made towards zero. This time they have to predict which number they will land on after each of the two throws of the dice, so it is possible to win three points on each turn: one for the first prediction, one for the second, and one if they finish up on the flagged number.

Activity 3.5: what did I do? (12, +, – version)
Objective   To give children experience of addition and subtraction as inverses of each other.
Materials   One calculator for each pair of children; plastic pennies as prizes.
Method   This is a game for two players and an umpire. The players take it in turns to challenge each other with the question 'What did I do?' The number 12 is entered on the calculator by the umpire. Player A takes the calculator and presses either '+' or '–', followed by a single digit and the equals key. The calculator is then passed to player B who has to (1) state which keys A pressed, and (2) press either '+' or '–', followed by a single digit and the equals key, in order to get the 12 back on display. The umpire awards B one penny for correctly stating which keys A pressed and a further penny for getting back to 12. It is then player B's turn to challenge A.
   An interesting discussion might ensue if, after performing an operation, the first player hands the calculator to the second player with 12 still on display.

Activity 3.6: more than/less than
Objective   To strengthen understanding of 'more than', 'less than', and to link these ideas with 'take away' and 'difference'.
Materials   A set of 40 plastic cubes that can be linked together; 20 cards, 10 saying 'more than' and 10 'less than'; two pots or boxes.

Method This is a game for two children plus a third acting as umpire. Each player has 20 cubes to start with. The pack of cards is placed face down on the table. Players play in turn as follows.

One player stands any number of cubes, joined together, on the table, stating how many have been played. (The first player in each turn must play two or more cubes, unless there is only one left.) The second player then plays any number of cubes different from the first. The top card is turned over. If it says 'more than' the player who has played more than the other wins. Similarly, if it says 'less than' the one playing less than the other wins.

The winning player actually wins the *difference* between the two columns of cubes. These cubes are then taken from the larger pile and placed in the winner's pot, where they stay until the game is over. The equal residues are then returned to the players and the game continues, until each player's supply of cubes is reduced to one. These remaining single cubes are put into the pots. The object of the game is to get the most cubes into your pot. Note that on a 'less than' card you win cubes from the other person's pile, but on a 'more than' card the winnings come from your own pile.

The umpire's job is to insist that the players say the appropriate words at each stage and to check on fair play. They must say, for example, 'I play two cubes', when putting out their cubes. The winner each time must use correctly the words written on the card (i.e. 'more than' or 'less than') and the word 'difference' – otherwise they forfeit their winnings. For example, they might say: 'My two is less than your five, and the difference is three.'

A variation is to give each player one pound in small change instead of cubes.

Activity 3.7: I have, who has? (addition and subtraction stories)
Objective To practise using all the models and language for addition and subtraction.
Materials Prepare a set of 16 cards with 'questions' on one side and the corresponding 'answers' on the other side, using the same cyclic scheme as explained in Activity 2.2, with the question on one card answered on the reverse side of the next. In this version use as questions a series of statements or stories covering a wide range of situations with different structures and associated language for addition and subtraction. Make sure that there are no duplicate answers. Here are some suggestions, with the corresponding answers in brackets after each one:

1. Start at 4 and count on 7. $(4 + 7)$
2. John has 3 apples, Peter has 8. How many more than John has Peter? $(8 - 3)$
3. Gill had 8 apples. She ate 5. How many left? $(8 - 5)$
4. Twelve subtract seven. $(12 - 7)$
5. The difference between 4 and 7. $(7 - 4)$
6. Eight add four. $(8 + 4)$
7. A plant 7 cm tall grows by 5 cm. How tall is it now? $(7 + 5)$
8. A 12p chocolate bar was reduced by 5p. What does it now cost? $(12 - 5)$
9. I want to buy a book costing £7. I only have £3. How much more do I need? $(7 - 3)$

10. John is 4, Jack is 8. How much younger is John? (8 – 4)
11. Start at 12 and count back 8. (12 – 8)
12. There are 12 children. If 4 are going on a school trip, how many are not going? (12 – 4)
13. One sweet costs 4p, another costs 3p. How much for them both? (4 + 3)
14. The sum of 7 and 4. (7 + 4)
15. I am 12. How old was I three years ago? (12 – 3)
16. How many less than 8 is 7? (8 – 7)

Method The cards are shuffled and dealt between three players, with the remaining card placed in the centre of the table. The game is then played in exactly the same way as in Activity 2.2.

SUMMARY OF KEY IDEAS IN CHAPTER 3

1. Two categories of situations to which the language and symbols of addition can be connected are those with the aggregation structure (including the union of two sets with no members in common) and those with the augmentation structure (including counting-on and increasing). These are the main addition structures, but not the only ones.
2. Five categories of situations to which the language and symbols of subtraction can be connected are partitioning, complement of a set, reduction (including counting-back), comparison, and inverse-of-addition. These are the main subtraction structures, but not the only ones.
3. Particularly important in understanding subtraction is the extensive language of comparison.
4. For any comparison statement that makes the greater quantity the subject of the sentence there is an equivalent statement that makes the smaller quantity the subject. Teachers should encourage children always to make both statements and to develop both sets of language.
5. Subtraction is not just 'take away'. This language applies only to partitioning. Since this is only one of a number of subtraction structures it should not be over-emphasised at the expense of the others.
6. The partitioning structure and the language of 'take away' cannot, for example, be used meaningfully in situations involving negative numbers. Subtraction in these situations is normally either comparison or inverse-of-addition.
7. When tackling word-problems children often respond incorrectly to words that cue 'addition' in situations that actually have a subtraction structure, and vice versa.

SUGGESTIONS FOR FURTHER READING

Boulton-Lewis, G. M. (1993) Young children's representations and strategies for subtraction, *British Journal of Educational Psychology*, 63, pp. 441–56. (The author discusses some of the difficulties that occur when teachers introduce procedures that are recommended in curriculum documents without being aware of the cognitive load that they impose on pupils.)

Boulton-Lewis, G. M. and Tait, K. (1994) Young children's representations and strategies for addition, *British Journal of Educational Psychology*, 64, pp. 231–42. (A similar discussion to the one above, with a focus on addition.)

Carpenter, T. P., Moser, J. M. and Romberg, T. A. (eds) (1982) *Addition and Subtraction: a Cognitive Perspective*, Lawrence Erlbaum Associates, Hillsdale, NJ. (This book provides a wide variety of useful readings written by eminent mathematicians and psychologists from all over the world. See especially the chapter by G. Vergnaud on the classification of the thinking involved in addition and subtraction problems, pp. 60–7.)

Haylock, D. (1995) *Mathematics Explained for Primary Teachers*, Paul Chapman Publishing, London. (Chapters 4 and 6 explain in detail the various structures and associated language of addition and subtraction.)

Hughes, M. (1986) *Children and Number: Difficulties in Learning Mathematics*, Blackwell, Oxford. (In Chapter 3 Hughes describes young children's understanding of the concepts of addition and subtraction in their early years. In subsequent chapters he considers the difficulties created by the formal demands of schooling.)

Nunes, T. and Bryant, P. (1996) *Children Doing Mathematics*, Blackwell, Oxford. (Chapter 6 of this recent review of research into children's understanding of mathematics deals with addition and subtraction structures.)

4

Multiply and Divide

A similar analysis of multiplication and division to that of addition and subtraction is undertaken in this chapter. It is as well for teachers of young children to have a clear understanding of the network of connections that will need to be established eventually for some understanding of what these operations are about, even though their pupils may be only at the stage of handling them informally. To help in this analysis we will make extensive use of stories written by 9–11-year-old children to go with multiplication and division statements. Although these are children a little older than many of those whose teachers are being addressed in this book, these stories nevertheless provide a number of significant insights into the confusions that might arise from the ways in which younger children first encounter the operations and symbols of multiplication and division.

WHAT IS MULTIPLICATION?

Children's difficulties in understanding multiplication

Some 9–11-year-old children are asked to write a story that goes with '9 × 3'. First they were given some examples of stories for '9 + 3' (e.g. 'Tom had 9 marbles, Katie had 3 marbles, how many altogether?') to ensure that they understood what was meant by a 'story'. These were some of their responses for '9 × 3':

- 9 and 3 stood in a shop they said please could we have a times sign. He said yes so they walked along with the times sign in the middle.
- Belinda could not work out 9 × 3 because it was too hard for her.
- 9 children were writing an essay and 3 more children joined them. That made 27 children altogether.
- The boy had 9 pens and the teacher asked him what would 9 × 3 be. He said 27 and the teacher said that's right.
- 9 said to 3 lets multiply together and see what it makes.

A quick look at these stories reveals some of the difficulties that children have in making sense of multiplication in real terms. Given this task, a few children do write valid stories – such as 'I had 9 cats and they each had 3 kittens' – but it does seem to be only a small proportion of 9–11-year-olds who have clear structures in their mind that they can associate with multiplication. This is even the case when the children apparently know their tables and can recall multiplication facts like '9 × 3 = 27' with confidence, as is shown in two of the stories above. It seems as though, for the majority of children, multiplication is something you do with numbers in mathematics sessions in school, but it is not connected with any confidence to the real world. For many children a multiplication statement is just a set of marks made on a piece of paper, which is either right or wrong, or an instruction to recall the appropriate response, which you can either do or not do.

The repeated-addition structure

So how do infant-teachers interpret multiplication?

- I must admit I just think of it as 9 times 3, something you do with numbers.
- It's nine sets of three isn't it?
- Or is it three sets of nine?
- No, surely that would be 3 times 9?
- I don't think it matters. It's both, isn't it?

Certainly one important category of situations to which multiplication must be connected is that to which these teachers are alluding: the idea that the multiplication sign means 'sets of'. So, one of the most obvious ways of interpreting the symbols '9 × 3' is by imagining situations where we have 9 sets of 3 things. These situations have what we will refer to as the *repeated-addition* structure (or to be more precise, the repeated-aggregation structure – see Chapter 3 for an explanation of the aggregation structure of addition). It is called repeated addition simply because 9 sets of 3, for example, can also be written in symbols as '3 + 3 + 3 + 3 + 3 + 3 + 3 + 3 + 3'. We should note at the outset that the language of 'so many sets of so many' that is central to this structure implies that we are dealing only with situations involving cardinal numbers – where the second number is the number of objects in a set and the first is the number of these sets.

Commutativity and rectangular arrays

There is a question here which causes some confusion, that we should try to sort out. Does '9 × 3' mean '9 sets of 3' or should it be '3 sets of 9'? Which of the pictures (a) or (b) in Figure 4.1 should be connected with these symbols?

The first thing to note is that it is by no means immediately obvious that nine sets of three objects and three sets of nine objects come to the same result. The two diagrams in Figure 4.1 do not immediately strike one as necessarily representing the same number. The fact that they do is an instance of the property of multiplication known as *commutativity*. Formally this is the rule that says that $a \times b$ is always equal to $b \times a$, whatever the two numbers a and b. As we indicate in Chapter 5, the principle of commutativity is one of the fundamental properties of number operations.

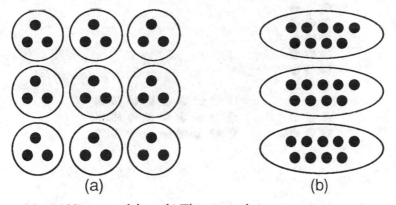

Figure 4.1   (a) Nine sets of three (b) Three sets of nine

The other operation for which commutativity holds is addition, since $a + b = b + a$, for any two numbers a and b. There is a stage in their development of understanding of addition in which young children gradually get hold of the idea that a set of five objects combined with a set of four objects is the same as a set of four combined with a set of five. At least with addition there does not appear to be much perceptual difference between, say, holding up four fingers on your left hand and five on your right hand, and holding up five fingers on your left and four on your right. Although there is a transformation involved between the two situations, the equivalence is clearly apparent. Eventually most children are able to switch freely between, say, '5 + 4' and '4 + 5'. But this is much more of a hurdle for multiplication. The equivalence between 'five sets of four' and 'four sets of five' is not clearly apparent, and, incidentally, many children would find the calculation of the first of these more difficult than the calculation of the second – because counting in fives is easier than counting in fours.

Now, strictly speaking, the words 'nine times three' mean that you have nine, three times. In other words, 'nine times three' is 'three sets of nine', as shown in Figure 4.1(b). Similarly, the formal language 'nine multiplied by three' also refers to the picture in Figure 4.1(b): a set of nine is reproduced three times. So in this strict interpretation, '9 × 3' represents '9 + 9 + 9', whereas '3 × 9' represents '3 + 3 + 3 + 3 + 3 + 3 + 3 + 3 + 3'.

Some primary textbooks take this very seriously and formally, and take children through the sequence: 3 sets of 9 = 3(9) = 9 × 3 = 27. We would not wish to be as formal or as pedantic as this. In fact, it would seem to us to be appropriate that the commutative nature of multiplication be established before the introduction of the formal representation in symbols. Then when the multiplication sign is introduced it really would be the case that both '9 × 3' and '3 × 9' could represent either nine sets of three or three sets of nine.

In order to establish commutativity it is most helpful if considerable attention is given to connecting one particular picture of multiplication into the network of experiences associated with this concept. This is the picture of a *rectangular array*, as shown in Figure 4.2(a) and (b).

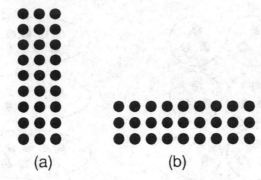

Figure 4.2   Rectangular arrays for '9 × 3'

It is our contention that pictures such as these should form a major component of our understanding of '9 × 3'. One of the reasons for this emphasis on the notion of rectangular array is that this picture of multiplication makes the commutative property transparent. So Figure 4.2(a) can be talked about as being both 'nine rows of three dots' (going across the page) and 'three rows (or columns) of nine dots' (going down the page). Clearly, in this case, nine threes and three nines are the same. In the same way, Figure 4.2(b) can be talked about as being both 'three rows of nine dots' (going across the page) and 'nine rows (or columns) of three dots' (going down the page). Later on, then, both '9 × 3' and '3 × 9' can be used as symbols to represent either of these diagrams.

Young children, before they start recording multiplication facts like '3 × 4 = 12' formally, can be encouraged to identify rectangular arrays in their environment – the world is full of them – and to record their observations with a diagram and an appropriate comment, as in Figure 4.3.

We are beginning to see again that understanding of a number operation is involving the establishment of a network of connections. Understanding multiplication would seem to involve connecting the language of 'multiplied by' and 'times', concrete situations such as repeated sets of objects, the symbols for multiplication statements and the important picture of the rectangular array.

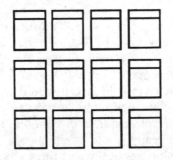

3 rows of 4 windows
3 fours make 12

4 rows of 3 windows
4 threes make 12

Figure 4.3   Recording arrays

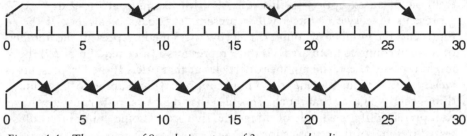

Figure 4.4   Three steps of 9 and nine steps of 3 on a number line

With this picture forming a major component of the multiplication network the child has something to which to connect later experiences in mathematics, such as finding areas of rectangles using multiplication.

One further important image to be built into the network of connections for multiplication is that of repeated steps on the number line. In this image, children learn to connect the symbols '9 × 3' with '3 steps of 9' or '9 steps of 3' along the number line, as shown in Figure 4.4. Before commutativity is firmly established it is quite a surprise when these two different procedures lead to the same point!

Extending the repeated-subtraction structure

The question we must consider now is whether repeated addition, the idea of 'so many sets of so many', is the only structure of situations to be connected with multiplication, or do we face a similar situation to that with addition and subtraction, where the symbols and the language had to be connected to a number of different categories of experiences. We asked our infant-teachers whether they could recall other situations in which multiplication is the appropriate operation – other occasions in real life in which we might press the multiplication key on the calculator?

M. We use it a lot when we're shopping, don't we? When you're working out the cost of 3 things at 9p each, for example.
E. But isn't that just three sets of nine again?
D. Not really. Nine pence isn't necessarily a set of nine things.
A. And what about 3 lengths of 9 cm, or 3 periods of 9 minutes, or 3 buckets each containing 9 litres?

From this discussion we can see first that the repeated-addition structure, which has so far been thought of as repeated sets, has to be extended to other contexts, such as money, length, weight, capacity, time, and so on. Each of the ideas suggested above in these various contexts has to be connected with '9 × 3' or '3 × 9'. This is a not too difficult extension of the repeated-addition structure, but we should note that now only one of the numbers is a cardinal number, representing the number of things in a set, and the other number is used for measuring a length or a value or a weight, and so on.

This highlights one of the inbuilt difficulties in interpreting multiplication in concrete terms, namely that the two numbers must normally represent different sorts of things. (Multiplying two lengths to obtain an area is an example of an exception to this rule.) So, for example, if the 9 in '9 × 3' represents nine sweets the 3 will represent, say, bags of sweets. If the 9 represents the number of counters in a row the 3 might represent the number of rows of counters in an array. If the 9 represents a price (e.g. 9p or £9) the 3 might represent, say, the number of articles at that price. If the 9 represents a weight (e.g. 9 kg or 9 stone) the 3 might represent the number of individual things each weighing that much. This idea that the two numbers usually have to represent different kinds of things clearly throws some children, as illustrated in some of their stories for '9 × 3':

- I had 9 footballs and I lost 3 footballs, then I got back 3 footballs, so I had 9 footballs × 3 footballs.
- The army had 9 tanks and the navy had 3 ships. When they timesed them together they were the biggest army in the whole world.
- John had 9 cars and his brother had 3 cars, so his dad asked him what was 9 times 3 and he told him 27.

The scaling structure

There is a further structure associated with multiplication to be considered, in which a quantity is *scaled* by a factor. Not surprisingly, we call this the *scaling* structure. This is the structure of the following story, for example, written by a child to go with the symbols '9 × 3': 'I have 3 pens. My friend has 9 times as many. How many has she got?' At a casual glance the reader may well think this is no different from the repeated-addition structure. But we should note that we are not dealing here with '9 sets of 3 pens'. The story is about two sets of pens. One is a set of 3 pens, the other is to be calculated as a set of 27 pens – and the '9 times as many' is used to express a relationship between them.

This scaling structure is an important component of the network of connections for multiplication because of later mathematical experiences that involve this idea of scaling. So, for example, it might be encountered when calculating a percentage increase, or when dealing with scale factors in mapwork and scale drawings.

WHAT IS DIVISION?

What image comes most readily to our minds when we see the symbols '12 ÷ 3'? The following conversation with some infant-teachers raises some important points about language and shows that there are at least two different structures associated with division:

D. If I put twelve cubes on the desk what would you expect me to do with them to demonstrate '12 ÷ 3'?
L. I expect you to share them into three piles. One for you, one for you and one for you. And so on.
D. So the answer is how many in each pile. What do you say when you have done this?
L. Twelve shared by three is four.
C. Twelve shared between three is four each, surely.

D. Or, what about twelve shared equally between four is three each?
L. I think I sometimes just say twelve share three is four, but I don't think it's right to say that.
C. I was thinking of something different. I had in mind sharing the twelve cubes into piles of three.
D. And if you do that where's the answer?
C. It's the number of piles you finish up with.
D. So twelve divided by three is also how many threes in twelve?
L. I'd never think of it like that. I'd only think of it as sharing between three.

Two structures for division: equal-sharing and inverse-of-multiplication

We are back on familiar ground. The elementary mathematical operation of division, represented by the symbol '÷', appears to represent more than one type of situation, as has been the case with all the mathematical symbols we have analysed so far.

On the one hand, the symbols '12 ÷ 3' are connected to the idea of sharing 12 equally between 3. A set of 12 objects would thus be arranged into 3 groups, as shown in Figure 4.5(a), and the answer is the number of objects in each group. Division situations of this kind have what is called the *equal-sharing* structure.

But just as valid is to interpret '12 ÷ 3' as 'how many threes make 12?' In this case the 12 objects are arranged into groups of 3, as shown in Figure 4.5(b), and the answer is the number of groups. Division situations of this kind have what is called the *inverse-of-multiplication* structure.

M. I'm not sure I ever really realised that division could mean two different things like that! I always think of it as sharing.
D. What's 72 divided by 9?
M. [*After some thought*] Eight.
D. What went on in your mind when you worked that out?
M. I was trying to remember how many 9s make 72.
D. So, you were using the inverse-of-multiplication structure!
C. How did we become teachers without knowing this?

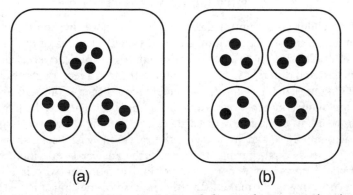

(a)   (b)

Figure 4.5   Interpretations of '12 ÷ 3': (a) Equal-sharing (b) Inverse-of-multiplication

Overemphasis on 'sharing'

In our experience, it seems that teachers of young children tend to emphasise the first structure, i.e. equal-sharing, when introducing division to young children, presumably because they perceive 'sharing' as an everyday concept with which children are familiar. There is a tendency therefore for the words 'shared between', 'shared by', or even just 'share' to be attached firmly to the symbol, as though this is what division really means. We must argue therefore – just as we argue in Chapter 3 that subtraction is not just 'take away' – that division is not just 'sharing'. In exactly the same way that we saw that the take-away (partitioning) structure of subtraction was a limited aspect of less long-term significance than, say, the comparison or the inverse-of-addition structure, we must note that the sharing structure of division is a limited view and of less significance in the long term than the inverse-of-multiplication structure.

Consider, for example, a division statement like '6 ÷ 0.25'. You can happily press the appropriate keys on your calculator and get the answer 24, but what might this mean in concrete terms? It certainly could not mean '6 cakes shared between 0.25 of a person makes 24 each'! However you might want to calculate 6 ÷ 0.25 if you needed to find out how many articles costing 25p each could be bought for £6. So, in this sense, '6 ÷ 0.25' means 'how many amounts of 0.25 make 6?' – in other words, it is interpreted using a situation with the inverse-of-multiplication structure.

When division is extended into contexts other than just sets of things, such as the money context example given above, both structures may be encountered. But the sharing structure makes sense only when the second number is a cardinal number, that is, a number representing a set of things, normally the number of people receiving a portion or the number of portions being measured out. So we might encounter the sharing structure of division in the context of liquid volume if we have 750 ml of wine to share out into five equal portions, or in the context of money if we have £750 to share equally between five people. On the other hand, we would encounter the inverse-of-multiplication structure of division if we needed to find how many 150 ml glasses of wine could be poured from a 750 ml bottle, or how many articles costing £150 each could be bought with £750.

Rectangular arrays and division

It will help children to connect these two structures of division together if they are encouraged to associate rectangular arrays with the idea of division, as well as with multiplication. A child could be given, for example, twelve counters and challenged to find different ways of arranging them in a rectangular array. Figure 4.6, showing one such possible arrangement, could then lead to discussion both about how many counters are in each of the three rows across the page and also about how many columns of three there are coming down the page. Hence, looked at one way this array answers the question 'what is 12 shared equally between 3?' (the equal-sharing structure) – the answer is provided by the fact each of the 3 rows has 4 counters. Looked at another way it answers the question 'how many 3s make 12?' (the inverse-of-multiplication structure) – with the answer provided by the fact that there are 4 columns of 3 counters.

Figure 4.6 One way of arranging twelve counters in an array

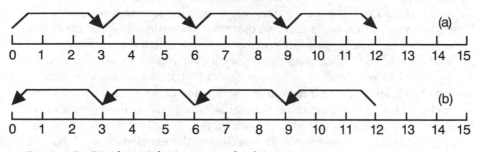

Figure 4.7 Dividing 12 by 3 on a number line

Division as repeated subtraction

The idea of division as the inverse of multiplication leads to a further interpretation. Since one structure of multiplication is repeated addition, it follows that a possible structure for division is *repeated subtraction*. In this interpretation '12 ÷ 3' might be thought of as: 'How many times can I take 3 away from 12 until there is nothing left?' This is clearly very similar to the question: 'How many 3s in 12?', so even if we regard it as a different structure it seems likely that there will not be much difficulty in learning to connect the same symbols with both questions. The number-line picture helps to connect these ideas together. In Figure 4.7, '12 ÷ 3' is experienced in two different ways: (a) starting at zero and moving in steps of 3 until 12 is reached – this answers the question 'how many 3s in 12?', i.e. the procedure incorporates the idea of inverse-of-multiplication; (b) starting at 12 and moving down in steps of 3 until zero is reached – this clearly incorporates the idea of repeated subtraction. Both of these experiences on the number line are important components of the network of connections for division.

Division as ratio

A more difficult aspect of division arises from the inverse of the scaling structure of multiplication. This is the *ratio* structure of division. In this structure, '12 ÷ 3' might be thought of as meaning something like: 'How many times bigger than 3 is 12?' This is using division to make a comparison between two quantities.

If, for example, A earns £12 an hour and B earns £3 an hour, there are, in fact, two ways of comparing their earnings. We could, on the one hand, use the *comparison* structure of *subtraction* – as discussed in Chapter 3 – and conclude that A earns £9 more than B (or B earns £9 less than A). In this way we would be considering the *difference* between the two quantities. On the other hand, we could consider the *ratio*, using this structure of *division* to conclude that A earns four times as much as B.

Which of these two ways of making the comparison (difference or ratio) should be used will depend on the context, although it is often a matter of subjective judgement. It is interesting to note, for example, that there was a time when teams in the English Football League table with the same number of points were ranked according to goal ratio. So a team with 12 goals for and 6 against would be ranked above a team with 17 goals for and 10 against, since the goal ratio of the first team is 2, whereas that of the second team is only 1.7. Nowadays goal difference is used, so that the two teams would be ranked in the reverse order since a goal difference of 7 is better than a goal difference of 6. Teachers will be familiar with this question as it applies to salary increases. A pay award in which all members get the same flat-rate increase is seen by some as being fair because it maintains the existing differences in salaries, but is seen by others as being unfair because it does not preserve the existing ratios between salaries. The latter would favour a pay award in which all get the same percentage increase because this preserves the existing ratios. This is a nice example of the way in which some mathematical transformations (the salary increases) preserve some equivalences and destroy others (i.e. the existing salary differences or ratios).

Children's stories for division

Children's stories for division statements again give us some very interesting insights into their understanding of the operation. Most use the sharing structure, as in these stories written to go with '12 ÷ 3':

- There was a boy and he had 12 stones so he shared them out into 3 piles. How many stones were there in each pile?
- There were 12 dollys. If there were 3 girls how many dolls would each girl get?
- The father won £12 on the lottery and shared it between his 3 children.

But others use the inverse-of-multiplication structure with equal confidence:

- Tom had 12 butterflies and he wanted them in sets of 3. How many sets?
- On the class outing 12 children were going. The head dived 3 children in each car. How many cars did he need?
- I had 12 chocolates and I put 3 on each plate and I used 4 plates.

There are, of course, those for whom division is something you do in school without any apparent meaning or purpose other than satisfying the teacher: 'One day in class the teacher asked Ben the answer to 12 shared by 3. Ben didn't know and he got an essay.'

Experiences of sharing that do not correspond to division

Other stories that children write for '12 ÷ 3' suggest that we might be deceiving ourselves in suggesting that sharing, in the way intended when doing division in school, is an experience with which children are familiar. Children have many experiences of sharing in their lives, but most of them are nothing like what we expect them to do when we give them '12 ÷ 3'. We can identify at least four examples of sharing experiences that are not actually division in the mathematical sense.

First, it is most unlikely that a child would share his or her twelve cakes between three friends and not have any for himself or herself. Parents and teachers share things out *between* children and seem happy to exclude themselves, but children share *with* their friends. Teachers should be alert to the subtle difficulties involved in mastering the use of prepositions such as 'between' and 'with' in the context of mathematical statements and language patterns. The fact that children normally 'share with' rather than 'share between' is no doubt the cause of the errors in stories such as this one for '12 ÷ 3': 'Tim had 12 cakes he shared them out with 3 of his friends.'

Second, sharing *equally* is a peculiarly mathematical process, not always reflected in the sharing experiences of everyday life, as shown in this child's story: 'The girl had 12 pens and her friend borrowed 3. Her other 2 friends had 1 each. How many did she have left?' This is certainly an example of sharing, it is even sharing between 3, but it is not 'sharing equally between 3' which is the language that must be connected with the symbols '÷ 3'.

Third, children experience sharing when they are told to share their possessions with another person. This can take a number of forms. For example, the child might have 12 items and agree to share 3 of them. This invalid interpretation of division is no doubt prompted by the unhelpful language pattern, 'twelve share three', as shown in these stories: 'The boy had 12 sweets and he ate one and gave 2 away to his friends. How many left?' 'I had 12 cars, I shared 3 of them.'

Finally, two children with unequal possessions might sometimes agree to share them by a process of pooling their resources, as occurs in this child's story, again written to go with the symbols '12 ÷ 3': 'One boy had 12 conkers the other had 3 conkers. When they shared the conkers they had equal amounts and they threw the remainder conker away.'

The language of division

So, in summary, we are suggesting that 'sharing equally between' is actually a more sophisticated and abstract idea than we might imagine, and also that it is not in the long term the most important structure of division. This then raises the question of the language that we as teachers use when we write the symbol. Now, of course, in real situations division is sometimes sharing. When this is the actual concrete situation being attended to then it is appropriate to use this language, although we must take note of the distinction between 'sharing equally between' and the other possible interpretations of sharing described above that are not what we want to connect with division. Children will need specific help in getting the pattern of language established: '12 shared between 3 is 4 each'.

But again there are two levels of language here, as was the case with subtraction. First there is the formal language that goes with the concept, such as '12 divided by 3'. But then there is the language appropriate to the physical situation. This might be '12 shared equally between 3', but it might equally well be '12 shared into groups of 3', depending on what we are actually doing with the counters on the table in front of us. So, in general terms we will say '12 divided by 3' and talk about the operation of 'division' and the process of 'dividing one number by another'. But in specific situations we will happily use the informal language appropriate to what we are actually doing in concrete terms.

CONTEXTS FOR MULTIPLICATION AND DIVISION

The range of contexts for experiencing multiplication and division

We encounter operations with numbers not just when dealing with sets of things, but also in a variety of measurement contexts. A major part of the development of understanding of the number operations is the establishment of connections between the symbols and language associated with the operation and the various structures of the operation as they are met in a wide range of real contexts. So, for example, we discuss in Chapter 3 the particularly complex network of connections involved in the comparison structure of subtraction as it is encountered in such diverse contexts as length, weight, time, and so on.

When we develop a similar scenario for multiplication and division we find that one of the reasons for the greater difficulty involved in understanding these operations is that often they arise in two different contexts simultaneously. We have already hinted at this problem in discussing multiplication earlier in this chapter, when we noted that the two numbers involved in a multiplication statement have to represent different sorts of things. This contrasts with addition and subtraction where the two numbers involved always represent the same sort of thing; we add a set to a set, a price to a price, a length to a length, and so on.

But if we consider possible contexts to be, for example, sets, money, length and distance, weight, liquid volume and capacity, and time, then any two of these might produce a possible real situation in which multiplication and division have some application and meaning.

We will illustrate this first with a number of examples of situations which might correspond to the calculation '9 × 3'. For example, using the two different contexts of money and weight, we encounter the repeated-addition structure of multiplication when finding the cost of 3 pounds of potatoes at 9p a pound. Using the two contexts of money and liquid volume we would encounter the same structure when calculating the cost of 9 litres of wine at £3 per litre. Using the two contexts of time and distance we might be calculating how far we can get in 3 hours if we cycle at 9 miles per hour.

Second, we might consider some examples of pairs of contexts in which '12 ÷ 3' might have an application and meaning – these all provide extensions of the equal-sharing idea of division. The two contexts of weight and money, for example, might give rise to an application of division when finding the equivalent price per kilogram of a 3 kg pack of some material which costs £12 – it is as though the 12 pounds are shared equally between each of the 3 kilograms. The two contexts of distance and time involve division when calculating average speed: 'What is my average speed if I walk 12 miles in 3 hours?' – here it is as though the 12 miles is being shared equally between each of the 3 hours. And the two contexts of money and time produce division problems such as calculating your rate of pay if you have earned £12 in 3 hours – this time the 12 pounds are being shared equally between each of the 3 hours.

Conclusion

The conclusion we come to then is that understanding of multiplication and division once again involves the building up of a complex network of connections between the symbols, the language, both formal and informal, the pictures associated with the operations, particularly rectangular arrays, but also steps up and down the number line, and the surprising variety of concrete situations, contexts and combinations of contexts in which they arise. We leave the last words on the subject of multiplication and division to some of our story-writers:

- Tanya was very brainy and worked out 9 times 3 in 2 secs.
- Once there was a boy at school and he was given some sums to do but when he got to number five he could not do it. The sum was 9 × 3.
- 12 ÷ 3 = 4 and the King of Scotland did not know what it ment.

Not just the King of Scotland, presumably.

SOME ACTIVITIES WITH CHILDREN

As in the previous chapters, the suggestions here are examples of the kinds of activities that aim to develop understanding. In this case the focus is on establishing the connections between the language, pictures, concrete situations and symbols of multiplication and division. Clearly, these kinds of activities would have to be supplemented, at an appropriate stage, by others that focus on computational skills.

Activity 4.1: stories (multiplication and division)
Objective To help children to connect the symbols for multiplication and division with a wide range of situations and language.

   Method Give children some multiplication and division statements (e.g. 8 × 3, 15 ÷ 5) and ask them to write stories to go with them. This is handled in the same way as Activity 3.1. Encourage children to use the different models and contexts for multiplication and division, by giving the beginnings of some stories. For example, children could be asked to write a story for '8 × 3' beginning 'Chocolate bars are 8p each . . . '; or a story for '15 ÷ 5' beginning 'Mary had £15 to spend on records. If a record costs . . . '

   Another approach is to specify contexts, for example by asking children to write a story for '8 × 3' that is about a farmer who sells potatoes at 8p a pound; or a story about '15 ÷ 5' that is about a person who walks for 15 miles.

Activity 4.2: swaps (multiplication and division)
Objective To develop connections between language, symbols, concrete experience and pictures, for the concepts of multiplication and division.

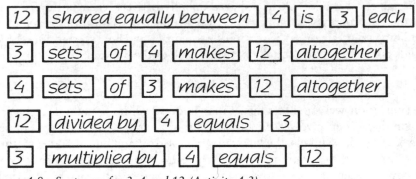

Figure 4.8   Sentences for 3, 4 and 12 (Activity 4.3)

Materials and method   The same as Activity 3.2, except using stories with multiplication and division examples. For example, a possible starting point might be the story: 'How many £16 chairs can my Mum buy with £80?'; this could then be swapped for coins, calculator, symbols, and a number-line drawing.

Activity 4.3: sentences (multiplication and division)
Objective   To develop language patterns for multiplication and division.

Materials   Several sets of strips of card with the following words or phrases written on them: divided by, multiplied by, times, shared equally between, makes, is, equals, sets, of, altogether, each; several sets of cards with appropriate numerals written on them; counting materials; a number line.

Method   As in Activity 3.3, a small group of children is given three numbers and challenged to use the cards to make up as many different sentences as they can using these three numbers. Figure 4.8 shows some examples of what might be achieved with the numbers 3, 4 and 12.

Activity 4.4: number-line multiplication
Objective   To provide experience of multiplication in the context of a number line.

Materials   Two conventional dice numbered from 1 to 6; a counter (or an appropriate small toy); a number line marked from 0 to 36; two small flags of some sort. (For a more advanced game, use dodecahedron dice with faces numbered from 1 to 12, and a number line marked from 0 to 144.)

Method   This is a multiplication version of Activity 3.4, for a small group of players. The player going first places the flags on the number line on any two numbers of his or her choosing. Each then plays in turn as follows. They place the counter on the zero mark and throw the two dice. One score represents the step size and the other the number of steps. Scores of 3 and 5, for example, might be '3 steps of 5' or '5 steps of 3'. (Children can discover for themselves the principle of commutativity in this context.) Once again they have to predict where they will land and score a point if they are correct. If they finish on a number with a flag on they get a bonus point. The positioning of the flags causes some interesting discussions – for example, 12 is a better bet than 13 if you are looking for bonus points!

Activity 4.5: what did I do? (36, +, −, ×, ÷ version)

Objective To give children experience of addition and subtraction, and multiplication and division, as inverse operations.

Materials One calculator for each pair of children; plastic pennies as prizes.

Method This is an extension of Activity 3.5 using all four operations. Players take it in turns to challenge each other with the question, 'What did I do?' The number 36 is entered on the calculator. Player A presses one operation key (36, +, −, ×, ÷) followed by a single digit and the equals key. The calculator is then shown to player B who has to (1) state which keys A pressed, and (2) press one operation key followed by a single digit and the equals key, in order to get the 36 back on display. B wins one penny for correctly stating which keys A pressed, and a further penny for getting back to 36. It is then player B's turn to challenge A.

Interesting discussions can arise in three particular cases: (1) when the first player has performed an operation that leaves 36 on display, since this could be achieved in four different ways! (2) if a player attempts to divide by zero; (c) when the first player divides by 7, the second player multiplies by 7 and then finds that instead of 36 the calculator displays 35.999999. (This is because the calculator can give the answer for '36 ÷ 7' to only 7 decimal places, thus giving a result slightly smaller than the true value. When this is then multiplied by 7 the result is just slightly short of the 36 we started with.)

Activity 4.6: arrays

Objective To connect multiplication and division with the picture of a rectangular array.

Materials Counters or cubes; a calculator.

Method First, as suggested earlier in this chapter, the children are sent to explore the environment in search of examples of rectangular arrays, recording their findings as shown in Figure 4.3. A calculator can be used to associate the array with the symbol for multiplication and to check the total number of objects in the array.

Then, back in the classroom – after discussing and sharing their examples of arrays with the teacher – children in small groups are given a pile of counters or cubes to use in a simple investigation. The challenge is to find out which numbers can be made into rectangular arrays and which ones cannot. For example, 7 cannot be made into an array, but 12 can be done in four different ways (3 rows of 4, 4 rows of 3, 2 rows of 6, 6 rows of 2). Note that a single line of objects does not count as an array. The numbers that cannot be made into arrays are *prime* numbers.

Activity 4.7: I have, who has? (multiplication and division stories)

Objective To practise using all the models and language for multiplication and division.

Materials Prepare a set of 16 cards with 'questions' on one side and the corresponding 'answers' on the other side, using the same cyclic scheme as explained in Activity 2.2 and Activity 3.7, with the question on one card answered on the reverse side of the next.

In this activity use as questions a series of statements or stories covering a wide range of situations with different structures and language associated with multiplication and division. Again, ensure that there are no duplicate answers. Here are some suggestions, with the corresponding answers in brackets after each one:

1. Four times three. (4 × 3)
2. How much for 4 apples at 5p each? (5 × 4)
3. Debbie shared 12p between 4 people. How much each? (12 ÷ 4)
4. How many sets of 3 make a set of 12? (12 ÷ 3)
5. 20 divided by 4. (20 ÷ 4)
6. 20 multiplied by 4. (20 × 4)
7. John has 4 sets of 12 stamps. How many altogether? (12 × 4)
8. How many times longer than 3 cm is 15 cm? (15 ÷ 3)
9. How many times can 5p be taken away from 15p until there's nothing left? (15 ÷ 5)
10. 4 rows of 15 seats. (15 × 4)
11. John is 12 years old. His Mum is 3 times as old as him. How old is John's Mum? (12 × 3)
12. How many 5p coins make 20p? (20 ÷ 5)
13. 20 add 20 add 20. (20 × 3)
14. Three fives. (5 × 3)
15. Half of 20. (20 ÷ 2)
16. Two people shared 12 sweets. How many each? (12 ÷ 2)

Method   As in Activities 2.2 and 3.7.

SUMMARY OF KEY IDEAS IN CHAPTER 4

1. One category of situations to which the language and symbols of multiplication can be connected is repeated addition. This structure is most clearly seen in the context of sets (so many sets of so many), but extends naturally to repeated steps along the number line and to measuring contexts.
2. Multiplication (like addition) is commutative. In other words, $a \times b$ is always equal to $b \times a$, whatever the two numbers a and b (just as $a + b$ is always equal to $b + a$).
3. The commutative property of multiplication is most clearly seen in a rectangular array. This image, together with the associated language, is an important component in the network of connections for understanding multiplication and division.
4. Strictly speaking, in the repeated-addition structure '9 × 3' means '3 sets of 9'. But once commutativity is established both '9 × 3' and '3 × 9' can be connected with either '3 sets of 9' or '9 sets of 3'.
5. Another category of situations to which the language and symbols of multiplication can be connected is scaling.
6. Four categories of situation to which the language and symbols of division can be connected are equal-sharing (between), inverse-of-multiplication, repeated subtraction and ratio.
7. Ratio and difference are two ways of comparing quantities, using division and subtraction respectively.
8. Children have many other experiences of sharing which do not correspond to the equal-sharing structure of division.
9. Multiplication and division often arise in situations involving two different contexts, such as money and weight, or distance and time.

SUGGESTIONS FOR FURTHER READING

Anghileri, J. (1995) Making sense of symbols. In J. Anghileri (ed.) *Children's Mathematical Thinking in the Primary Years*, Cassell, London, pp. 74–91. (Anghileri considers the meaning of multiplication and division and methods of teaching them to avoid later confusion.)

Desforges, A. and Desforges, C. (1980) Number-based strategies of sharing in young children, *Educational Studies*, 6, pp. 97–109. (A rare account, full of insights into pre-schoolers' understanding of the concept of sharing.)

Haylock, D. (1995) *Mathematics Explained for Primary Teachers*, Paul Chapman Publishing, London. (Chapters 8 and 10 consider in detail the structures and associated language of multiplication and division.)

Kouba, V. L. and Franklin, K. (1995) Multiplication and division: sense making and meaning, *Teaching Mathematics*, May, pp. 574–7. (Kouba and Franklin argue that young children should be given plenty of practical experience in solving and creating multiplication and division problems if they are to develop a sound understanding of the concepts. They also provide some strategies to assess this understanding.)

Newman, C. (1985) How children divide, *Mathematics Teaching*, 112, pp. 18–19. (Newman describes how her class of 10-year-olds solved division problems. She concludes that it is essential that teachers talk to their pupils individually about their work in order to evaluate their mathematical thinking.)

Nunes, T. and Bryant, P. (1996) *Children Doing Mathematics*, Blackwell, Oxford. (Chapter 7 of this recent review of research into children's understanding of mathematics deals with multiplication and division structures.)

Weiser, W. (1995) Semantic structures of one-step word problems involving multiplication or division, *Educational Studies in Mathematics*, 28, no. 1, pp. 55–72. (Weiser provides a research-based classification of the structures of word problems involving multiplication and division and compares this with the structures of addition and subtraction problems.)

5

Number Patterns and Calculations

Sam, aged 6, had drawn a block graph showing how many children in the class had a cat as a pet and how many had a dog. He had coloured in the squares in the columns of his graph alternately blue and red. His teacher asked him to write about his graph:

> Cats beat dogs. There are 13 squares in the cat row and only 8 squares in the dog row. There are 5 more cats than dogs. 13 is 2 + 2 + 2 + 2 + 2 + 2 + 1. 13 is 6 twos and 1 odd one. 13 is an odd number. 8 is an even number. 8 is 4 twos and none left over.

Sam is clearly a child with the kind of grasp of number relationships and fascination with pattern in number that teachers should aim to develop as the basis for confidence and success in manipulating numbers. In the previous chapters we have considered understanding of number and number-operations in terms of the connections between the symbolic representation of the operations and various categories of concrete situations, language and pictures. In this chapter we turn our attention to developing understanding of the relationships between numbers themselves. As is shown by the example of 6-year-old Sam writing about odd and even numbers, central to our understanding of number relationships is the notion of *pattern*. We aim also to demonstrate that it is this sense of pattern in number that is the foundation for success and confidence in handling calculations, whether written or mental, or a combination of the two. In this chapter we are not considering fractions or negative numbers, so when we refer to 'a number' in the discussion below we mean 'a positive integer' (whole number).

PATTERN IN NUMBER

Spatial patterns and visual images related to numerical patterns

How do you think about the concepts of 'odd' and 'even'? What ideas dominate your image of odd and even numbers? These are some responses from infant-teachers:

• Even numbers are nice. Odd numbers are a pain in the neck. You can't line children up in twos if there's an odd number.

- I think about the patterns they make if they were, say, scones arranged on a tray.
- I think of even numbers as things arranged in pairs. With odd numbers there's an odd one stuck out at the end.
- I just think of even numbers as those that end in 0, 2, 4, 6 or 8, and odd numbers those that end in 1, 3, 5, 7 or 9.
- I imagine the odd numbers on one side of the road and the even numbers on the other side.
- Then there's the pattern you get when you count: odd, even, odd, even, odd, even, and so on, going on for ever.

These responses show how strong is the idea of pattern in our understanding of such simple numerical concepts as odd and even. It is significant that one of the main uses of the word 'pattern' is to refer to a spatial or geometric design, particularly one in which certain key features are repeated and linked together in a systematic fashion. It is not surprising therefore that when we talk about a 'number pattern' or make any kind of comment about patterns in the context of number, what we are doing more often than not is drawing attention to some connection between the relationships between numbers and a visual image, a picture, or a spatial or geometric arrangement of some kind. For example, nearly all the comments given above by infant-teachers about odd and even numbers contain visual or spatial imagery: lining up in twos, patterns of scones on a tray, an odd one sticking out, opposite sides of a road, and so on. Even the comment about the counting pattern of 'odd, even, odd, even, odd, even' can be thought of as a spatial observation, by visualising a line of alternately odd and even numbers arranged in order. When 6-year-old Sam looked at the 13 squares coloured alternately blue and red – in the example at the head of this chapter – the visual image immediately prompted the connection with the notion of 'odd'. A strong part of his concept of 'odd' is clearly this connection between these numbers and the spatial pattern of pairs of items with an extra one added on. One suspects also that for Sam, as for many children (and adults, for that matter), the aesthetic aspect of pattern in numbers, that comes through most strongly in visual imagery, is an important motivating factor in exploring, using and just playing with numbers.

Consideration of number patterns is often, therefore, another example of the importance of making connections between symbols and pictures in developing understanding. Many of the key relationships between numbers that contribute to a person having what is sometimes called a 'feel for number' are more securely understood if we make the connections with visual patterns or images. We have already done this, for example, in our discussion of understanding the principle of commutativity in multiplication in Chapter 4 (see Figure 4.3). The imagery of a rectangular array – a neatly arranged geometric pattern of dots – makes the numerical pattern transparent and contributes strongly to our understanding of the principle.

At a more elementary level, even the patterns of dots that appear on dice or dominoes for the numbers zero to six (see Figure 5.1) are an important part of our feel for the various numbers. For example, many people when asked to visualise 'five' will bring to mind the spatial arrangement of dots for this

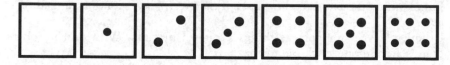

Figure 5.1   Patterns of dots for 0 to 6 on dice or dominoes

number that is shown in Figure 5.1. It is as though this visual arrangement is very much part of what makes five the number it is and distinguishes it from other numbers. These and other such patterns of dots also help us to relate one number to other numbers. For example, the visual image of five dots makes clear how 5 is made up of two 2s and a 1, or a 4 and a 1; and, being a rectangular array, the image of six dots connects six with both 'two 3s' and 'three 2s'.

Ten-complements

For young children developing their ability to handle number, one category of important number relationships to be grasped is what are sometimes called *complements*, particularly, to begin with, *ten-complements*. For example, 3 and 7 are ten-complements, because they add up to 10. The simple idea here is that of 'making a number up to 10': 7 is the number that makes 3 up to 10, and 3 is the number that makes 7 up to 10. We have already introduced the idea of a complement of a set in Chapter 3, as one of the important subtraction structures – in Figure 3.6, for example, with a total set of 12 counters, subsets of 3 and 9 are complements of each other (with respect to 12). Because of our base-ten number-system, ten-complements are particularly significant in manipulating numbers and require special emphasis in teaching young children. We should aim for children to be able to recall them instantly and to use them freely. The patterns inherent in these ten-complements are very important and are a vital part of understanding the relationships involved. So, when we look at the sequence of ten-complements (0 + 10, 1 + 9, 2 + 8, 3 + 7, 4 + 6, 5 + 5, and so on) we can observe the first number in each pair going down by one and the second number going up by one. But this numerical pattern is made so much stronger if it is associated with discussion of various spatial representations, such as those using blocks or colouring squares, as shown in Figure 5.2.

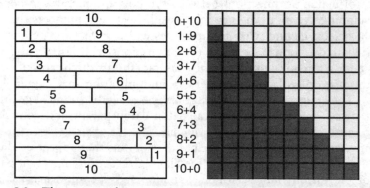

Figure 5.2   The pattern of ten-complements using blocks or colouring squares

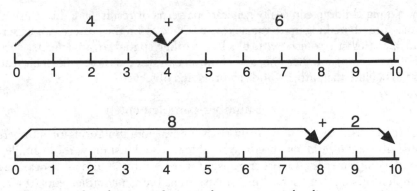

Figure 5.3 *Examples of ten-complements shown on a number line*

Then, of course, the visual images of ten-complements provided by appropriate drawings on the number line also promote a deeper understanding of the relationships, as shown in Figure 5.3.

The visual images of 'ten-complements' shown in Figures 5.2 and 5.3 are crucial in promoting a mental structure that facilitates the processing of operations with numbers. For example, when learning the number bonds to 20, a child can draw on these images to support their reasoning. For instance, given '8 + 7', many young children find it helpful to imagine 'making the 8 up to 10', by using 2 of the 7. In other words, they transform '8 + 7' to '8 + (2 + 5)', which can be reorganised as '(8 + 2) + 5', which is '10 + 5', which is easy. (This reorganisation uses the principle of *associativity*, discussed towards the end of the chapter.)

The pattern of ten-complements can then be extended from 'making a number up to ten' to 'making a number up to the next ten'. For example, we discover this pattern for making numbers in the thirties up to 40: 31 + 9, 32 + 8, 33 + 7, 34 + 6, 35 + 5, 36 + 4, 37 + 3, 38 + 2, 39 + 1. Young children can again represent this pattern of symbols with number line drawings, or patterns of blocks or coloured squares, and discuss how it is related to the pattern of ten-complements. Figure 5.4 shows how this might be set out with blocks. With this pattern securely grasped the learner can then freely transform a calculation such as '38 + 7' to '38 + (2 + 5)', then to (38 + 2) + 5, using the 2 to make the 38 up to 40, leading to the sum of 45.

Then we find another pattern emerging when we consider this sequence of additions: 8 + 7 = 15, 18 + 7 = 25, 28 + 7 = 35, 38 + 7 = 45, 48 + 7 = 55, and so

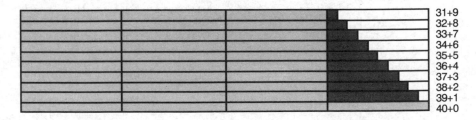

Figure 5.4 *The pattern of 40-complements*

on. Young children can easily generate patterns of results like these, using the procedure of 'making up to the next ten'. Once again the pattern can be set out and made even stronger with blocks or other spatial arrangements, such as drawings on the number line, and children can discuss these with their teacher and articulate the patterns and relationships observed.

Other number-complements

But, of course, to perform freely such mental manipulations of numbers as those above the child also needs to be able to recall instantly, for example, the 'seven-complements', in order to split the 7 into 2 and 5. These seven-complements have the same kind of pattern as the ten-complements (0 + 7, 1 + 6, 2 + 5, 3 + 4, and so on) and, in the same way, they can be experienced, explored and discussed with appropriate visual and spatial arrangements such as blocks, colouring squares and number lines. Clearly, we need to know the complements not just for making numbers up to 10 and up to 7, but for every number at least from 0 to 20. In Table 5.1, for example, is the list of pairs of numbers that sum to 0, 1, 2, 3, 4, 5, 6, 7, 8, 9 and 10, arranged in a systematic way that makes clear the extensive range of patterns involved here.

So, what are some of the aspects of pattern that strike you about this arrangement of additions? What observations about the number and spatial relationships here would you like to hear children making?

- The first number as you go along a row is the same for every sum, and the second number goes up by one each time.
- As you go down a column the first number goes up by one and the second number goes down by one each time.
- All the sums in any column give the same answer.
- The number of combinations in each column increases by one each time.
- And the number in each row reduces by one each time.
- So the pattern makes a triangle shape – and this would carry on if you went on to 20, or any number.

This arrangement is typical of the amazing amount of fascinating pattern inherent in number relationships that is waiting to be discovered by young

Table 5.1 Pairs of complements with respect to numbers from 0 to 10

0	1	2	3	4	5	6	7	8	9	10
0 + 0	0 + 1	0 + 2	0 + 3	0 + 4	0 + 5	0 + 6	0 + 7	0 + 8	0 + 9	0 + 10
	1 + 0	1 + 1	1 + 2	1 + 3	1 + 4	1 + 5	1 + 6	1 + 7	1 + 8	1 + 9
		2 + 0	2 + 1	2 + 2	2 + 3	2 + 4	2 + 5	2 + 6	2 + 7	2 + 8
			3 + 0	3 + 1	3 + 2	3 + 3	3 + 4	3 + 5	3 + 6	3 + 7
				4 + 0	4 + 1	4 + 2	4 + 3	4 + 4	4 + 5	4 + 6
					5 + 0	5 + 1	5 + 2	5 + 3	5 + 4	5 + 5
						6 + 0	6 + 1	6 + 2	6 + 3	6 + 4
							7 + 0	7 + 1	7 + 2	7 + 3
								8 + 0	8 + 1	8 + 2
									9 + 0	9 + 1
										10 + 0

children and to be built into their networks of connections. Time spent discovering and discussing patterns such as these will not be wasted. And, of course, as you would by now expect us to say, the patterns in this table become even stronger when connected with spatial patterns of dots, or blocks or coloured squares.

Hundred-complements

Having instant recall of the complements to any number is potentially useful knowledge. But particularly important in developing confidence in handling two-digit numbers is knowledge of hundred-complements. For example, in handling money a useful skill is to be able quickly to make a number of pence (e.g. 37p) up to £1 by recalling its hundred-complement (in this case, 63p). This is helpful when giving or checking change from £1. It also helps in mental calculations, particularly in subtraction situations with the comparison structure (see Chapter 3) – such as in finding differences in prices or lengths – when one number is less than 100 and the other is greater than 100. For example, to find the difference in height between two children of heights 123 cm and 88 cm someone who is confident with hundred-complements might reason: we need 12 to make the 88 up to 100, and then another 23, giving 35 cm in all. This kind of reasoning is supported enormously by representations of the situation on the number line, where the gap between 88 and 123 can be seen clearly as a combination of two bits: the bit needed to get from 88 to 100 (the hundred-complement of 88) and the bit needed to get from 100 to 123. (In the classroom a readily accessible and useful version of the number line from 0 to 100 is a metre-rule marked in centimetres – provided the children can find enough space to use it!) So, once again, the pictorial imagery promotes appropriate mental structures for manipulating numbers with confidence.

There is a common error in reasoning that occurs here – with which all primary teachers will be familiar – that leads a child to write, for example: '100 – 63 = 47'. This is typical of children's errors in arithmetic when they respond to the individual symbols merely as a set of marks on the paper without relating them to anything concrete or visual. So, they might reason: '100 take away 60 is 40, . . . 10 take away 3 is 7, . . . 40 add 7 is 47.' Or they might set out the calculation in vertical layout as shown in Figure 5.15 (j) and respond to this arrangement of symbols in a way that produces the same wrong answer. But if they have learnt to associate hundred-complements with the image on the number line, as shown in Figure 5.5, then they are much more likely to see

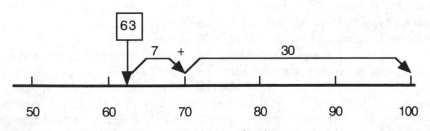

Figure 5.5   Connecting '100 – 63' with a number-line image

'100 – 63' as 'making 63 up to 100' and thus to see it as 'making up to 70 and then up to 100', i.e. '7 + 30'. It is significant that we used the word 'see' twice in that last sentence. This is our main argument here. We want children (and their teachers) to 'see' numbers and number relationships – to make the connections between the symbols and the various visual images and spatial representations available.

Just as we extended the idea of 'making up to 10' to 'making up to the next ten', in the same way we can extend the idea of 'making up to 100' to 'making up to the next hundred'. So, for example, if the problem is to find the difference between 388 cm and 423 cm, the reasoning would be along these lines: 'We need 12 to make the 388 up to 400, and then another 23', giving the same answer, 35 cm, as was obtained above when finding the difference between 88 cm and 123 cm. This then can lead to the identification of a pattern of similar differences. Children can discover and discuss the pattern in sequences of results like the following example and how these results are obtained by the procedure of making the second number up to the next hundred: 123 – 88 = 35, 223 – 188 = 35, 323 – 288 = 35, 423 – 388 = 35, 523 – 488 = 35, and so on.

Sixty-complements and time calculations

One other set of complements that are particularly important to learn are the sixty-complements (e.g. 25 and 35, 15 and 45, 28 and 32). Because we have 60 minutes in an hour, these are significant initially in learning to tell the time – for example, we need to be able to link the '35' in 'three thirty-five' with the '25' in 'twenty-five to four'. Then later they are crucial in handling time-calculations. For example, if we have to find the length of time of a train journey starting at 3.28 p.m. and finishing at 4.17 p.m., the most appropriate procedure is to make the 28 up to 60 (i.e. 32 minutes to get from 3.28 to 4 o'clock) and then to add on the 17 minutes, giving '32 + 17', i.e. a journey time of 49 minutes. (The 32 here is the sixty-complement of 28.) We hope that by now the reader can envisage this procedure as two steps on a number line (or, in this case, a time line). This is again precisely the kind of reasoning supported by mental visual imagery that is a good basis for confident manipulation of numbers.

Use of fives and doubles

The combinations of the numbers from 6 to 9 seem to be the trickiest of all the additions of two single-digit numbers for young children to learn: 6 + 6, 6 + 7, 6 + 8, 6 + 9, 7 + 7, 7 + 8, 7 + 9, 8 + 8, 8 + 9, 9 + 9. There are, however, two elementary patterns of relationships between numbers that are particularly useful for these children when they are learning these particular number bonds. These are (1) reference to fives, and (2) reference to doubles.

First, it seems as though many young children find it helpful to relate these numbers to *five*, for example to think of 7 as '5 + 2'. This procedure is presumably linked to the strong visual image of five fingers on one hand. Using this strategy, for example, '6 + 8' can be envisaged as '(5 + 1) + (5 + 3)', which is then mentally rearranged, imagining the two handfuls of fingers put together to make a ten, as '(5 + 5) + (1 + 3)' to give the response 14. Written down this

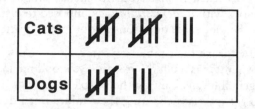

Figure 5.6   Tallying with numbers grouped in fives

sounds somewhat laborious, but in practice, with the support of appropriate mental imagery, the mental processing can be very rapid. Two young children working together on additions like '6 + 8' can make the link between the symbols and the visual image very strong. For example, one child puts out 6 fingers (one handful plus one finger), the other puts out 8 fingers (one handful plus three fingers), they put together the two handfuls to make 10 and then add on the other fingers. When recording statistical data, such as how many children have cats and how many have dogs, as in the example at the head of this chapter, the process of *tallying* can be taught to children to capitalise on this tendency to relate numbers to five. This is shown in Figure 5.6, with the marks corresponding to the numbers of children grouped in fives. This is not just a useful skill for handling data – it also provides a strong pictorial image of numbers grouped in fives, which, as we have seen, seems to be a strategy that many children find helpful in manipulating the more difficult numbers.

Second, it seems as though children often pick up the *doubles* more quickly and more securely than any of the others in the list of number bonds. The reason for this is possibly that there is just less to remember! If you are doing '6 + 6', for example, you can imagine it as '(5 + 1)' and the same thing again, rather than '(5 + 1)' and then something different, as it would be with, say, '6 + 8'. The doubles also have a strong pattern (that can be made even stronger, of course, by appropriate pictorial or spatial representation with blocks or coloured squares) of going up in twos: $1 + 1 = 2, 2 + 2 = 4, 3 + 3 = 6, 4 + 4 = 8, 5 + 5 = 10, 6 + 6 = 12$, and so on – and children seem to pick up the pattern and rhythm of counting in twos fairly quickly. Whatever the reason, it seems that many children have greater fluency in instant recall of the doubles than many of the other addition bonds. So, another useful strategy for many children is to relate additions to these doubles. Using this procedure many children will relate '6 + 8' to '6 + 6', transforming it mentally as follows: $6 + 8 = 6 + (6 + 2) = (6 + 6) + 2 = 12 + 2 = 14$. Again the actual mental processing for many young children is more fluent than this long-winded explanation might suggest. Which strategy children use – reference to fives or reference to doubles – will depend partly on the actual sum being tackled and partly on what particular number knowledge is most secure.

Patterns in multiplication tables

I like the story of the boy who was asked whether he knew his tables and replied, 'I know the tune, but I can't remember the words!'

Whenever we talk to teachers and student-teachers about the importance of learning mathematics with *understanding*, as opposed to just learning by rote, we invariably get the inevitable questions about multiplication tables:

- Shouldn't children learn their tables by rote?
- I'm glad I did when I was a child – it's always stood me in good stead.
- Is it wrong to get children chanting their tables?
- I would like to get my class chanting their tables but I daren't do it in case the teacher next door hears!

So let us make this absolutely clear: we are all in favour of children memorising their multiplication tables! Obviously, the more number facts that one can recall instantly the better – and the number facts in the multiplication tables (up to 10 × 10) are some of the most useful to have at your fingertips. If chanting the tables helps to commit them to memory, that's fine by us. (We recommend that when you do this you say each result twice, so that the child who doesn't get it first time at least says it correctly the second time: one 3 is 3, one 3 is 3; two 3s are 6, two 3s are 6; three 3s are 9, three 3s are 9, . . . and so on.) But teachers would be failing their pupils if they did nothing more than to get them to commit these results to memory. We want children to memorise them by all means – but also to learn them with understanding! This means making connections – relating together the results within the tables, connecting them to concrete situations and pictures, and, above all, discovering, articulating and using the amazing amount of pattern that is built into them. A number of activities for focusing children's attention on some of the patterns in the multiplication tables are given at the end of this chapter, particularly patterns related to counting in steps other than 1 on a hundred-square.

The most obvious patterns are those that emerge when you count in tens, fives, twos, and nines. Because ten is the base of our number system, counting in tens produces only numbers that end in zero, i.e. numbers without any units: 10, 20, 30, 40, . . . and so on. Counting in fives produces numbers in which the last digit is alternately 5 and zero: 5, 10, 15, 20, 25, 30, 35, . . . and so on. Figure 5.7 shows how this pattern can be interpreted visually for discussion with young children, using rods representing 5s and 10s: when there is an even number of 5-rods this is equivalent to a collection of 10-rods, but when there is an odd number there is one extra 5-rod each time. The last digit in the number is what you are left with after you have exchanged as many rods as you can for 10-rods. The same connection can – and should – be made with 5p and 10p coins.

Counting in twos produces a sequence of numbers in which the last digits follow the pattern 2, 4, 6, 8, 0, 2, 4, 6, 8, 0, 2, 4, 6, 8, 0, . . . repeated for ever. This is, of course, another manifestation of the set of even numbers. We should

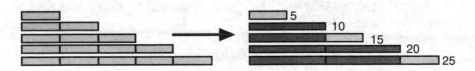

Figure 5.7   The pattern of counting in fives shown with blocks

Table 5.2 The counting-in-nines pattern

$$1 \times 9 = 9$$
$$2 \times 9 = 18$$
$$3 \times 9 = 27$$
$$4 \times 9 = 36$$
$$5 \times 9 = 45$$
$$6 \times 9 = 54$$
$$7 \times 9 = 63$$
$$8 \times 9 = 72$$
$$9 \times 9 = 81$$

not consider patterns like this to be trivial and not worthy of comment – they are crucial for a child's developing confidence with number and we should do all we can to make them explicit and meaningful. We might ask, for example, whether the reader has ever considered the relationship between the fact that '$2 \times 5 = 10$' and the observation that there are five numbers in the pattern for the last digits when counting in twos (2, 4, 6, 8 and 0) and two numbers in the pattern for the last digits when counting in fives (5 and 0)? And why when you count in 3s do the last digits include all ten digits from 0 to 9 before repeating: 3, 6, 9, 2, 5, 8, 1, 4, 7, 0, 3, 6, 9, 2, 5, 8, 1, 4, 7, 0, . . . ? And why does the same thing happen with the last digits when counting in 7s (7, 4, 1, 8, 5, 2, 9, 6, 3, 0, repeated) and in 9s (9, 8, 7, 6, 5, 4, 3, 2, 1, 0 repeated)? We will leave readers to explore these questions themselves, encouraging them to interpret the patterns with visual or spatial representations. (Hint: think about, for example, collections of 3-rods, 7-rods or 9-rods and how many you would need before you could replace the whole collection by 10-rods – and contrast this with what happens with 2-rods, 5-rods, or even 4-rods, 6-rods and 8-rods.)

One of the strongest patterns in the multiplication tables is that for counting in nines, shown in Table 5.2. Every possible means should be employed to make this pattern explicit and meaningful to children.

D. What's the pattern you notice here?
C. I can see that the tens go up by one each time and the units go down by one. But why does that happen?
D. If you buy something for 9p using a 10p coin what happens?
C. You get a penny change!
D. So the shopkeeper's collection of coins has gone up by one 10p and . . . ?
C. . . . down by one penny!
E. So counting in nines is going up by 10 and down by 1 each time.
A. So if you want 7 nines, it's 7 tens take away 7. That's 70 take away 7 . . . 63.
B. Why do the two digits always add up to 9?

Figure 5.8 shows the beginning of the 9-times table set out with ones and tens. This is another way of making the pattern explicit. You start with 9 ones. Adding another 9 each time is equivalent to adding a ten and removing a one. So the total number of pieces remains the same (up to $10 \times 9 = 90$) – which answers the question raised at the end of the conversation above! Further activities related to the pattern in the 9-times table are given at the end of the chapter.

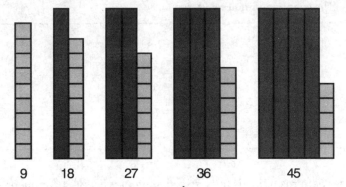

9   18   27   36   45

Figure 5.8   Counting in nines using ones and tens

In the context of learning the multiplication facts, we should mention again the importance of commutativity. This property means that if you know, say, '8 fives' (which is fairly easy because of the pattern in the 5-times table), you also know '5 eights' (which is more difficult). Similarly, if you know, say, '7 nines' (which is not too difficult because of the pattern in the 9-times table), you also know '9 sevens' (which, being from the tricky 7-times table, is obviously much more difficult!). Clearly the ability to employ the commutativity principle strategically cuts down the number of 'difficult' results substantially.

Finally, in this section, we mention how some other potentially difficult results can be derived instantly from easier ones, by the process of *doubling*. Doubling is really easy if there is no carrying involved. So, if you can instantly recall, say, '3 × 4 = 12', you can quickly deduce '6 × 4 = 24' and '3 × 8 = 24' by doubling the 12, and then '6 × 8 = 48' by doubling the 24. Back in the 7-times table, '4 × 7' and '6 × 7' might cause some difficulty – so do we know a related simpler result? Well, we may know '2 × 7 = 14' and '3 × 7 = 21', in which case the doubling procedure quickly and easily gives us '4 × 7 = 28' (doubling 14) and '6 × 7 = 42' (doubling 21). Learning the hundred results in the tables from '1 × 1' to '10 × 10' becomes much easier if these kinds of relationships and patterns are understood and utilised.

THE HUNDRED-SQUARE

In this section we set out to convince infant-teachers that much more emphasis should be placed on children learning to add and subtract using a hundred-square than is currently the practice in many schools. An example of a hundred-square is shown in Figure 5.9.

Significant characteristics of the hundred-square

The hundred-square is a spatial arrangement of numbers that makes transparent (a) the ordinal aspect of number, and (b) the relationships associated with place value. So, for example, 43 is defined by its *position* in the hundred-square. What is significant about 43 is that it comes in a row between 42 and 44. This emphasises the ordinal aspect of number, which, as we have argued in

1	2	3	4	5	6	7	8	9	10
11	12	13	14	15	16	17	18	19	20
21	22	23	24	25	26	27	28	29	30
31	32	33	34	35	36	37	38	39	40
41	42	43	44	45	46	47	48	49	50
51	52	53	54	55	56	57	58	59	60
61	62	63	64	65	66	67	68	69	70
71	72	73	74	75	76	77	78	79	80
81	82	83	84	85	86	87	88	89	90
91	92	93	94	95	96	97	98	99	100

Figure 5.9   A hundred-square

Chapter 2, is often insufficiently emphasised in infant schools, with a consequent overemphasis on the cardinal aspect. The number 43 here is not a set of things (i.e. it is not a cardinal number) – it is a label for one square in an ordered arrangement of squares. The number 43 also refers to the square that comes between 33 and 53 in the column of numbers all ending in the digit 3 – this pattern is, of course, significant in terms of our base-ten place-value system and is related to the fact that there are ten squares in each row. So, what patterns can you see in the hundred-square?

- All the numbers in a column end in the same digit.
- That's because you're adding 10 each time as you go down the columns.
- And you add 1 each time as you go along the rows.
- The numbers in the column on the right are the 10-times table.
- There's a diagonal line of squares starting at 9 that gives the 9-times table!
- And one starting at 11 that gives the 11-times table!
- If you do something like 'add 23' it's the same move each time – down two squares and along three.
- And it's the same if you do 'subtract 23' – only then it's up two squares and back three.

● Do the 2 and the 3 that you move when you're doing these correspond to the 2 tens and 3 ones in 23?

Yes, of course they do! This is a very good example of the way in which the hundred-square can be a powerful aid for developing mental structures that support the mental manipulation of numbers. We will make explicit then some of the steps that children might go through in developing such mental strategies through calculations based on the hundred-square.

Adding ones and adding tens

First, just as with a number line, there is the obvious feature that 'adding 1' corresponds to moving 1 step along, 'adding 2' to moving 2 steps, 'adding 3' to moving 3 steps, and so on. The only difference with the hundred-square is that you have to move to the beginning of the next row when you reach a multiple of 10. This might seem a disadvantage compared to working on a number line, in terms of the image of number as a continuous line going on for ever in both directions. But the hundred-square has the practical advantage of being more compact than a number line labelled from 1 to 100, and the procedure of moving to a new line every time you reach a 10 does emphasise clearly the base-ten aspect of our place-value system. Just as with the number line, children can handle '46 + 7', for example, by doing '46 + 4' to get to the end of the line (making the 46 up to the next ten) and then adding another 3. So, using the procedure for 'adding 2', children can discover, articulate and discuss patterns such as: 6 + 2 = 8, 16 + 2 = 18, 26 + 2 = 28 , 36 + 2 = 38, and so on. Or, with 'adding 7', going over the end of a line each time: 6 + 7 = 13, 16 + 7 = 23, 26 + 7 = 33, 36 + 7 = 43, and so on. These patterns are illustrated in Figure 5.10.

Probably the most significant pattern in the hundred-square is one picked up by some of the infant-teachers in their comments above: the 'adding-10' pattern. If you move down one step this corresponds to 'adding 10'. Then, of course, this extends to 'adding 20' (move down 2 steps), 'adding 30' (move down 3 steps), and so on. So, starting at any square we choose (e.g. 26), children can discover and articulate patterns like this: 26 + 10 = 36, 26 + 20 = 46, 26 + 30 = 56, and so on.

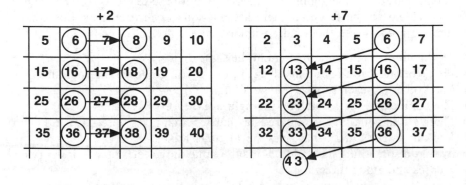

Figure 5.10   Some patterns for adding 2 and adding 7 on the hundred-square

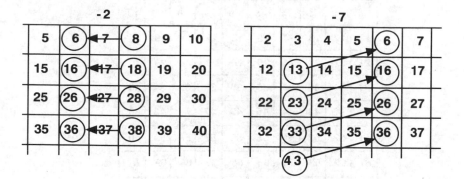

Figure 5.11   Some patterns for subtracting 2 and subtracting 7 on the hundred-square

Subtracting ones and subtracting tens

Clearly, all the adding procedures described above have their inverses in sub-traction procedures, where you move back along a row (rather than forwards) or move up (rather than down) the numbers of steps in question. The same range of patterns is there to be discovered, articulated and discussed by children. For example, there is this kind of pattern for subtracting 2, corresponding to moving 2 steps back along a line: $8 - 2 = 6$, $18 - 2 = 16$, $28 - 2 = 26$, $38 - 2 = 36$, $48 - 2 = 46$, etc. And there is this kind of pattern where the number of steps backward moves you to the line above: $13 - 7 = 6$, $23 - 7 = 16$, $33 - 7 = 26$, $43 - 7 = 36$, and so on. These two examples are illustrated in Figure 5.11. Comparison with the processes in Figure 5.10 makes clear how adding 2 and subtracting 2 (or adding 7 and subtracting 7) are inverse processes.

Subtraction also produces this kind of pattern for subtracting multiples of 10, corresponding to moving up 1 step, 2 steps, 3 steps, and so on: $86 - 10 = 76$, $86 - 20 = 66$, $86 - 30 = 56$, $86 - 40 = 46$, etc. Once again, these kinds of activities on the hundred-square provide mental structures that are helpful for the learner. With these procedures pupils are much more likely to see subtraction and addition as inverse processes than they are if they are using some of the standard written procedures for addition and subtraction.

Patterns for nines and eights

Other patterns in the hundred-square can be helpful in developing a feeling for number. For example, one of the infant-teachers above spotted the pattern for the 9-times table: 9, 18, 27, 36, and so on, all lying on a diagonal line. This is an instance of a more general 'adding 9' pattern. 'Adding 9' can be interpreted as 'move forward 9 steps' – but it can also be interpreted as 'move down 1 step and back 1 step'. This corresponds, of course, to adding 10 and subtracting 1, which, as we saw earlier in this chapter in the discussion of the pattern in the 9-times table, is a really helpful way of thinking about counting in nines. It provides the mental structure for the addition of 9 to any number. For example, '57 + 9' is transformed to '57 + 10 – 1', i.e. '67 – 1'. This pattern for adding 9 then extends naturally to adding 19 (add 20, subtract 1), adding 29

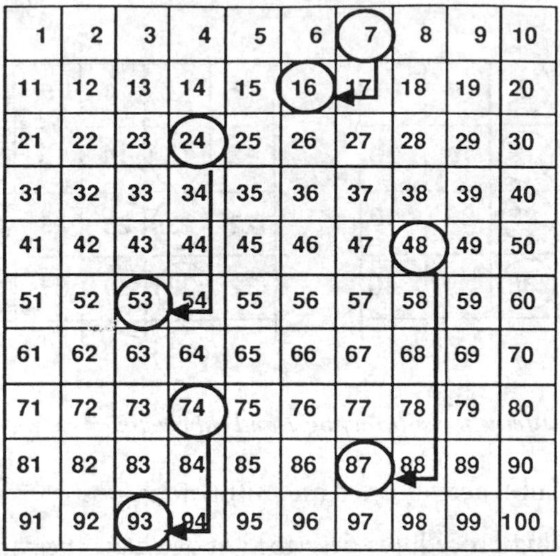

1	2	3	4	5	6	7	8	9	10
11	12	13	14	15	16	17	18	19	20
21	22	23	24	25	26	27	28	29	30
31	32	33	34	35	36	37	38	39	40
41	42	43	44	45	46	47	48	49	50
51	52	53	54	55	56	57	58	59	60
61	62	63	64	65	66	67	68	69	70
71	72	73	74	75	76	77	78	79	80
81	82	83	84	85	86	87	88	89	90
91	92	93	94	95	96	97	98	99	100

Figure 5.12 '7 + 9', '74 + 19', '24 + 29' and '48 + 39' on the hundred-square

(add 30, subtract 1), and so on. Figure 5.12 shows some examples of these processes on the hundred-square in action for various calculations. In the same way, 'add 8' can be seen as a move of '1 step down and 2 steps back', corresponding to 'add 10, subtract 2', which supports a mental process that some people find helpful. For example, '27 + 8' can be transformed to '27 + 10 − 2'. This then extends to adding 18 (add 20, subtract 2), adding 28 (add 30, subtract 2), and so on. And, of course, both the 'add 9' and 'add 8' procedures have their inverses in 'subtract 9' (one step up and one step forward, corresponding to 'subtract 10, add 1') and 'subtract 8' (one step up and two steps forward, corresponding to 'subtract 10, add 2'). These are just the kinds of patterns that we would urge teachers to encourage their pupils to discover, to articulate and then to use in their mental and informal calculations.

Additions with two-digit numbers on the hundred-square

With this background of activities helping to shape appropriate mental structures for visualising addition and subtraction strategies on the hundred-square, children will have the basis for developing effective mental methods for the addition and subtraction of two 2-digit numbers. So, for example, on the hundred-square '26 + 32' is transformed to '26 + 30 + 2', which means: 'Start at 26, move down three steps (adding 30) and along 2 steps (adding 2).' This spatial procedure should then provide pupils with mental structures that will enable them to carry out such calculations mentally, by the same strategy: 26, . . . add 30, . . . 56, . . . add 2, . . . 58. As we argue below, this is so much more valuable to children than introducing them too early to formal written methods of calculation that encourage them to treat the 2 and 6 in 26 and the 3 and 2 in 32 as separate entities. In the hundred-square approach, the number 26 is seen first in terms of its *position* in the ordering of numbers. And 'add 32' is seen as a combination of 'add 30' and 'add 2'.

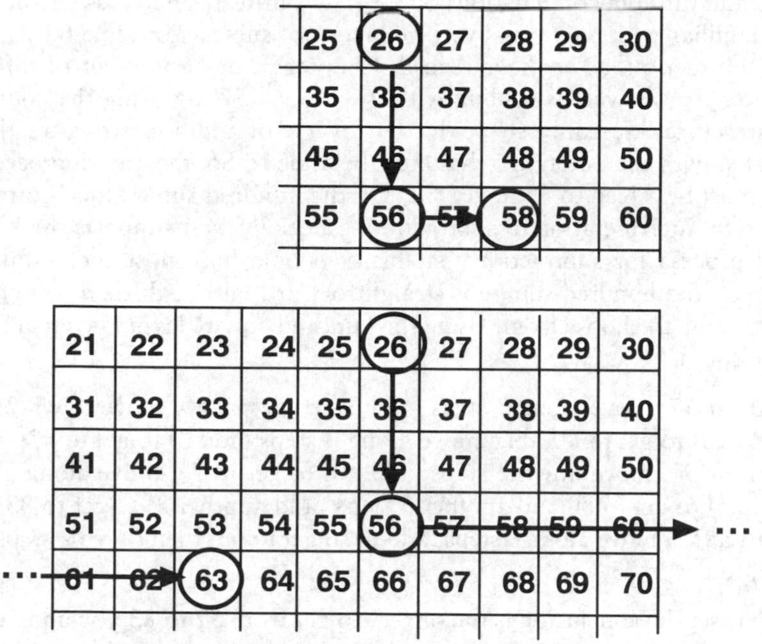

25	(26)	27	28	29	30
35	36	37	38	39	40
45	46	47	48	49	50
55	(56)	57	(58)	59	60

21	22	23	24	25	(26)	27	28	29	30
31	32	33	34	35	36	37	38	39	40
41	42	43	44	45	46	47	48	49	50
51	52	53	54	55	(56)	57	58	59	60
61	62	(63)	64	65	66	67	68	69	70

Figure 5.13 '26 + 32' and '26 + 37' on the hundred-square

Errors in addition are most likely when children tackle an addition such as '26 + 37' by a formal written method involving 'carrying 1'. Using the hundred-square procedure such errors just do not arise. The child starts at 26, adds 30 (3 steps down) to get 56, and then adds 7 to this (7 steps along – possibly by first making up to 60 with 4 steps and then a further 3). Eventually this kind of activity leads to facility with the corresponding mental strategy for '26 + 37': 26, . . . add 30, . . . 56, . . . add 4, . . . 60, . . . add 3, . . . 63. The procedures on the hundred-square corresponding to '26 + 32' and '26 + 37' are illustrated in Figure 5.13.

Subtractions with two-digit numbers on the hundred-square

Subtraction of a two-digit number can be experienced first as simply the re-verse process of addition, using the counting-back principle. So, to deal with '83 – 57' – a tricky subtraction, involving exchanging tens for ones if set out as a vertical calculation – we can simply interpret the 'subtract 57' as '5 steps up' (which takes us to 33) and '7 steps back' (which takes us to 26). Of course, we are assuming here that the procedures for subtracting 50 and for subtracting 7 have already been thoroughly grasped. For most children it is then an achiev-able step from carrying out the process on the hundred-square to performing the task mentally – or informally with paper and pencil – using this kind of strategy: 83, . . . subtract 50, . . . 33, . . . subtract 3, . . . 30, . . . subtract 4, . . . 26. Again, note how the procedure leads the child to deal with 83 as a number in its own right defined by its position in the hundred-square – not as an 8 and a 3, with a 5 and a 7 to be taken away, and with all the potential for bizarre and random combinations of 8, 3, 5, 7, little 1s and crossings-out that are so familiar with the formal vertical layout of subtractions like this.

But subtraction, as we have seen in Chapter 3, has a number of different structures. So, as well as dealing with, say, '83 – 57' by using the counting-back structure, we can also apply the inverse-of-addition structure that is associated with the question 'what must be added?' So, the question becomes: 'What must be added to 57 to get 83?' On the hundred-square this is often the most useful interpretation of subtraction, especially as it supports the kind of mental process for subtraction that many people find most successful. The process on the hundred-square is straightforward, although there are at least three variants to choose from! Using the hundred-square layout given in Figure 5.9, we could:

(a) start at 57, move along 3 steps (add 3), to get to 60, move down 2 steps (add 20) to get to 80, then move along 3 steps (add 3) to get to 83;
(b) start at 57, move down 2 steps (add 20) to get to 77, move along 3 steps (add 3) to get to 80 and another 3 steps (add another 3) to get to 83;
(c) start at 57, move along 6 steps (add 6) to get to 63, then down 2 steps (add 20) to get to 83.

In each case, the conclusion is the same – to get from 57 to 83 you add 26. For many people, variant (a) is a strategy that might be used quite often. Mentally the process may be something like this: 57, . . . add 3 makes 60, . . . 70, 80, . . . that's another 20, . . . that makes 23, . . . and another 3 to get to 83, . . . that makes 26. This kind of mental reasoning can, of course, be supported by whatever informal jottings are helpful to aid the memory. It should also be supported by corresponding moves on a number line marked from 0 to 100, such as a metre-rule.

The two-hundred-grid

The astute reader will be wondering about additions of two-digit numbers where the answer is greater than 100. How do you learn to do these using a hundred-square? The answer is simple: extend it to a two-hundred-grid! Figure 5.14 shows a possible layout for a 200-grid and, as an example, the steps involved for the addition '76 + 57': start at 76, move down 5 steps (add 50) to 126, and move along 7 steps (add 7) to 133. An alternative approach is for the children to use the hundred-square, but to continue back at the top when they get to the bottom, simply remembering to say 'one hundred and . . . '. So, for example, in tackling '76 + 57' they would move from 76, to 86, to 96, then up to the top again to 6 (but saying 'one hundred and six'), then to 16 (but saying 'one hundred and sixteen'), and so on.

To get to the stage where this level of addition can be carried out confidently we have to extend two kinds of patterns. First, we have to be able to extend an 'adding-10' pattern beyond 100. For example: 76 + 10 = 86, 76 + 20 = 96, 76 + 30 = 106, 76 + 40 = 116, and so on. Then, we have to be able to extend a sequence such as '6 + 7 = 13, 16 + 7 = 23, 26 + 7 = 33, 36 + 7 = 43, . . . 86 + 7 = 93' beyond 100: 96 + 7 = 103, 106 + 7 = 113, 116 + 7 = 123, and so on. Of

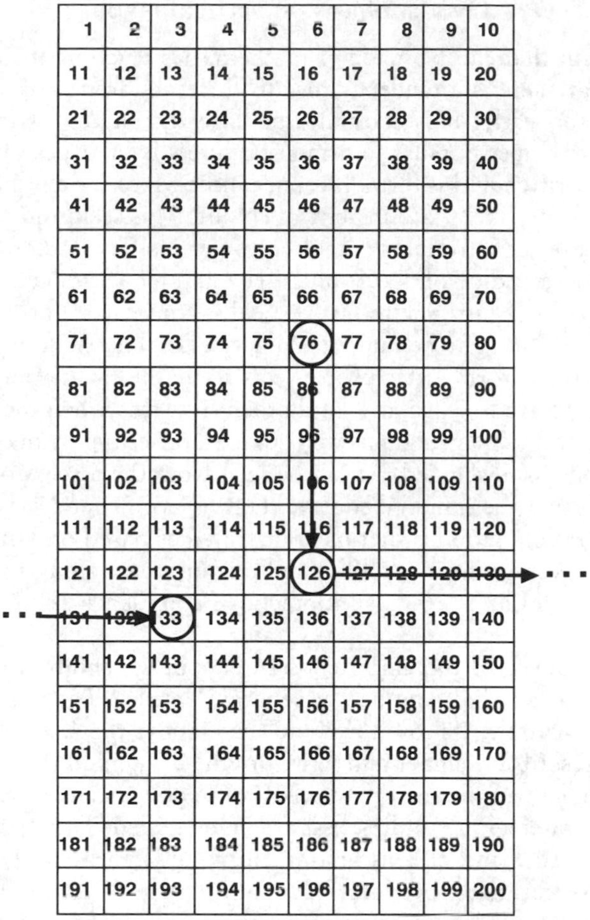

1	2	3	4	5	6	7	8	9	10
11	12	13	14	15	16	17	18	19	20
21	22	23	24	25	26	27	28	29	30
31	32	33	34	35	36	37	38	39	40
41	42	43	44	45	46	47	48	49	50
51	52	53	54	55	56	57	58	59	60
61	62	63	64	65	66	67	68	69	70
71	72	73	74	75	76	77	78	79	80
81	82	83	84	85	86	87	88	89	90
91	92	93	94	95	96	97	98	99	100
101	102	103	104	105	106	107	108	109	110
111	112	113	114	115	116	117	118	119	120
121	122	123	124	125	126	127	128	129	130
131	132	133	134	135	136	137	138	139	140
141	142	143	144	145	146	147	148	149	150
151	152	153	154	155	156	157	158	159	160
161	162	163	164	165	166	167	168	169	170
171	172	173	174	175	176	177	178	179	180
181	182	183	184	185	186	187	188	189	190
191	192	193	194	195	196	197	198	199	200

Figure 5.14   '76 + 57' on a two-hundred-grid

course, in terms of movements on the 200-grid these are not difficult extensions. With these ideas secure, we can handle the two steps of '76 + 50' and '126 + 7' that are involved in '76 + 57'.

Then, of course, with the provision of a 200-grid, pupils can handle the corresponding subtractions, such as '133 – 57' – either by counting back 57, or by starting at 57 and adding on. To deal with these mentally by counting back they will need to be able to subtract 10, 20, 30, 40, and so on, from any number up to 200, particularly those that cross over the 100 mark, such as '133 – 50'. Appropriate activities on the 200-grid can establish patterns of results like: 133 – 10 = 123, 133 – 20 = 113, 133 – 30 = 103, 133 – 40 = 93, and so on.

CHILDREN'S ERRORS AND VERTICAL LAYOUT

I couldn't do any of the sums in the test. They were all flat sums like 26 + 37. We've only been taught how to do the ones that go up and down. (*11-year-old boy complaining about the Key Stage Two National Curriculum Mathematics test.*)

Overemphasis on vertical layout

A fair criticism that can be made of mathematics teaching in British primary schools is that there is a tendency to introduce children to vertical layout of calculations too early. It is certainly the case that many of the commercial mathematics schemes popular in primary schools have pages of additions and subtractions written in this form. It is not unknown to see children as young as 5 writing out sums like '6 + 2' in vertical layout! This seems quite bizarre to us. There is no case for introducing children to vertical layout before they have a thorough understanding of place value (see Chapter 1). Indeed our experience is that the too early introduction of vertical layout can be positively harmful. Presumably the thought behind this practice is that writing additions and subtractions in this form is the 'proper' way to do the calculations, the children will eventually have to learn how to do them like this when they get on to the harder sums, and so they might as well get used to setting them out in this form now! Such logic is misguided. As can be seen from the discussion above about calculations using the hundred-square, there is no 'proper' way of doing calculations. Our contention is that mental strategies based on visual or pictorial images, such as movements on the hundred-square or along the number line, are the major priority for the development of confidence and success in handling numbers.

Vertical layout used too early tends to encourage children to think of the digits in, say, a two-digit number, as separate entities. They may well set out, say, '13 + 24' with the 1 above the 2 and the 3 above the 4, add the 3 and the 4 first in the prescribed manner and write down 7, then add the 1 and the 2 and write down 3, getting the correct answer, but in doing so have no conception at all of the two numbers 13 and 24 that are being added. They have just added 3 and 4 and added 1 and 2! This kind of thinking is particularly encouraged if pupils are just learning procedures for manipulating the symbols without substantial experience of relating them to the concrete embodiments of place value, such as base-ten blocks and 1p, 10p and 100p coins.

Some typical errors in vertical layout

Not surprisingly then, vertical layout leads to all manner of errors, many related to the tendency to treat the digits as separate numbers and then to combine them in various ways that ignore or apply wrongly the place-value principle. Figure 5.15 shows some of the many common errors that children make in addition and subtraction using vertical layout.

In examples (a) and (b) in Figure 5.15 the child concerned has in each case just added up the three digits in the two numbers. In example (c) the child has made a common mistake associated with failing to write the units in the same column. In example (d) the child has added the 6 and 7 to get 13, written this down, then added the 2 and 3 to get 5, without remembering to 'carry one'. In example (e), another child has tried to apply the principle of carrying but has carried the wrong bit of the 13. In example (f) the pupil has worked from left to right, rather than from right to left and consequently misapplied the carrying procedure. Example (g) is the most familiar subtraction error: simply

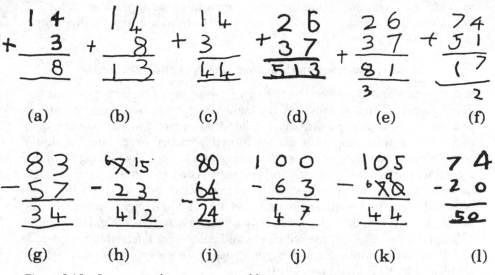

Figure 5.15   Some typical errors in vertical layout

taking the smaller digit from the larger one each time. Children have many original ways of muddling up the decomposition process in subtraction. Example (h) is a case where the child has used the idea of exchanging a ten for ten ones unnecessarily and finished up writing 12 in the units column! Zeros in subtraction questions have huge potential for generating all kinds of errors, such as those shown in examples (i), (j), (k) and (l). Sometimes children just ignore a zero, as in example (i). Other times they treat it like 10, as in example (j). And sometimes, because they remember that you have to apply a different procedure when there is a zero in the top number of a subtraction they will try to apply this to a zero in the bottom number, as shown in example (k). Finally, it is not uncommon for children always to write down 0 as the result whenever they have to subtract 0, as shown in example (l).

Now this is not intended to be a comprehensive analysis of all the errors that children can and do make in written calculations. But we have provided these typical examples because we are convinced that they are all errors that just would not occur if these pupils had not yet seen vertical layout and if they had been encouraged to develop mental and informal strategies based on the hundred-square or the number line, for what the 11-year-old quoted above calls 'flat sums'. Faced with '26 + 37' the mental strategies encouraged by the hundred-square (26, . . . add 30, . . . 56, . . . add 4, . . . 60, . . . add 3, . . . 63) would never lead to answers like 513 or 81! And, given the subtraction '75 − 23', we would expect an average 7-year-old brought up on activities on the hundred-square and the number line to reason along these lines: 75, . . . subtract 20, . . . 55, . . . subtract 3, . . . 52, with these mental steps supported by images of moving up and back along the rows of the hundred-square – not to launch themselves into a process of random borrowing or exchanging! Of course, children will make errors in using these mental strategies – mainly through recalling number bonds incorrectly or forgetting where they have got to – which is why they should be encouraged to make appropriate informal jottings as they go along. But they are less likely to apply a totally wrong procedure.

Standard written methods for addition and subtraction

In this section and in previous sections we have argued strongly the case for the development of mental processes for manipulating numbers based on visual and pictorial images, particularly the hundred-square and the number line, rather than emphasising too early the formal, standard procedures for doing additions and subtractions. There is a strong case for not introducing at all the formal written methods for addition and subtraction to children up to the age of about 8 years. Readers who wish nevertheless to get to grips with these standard procedures – and are interested in how children might come to *understand* them by making connections with concrete materials embodying place-value principles, such as base-ten blocks and coins – are referred to Chapters 5 and 7 of *Mathematics Explained for Primary Teachers* by Derek Haylock (published by Paul Chapman, 1995).

SOME FUNDAMENTAL PROPERTIES OF NUMBER-OPERATIONS

In this final section we summarise and state explicitly and in general terms some of the fundamental properties of number-operations that underpin much of our manipulation of numbers.

Commutativity

We have already discussed extensively – both in Chapter 4 and in this present chapter – the principle of *commutativity* that applies to addition and multiplication. We have seen how the principle is important both in terms of understanding the structure of the operations and also for making certain calculations more accessible. Most people, for instance, given '5 + 88' would automatically change it to '88 + 5', so that they can start with the 88 and add on 5, which is much easier to conceptualise than to start with the 5 and add on 88. In doing this they are, no doubt unconsciously, making use of the commutativity of addition. Likewise, if you needed to find the value of '5 × 46' you would be well advised to think of it as '46 fives' rather than '5 forty-sixes'. The commutative properties of multiplication and addition are expressed in general terms as follows:

$$a + b = b + a \qquad \text{(commutativity of addition)}$$
$$a \times b = b \times a \qquad \text{(commutativity of multiplication)}$$

This means that in practice the order in which you write down a sum or a product makes no difference to the result. We should note, however, that the operations of subtraction and division are not commutative, since, in general, '$a - b$' does not equal '$b - a$' and '$a \div b$' does not equal '$b \div a$'. (We say 'in general' because these are equal if a and b happen to be the same number!)

These are clearly important and fundamental principles that children must learn and get into their mental structures for manipulating numbers – at the basic level they should know, for example, that it makes a big difference whether you enter '28 ÷ 4' on a calculator or '4 ÷ 28', but it makes no difference whether you enter '28 × 4' or '4 × 28'.

The principle of complements

Subtraction and division do satisfy, however, what we will call the *principle of complements*. In terms of subtraction, in a nutshell this says that if a is the complement of b with respect to some number, then b is the complement of a. Here are some examples of what we mean:

$10 - 4 = 6$	$10 - 6 = 4$	(4 and 6 are 10-complements)
$60 - 35 = 25$	$60 - 25 = 35$	(35 and 25 are 60-complements)
$100 - 24 = 76$	$100 - 76 = 24$	(24 and 76 are 100-complements)
$113 - 47 = 66$	$113 - 66 = 47$	(47 and 66 are 113-complements)

There is a similar pattern of relationships for division. A number that divides exactly into another number is called a *factor*. So, for example, 3 is a factor of 12 and 4 is also a factor of 12. But these two factors (3 and 4) are what might be called *complementary factors*, because 12 ÷ 4 is 3 and 12 ÷ 3 is 4. Here are a number of examples of what we are referring to here:

$12 ÷ 4 = 3$	$12 ÷ 3 = 4$	(3 and 4 are complementary factors of 12)
$28 ÷ 4 = 7$	$28 ÷ 7 = 4$	(7 and 4 are complementary factors of 28)
$90 ÷ 5 = 18$	$90 ÷ 18 = 5$	(18 and 5 are complementary factors of 90)
$17 ÷ 1 = 17$	$17 ÷ 17 = 1$	(17 and 1 are complementary factors of 17)

These patterns of results are clearly very useful in our understanding and manipulation of subtraction and division. Expressed in general terms they look like this:

if $x - a = b$ then $x - b = a$ (the principle of complements for subtraction)
if $x ÷ a = b$ then $x ÷ b = a$ (the principle of complements for division)

Associativity

Earlier in this chapter, when discussing the use of complements in addition, for making up to 10, we happily transformed something like '8 + (2 + 5)' into '(8 + 2) + 5', without comment. The brackets mean 'do this bit first'. So, '8 + (2 + 5)' is '8 + 7' and '(8 + 2) + 5' is '10 + 5'. We used this procedure because '10 + 5' is an easier sum than '8 + 7'. This is, incidentally, another example where a transformation is applied to a mathematical situation and an equivalence emerges – one of the themes we discussed in Chapter 1. We wish now to make explicit the mathematical principle behind this transformation. This is the principle of *associativity*, which, like commutativity, applies to addition and multiplication but not to subtraction and division. In relation to the example above the principle asserts that the 2 can be 'associated' with either the 8 on the left or the 5 on the right and it makes no difference to the answer. With multiplication, we get a similar pattern. For example, '(3 × 5) × 2' gives the same result as '3 × (5 × 2)' – i.e. 15 × 2 = 3 × 10.

Here are some further examples of the principle applied to addition and multiplication:

$$3 + (7 + 4) = (3 + 7) + 4$$
$$(5 + 8) + 12 = 5 + (8 + 12)$$
$$(3 \times 4) \times 5 = 3 \times (4 \times 5)$$
$$7 \times (10 \times 2) = (7 \times 10) \times 2$$

The readers should convince themselves that the same is not true for subtraction and division. For example, '10 – (5 – 3)' is not equal to '(10 – 5) – 3', and '24 ÷ (6 ÷ 2)' is not equal to '(24 ÷ 6) ÷ 2'. The patterns of results for addition and multiplication are expressed in general terms as follows:

$$a + (b + c) = (a + b) + c \qquad \text{(associativity of addition)}$$
$$a \times (b \times c) = (a \times b) \times c \qquad \text{(associativity of multiplication)}$$

For addition, like commutativity, this principle of associativity is not difficult to grasp. It is really quite apparent that, say, 'a 3-rod' on one side combined with 'a 7-rod and a 4-rod' on the other side gives you the same arrangement of rods as 'a 3-rod and a 7-rod' on one side and 'a 4-rod' on the other. When used along with the principle of commutativity, associativity allows you to write a string of numbers to be added without brackets and to combine them in any order you like. The fact that most children pick up this trick fairly easily supports the suggestion that the principles of commutativity and associativity in addition are self-evident.

But, again like commutativity, associativity is by no means an obvious principle when it comes to multiplication. It would seem not to be self-evident that '(3 × 4) × 5' should give the same answer as '3 × (4 × 5)'. Figure 5.16 provides a concrete embodiment of the principle, using this example. The rectangular block in Figure 5.16(a) is made up of 5 layers each of which is a 3 × 4 rectangle of cubes, whereas the rectangular block in (b) is made up of 3 layers each of which is a 4 × 5 rectangle of cubes. Clearly the two blocks have the same number of cubes – because they are actually the same block but standing with a different face uppermost. As with addition, once established the principle of associativity for multiplication combined with commutativity allows you to write a string of numbers to be multiplied without brackets and to combine

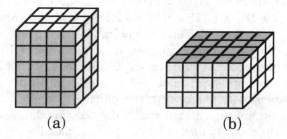

(a)   (b)

Figure 5.16   Showing associativity in multiplication: (a) (3 × 4) × 5; (b) 3 × (4 × 5)

them in any order you like. This is a useful trick. For example, '5 × 7 × 4' is probably easier if transformed to '5 × 4 × 7', i.e. '20 × 7'.

The distributive laws

The distributive laws may appear to be rather advanced mathematics for teachers of young children, but they are included here for the sake of completeness. They state essentially that both multiplication and division can be *distributed* across either an addition or a subtraction. Here are some examples – the reader is encouraged to check that the calculations on the left and right sides of the equals sign do come to the same answer in each case:

$(30 + 2) \times 3 = (30 \times 3) + (2 \times 3)$
Here multiplication by 3 is distributed across the addition of 30 and 2.
$(10 - 1) \times 7 = (10 \times 7) - (1 \times 7)$
Here multiplication by 7 is distributed across the subtraction '10 – 1'.
$(60 + 9) \div 3 = (60 \div 3) + (9 \div 3)$
Here division by 3 is distributed across the addition of 60 and 9.
$(700 - 14) \div 7 = (700 \div 7) - (14 \div 7)$
Here division by 7 is distributed across the subtraction '700 – 14'.

In fact, these are not as complicated as they look! The first example here is what most of us would do if asked to multiply 32 by 3: we would envisage it as 3 thirties and 3 twos. The second example simply expresses in formal terms the reasoning that emerged in the conversation earlier in this chapter about counting in nines: because '9 = 10 – 1', '7 × 9' can be transformed into '7 tens subtract 7 ones', i.e. '70 – 7'. The third and fourth examples make explicit the way in which some of us might tackle '69 ÷ 3' and '686 ÷ 7', by transforming the 69 into '60 + 9' and the 686 into '700 – 14'. For further discussion of the distributive laws and for examples of the principle in use in multiplication and division calculations, the reader is referred to Chapters 9 and 11 of *Mathematics Explained for Primary Teachers*. In summary, the generalisations of these distributive laws are as follows:

$(a + b) \times c = (a \times c) + (b \times c)$
(multiplication is distributive across addition)
$(a - b) \times c = (a \times c) - (b \times c)$
(multiplication is distributive across subtraction)
$(a + b) \div c = (a \div c) + (b \div c)$
(division is distributive across addition)
$(a - b) \div c = (a \div c) - (b \div c)$
(division is distributive across subtraction)

Identities

Zero (0) and one (1) are arguably the two most important numbers in the whole number system. Because of its special properties in relation to addition, zero is sometimes referred to as the *additive identity*. This refers to the observation that if you add zero to any number the result is identical to what you had to start with. 'Add 0' means 'do nothing'. The same thing applies to subtracting zero, of course. Similarly, the number one (1) is sometimes referred to as the *multiplicative identity*, because multiplying by 1 leaves a number unchanged. So, 'multiply by 1' also means 'do nothing'. And, of course, the same is true of dividing by 1 – for example, $7 \div 1 = 7$. In summary these are the four basic properties of 0 and 1 to be grasped, expressed as generalisations for any number a:

$$a + 0 = a$$
$$a - 0 = a$$
$$a \times 1 = a$$
$$a \div 1 = a$$

Zero also has some tricky properties in relation to multiplication and division that take a little thought. Explaining '$7 \times 0 = 0$' and '$0 \times 7 = 0$' is not too difficult – thinking of these as '7 sets of 0 items' or '0 sets of 7 items', using the repeated-addition structure of multiplication is straightforward enough. But children do need to think these through and discuss them, otherwise they will apply wrongly the additive-identity principle to multiplication, giving, for example, the answer 7 for '7×0' – on the (incorrect) basis that '$\times 0$' means 'do nothing'. Divisions involving zero are rather more puzzling. What do you make of '$0 \div 7$' and '$7 \div 0$'? The first can be understood using the equal-sharing structure of division: a set of 0 items shared between 7 people results in each person getting 0. So '$0 \div 7 = 0$'. However, '$7 \div 0$' makes no sense in terms of equal-sharing – you cannot envisage sharing 7 items between no people! However, we can interpret it as 'how many sets of 0 items make a total of 7 items?' Well, you can go on accumulating sets of 0 items as long as you like and you will never reach a total of 7. For example, we have put two thousand sets of zero elephants inside these brackets: [   ] – and we're still nowhere near to getting 7 elephants! The conclusion of this line of reasoning is that you cannot do '$7 \div 0$'. It is a calculation without an answer. Mathematicians say that division by zero is not allowed. So does any calculator – try it and see. (You may have heard somewhere that '$7 \div 0$' is equal to infinity – there is a branch of number theory that uses that kind of language, but please do not think that there is a real number called 'infinity'.) So, in summary, for any number a, the following generalisations can be made for multiplications and divisions involving zero:

$$a \times 0 = 0$$
$$0 \times a = 0$$
$$0 \div a = 0$$
$$a \div 0 \text{ cannot be done}$$

Inverses

Finally, in our review of some fundamental properties of number operations we summarise the idea of *inverses*. Most mathematical operations have an inverse operation. An inverse operation 'undoes' or reverses the effect of the first operation. The idea of inverses is central to concepts such as up and down, on and off, forward and back, left and right, clockwise and anticlockwise, and so on. A more advanced example might be finding the square root of a number (e.g. 6 is the square root of 36), which is the inverse operation of finding the square (e.g. 36 is the square of 6). Scaling a diagram by a factor of 3 (enlarging it), is the inverse of scaling it by a factor of one-third (reducing it). Applied to the four basic operations with numbers, we have already seen (in Chapters 2 and 3) that addition and subtraction are inverses. Children should discuss and articulate the pattern of relationships in examples such as these:

$3 + 4 = 7$	$7 - 4 = 3$	(subtracting 4 is the inverse of adding 4)
$15 - 8 = 7$	$7 + 8 = 15$	(adding 8 is the inverse of subtracting 8)
$57 + 24 = 81$	$81 - 24 = 57$	(subtracting 24 is the inverse of adding 24)

As we have seen in this chapter, these relationships are reinforced by movements on the number line and on the hundred-square. For example, adding 24 is achieved by 2 steps down and 4 along, subtracting 24 is the reverse process, 2 steps up and 4 back.

In Chapters 2 and 4 we described the operations of multiplication and division as inverses. So, using a calculator if necessary in order to focus on the mathematical structure, children should discuss and articulate the pattern of relationships in examples such as these:

$3 \times 4 = 12$	$12 \div 4 = 3$	(dividing by 4 is the inverse of multiplying by 4)
$56 \div 7 = 8$	$8 \times 7 = 56$	(multiplying by 7 is the inverse of dividing by 7)
$23 \times 5 = 115$	$115 \div 5 = 23$	(dividing by 5 is the inverse of multiplying by 5)

So, in summary, we can generalise these patterns for any numbers a, b and c, as follows:

if $a + b = c$ then $c - b = a$	(subtraction is the inverse of addition)
if $a - b = c$ then $c + b = a$	(addition is the inverse of subtraction)
if $a \times b = c$ then $c \div b = a$	(division is the inverse of multiplication)
if $a \div b = c$ then $c \times b = a$	(multiplication is the inverse of division)

SOME ACTIVITIES WITH CHILDREN

Throughout this chapter we have made suggestions for activities that might be used to enable children to build up their confidence in manipulating numbers through the development of the sense of pattern in numbers. Teachers should take every opportunity to encourage children to identify, to articulate and to use pattern in numbers. As we have seen, children can search for patterns in the addition and multiplication tables. They can interpret additions and subtractions with one- and two-digit numbers on a number line and on the hundred-square. They can discuss how to use ten-complements and hundred-complements, and how to relate sums to fives and doubles. Teachers should also give time for children to share different ideas for informal methods of doing calculations, whether these be mental, written or a combination of the two. Below we offer a few further suggestions for developing confidence with number through a greater awareness of pattern.

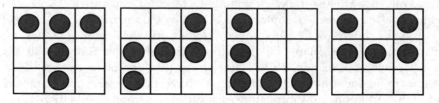

Figure 5.17   Some dot patterns for 5 (Activity 5.1)

Activity 5.1: dot patterns
Objective   To develop children's sense of the different ways in which the numbers from 1 to 9 can be made up.
   Materials   Each child needs a 3 × 3-square grid drawn on a square piece of card and 10 counters. They also require some sheets of centimetre-squared paper on which several 3 × 3-square grids have been drawn.
   Method   Starting with, say, 5, the children make as many different patterns as they can by putting five counters on the 3 × 3 grid. They record each different pattern by drawing dots on the grids on the squared paper. Discussion about what counts as a different pattern is valuable. This will involve picking up the sheet of paper with the patterns recorded so far and rotating it – or even looking at in in a mirror. Figure 5.17 shows some of the patterns for 5. The children do this for all numbers from 1 to 9. Each child then chooses his or her 'favourite' pattern for each number. They cut these out and arrange them for display, with the appropriate numerals written underneath.

Activity 5.2: rhythmic counting
Objective   To emphasise the rhythmic pattern of counting in twos, threes, fours, and so on.
   Materials   A drum or a tambour.
   Method   The class counts rhythmically in unison from 1 to, say, 50, while the teacher (or a child with a good sense of rhythm) beats in time on the drum or tambour. For counting in twos, they stress every second number: one, *two*, three, *four*, five, *six*, . . . and so on. When this is mastered they do the same thing again, whispering the numbers that are not being stressed; and then once again not saying them at all, but still maintaining the same rhythm. Then move on to counting in threes, stressing every third number, then counting in fours, stressing every fourth number.
   As an extension, the whole activity can then be done to the accompaniment of appropriate music – with 2 beats in a bar (e.g. a polka), 3 beats in a bar (e.g. a waltz), or 4 beats in a bar (e.g. a march).

Activity 5.3: how many trains?
Objective   To connect number combinations with visual images.
   Materials   A collection of coloured rods for 1 to 9; squared paper and colouring pens.
   Method   The children take one of the rods and find all the ways they can of making up a train of rods of the same length, using first two rods, then three

rods, and so on. For example, they could make a train of length 5 in 15 different ways: 1 + 4, 2 + 3, 3 + 2, 4 + 1, 1 + 1 + 3, 1 + 2 + 2, 1 + 3 + 1, 2 + 1 + 2, 2 + 2 + 1, 3 + 1 + 1, 1 + 1 + 1 + 2, 1 + 1 + 2 + 1, 1 + 2 + 1 + 1, 2 + 1 + 1 + 1, 1 + 1 + 1 + 1. Children should be encouraged to be systematic and to look for and use pattern. Discussion of whether, e.g., '1 + 1 + 3' is the same as '1 + 3 + 1' involves the principles of commutativity and associativity. This would lead to reduction of the list above to only 6 possibilities. These can then be copied on to squared paper, by colouring squares, and recorded in symbols.

Activity 5.4: Oddtown and Eventown
Objective To reinforce the concepts of odd and even.
Materials Red and white (or any two colours) Lego bricks, or similar materials that click together and can be used to build towers; small model cars numbered from 1 to 10; model people.
Method As part of their learning about the patterns of odd and even in number, a group of younger children assemble two model towns. In Oddtown all the buildings are made from an odd number of bricks and in Eventown from an even number. They should use red and white bricks alternately in their buildings, so, for example, a building with seven bricks will be made from four red and three white. They then put cars in the two towns according to whether they are odd-numbered or even-numbered. They also put a group with an odd number of model people in Oddtown and a group with an even number in Eventown. This can then be continued by adding other items that can be classified as odd or even – we leave this to the creativity of the teacher and the children.

Activity 5.5: making tables
Objective To introduce the multiplication tables through spatial arrangements of numbers.
Materials For each child: ten different grids cut from squared paper, each with rows of 10 squares, but with the number of rows ranging from 1 to 10 (Figure 5.18(a) shows the grid with 4 rows); a further ten grids each with columns of 10 squares, but with the number of columns ranging from 1 to 10 (Figure 5.18(b) shows the grid with 4 columns).
Method The children fill up each of the ten grids in the first set with numbers, counting from 1 in the top left-hand corner, down the columns, until they have filled up the whole grid. Figure 5.18(a) shows the completed grid with 4 rows. Discuss with the children the patterns in the arrangement of numbers and especially how the bottom row of numbers is 'counting in 4s' (or whatever the number of squares in the columns). They then cut out the bottom row from each of the ten grids and assemble them in order to make a multiplication square.

They should then repeat this with the other set of grids, with all the columns having 10 squares but the numbers of columns ranging from 1 to 10. This time they write the numbers in order along the rows, as shown in Figure 5.18(b), and cut out and assemble the final columns. They should finish up with two identical multiplication tables and a considerable amount of material for discussion of pattern in number.

1	5	9	13	17	21	25	29	33	37
2	6	10	14	18	22	26	30	34	38
3	7	11	15	19	23	27	31	35	39
4	8	12	16	20	24	28	32	36	40

(a)

1	2	3	4
5	6	7	8
9	10	11	12
13	14	15	16
17	18	19	20
21	22	23	24
25	26	27	28
29	30	31	32
33	34	35	36
37	38	39	40

(b)

Figure 5.18   Making tables (Activity 5.5)

Activity 5.6: table patterns on the hundred-square
Objective   To explore patterns on the hundred-square and to develop the patterns of counting in 2s, 3s, 4s and so on.

Materials   Photocopied sheets of hundred-squares (see Figure 5.9).

Method   This is a basic activity that emphasises pattern in number. On one of the hundred-squares the children count in 2s, touching every second number as they say them (2, 4, 6, . . .). They then go back and colour in each of these numbers, using just one colour, and discuss the pattern that emerges. Repeat this, counting in 3s, 4s, 5s, . . . , and so on, using a different colour for each pattern. Compare the patterns and discuss the relationships that emerge. Notice the simple arrangements of 2, 5 and 10, the diagonal patterns for 3, 6 and 9, the awkwardness of 7, the way in which the pattern for 4 is part of the pattern for 2 and the pattern for 9 is part of the pattern for 3, and so on.

Activity 5.7: the 9p shop
Objective   To strengthen understanding of the patterns in the tables through connections with money.

Materials   A pretend shop and a supply of plastic coins (10p, 1p, 2p, 5p).

Method   In the class shop, have a day when each item for sale costs 9p. Shoppers have only 10p coins and the shopkeeper has only 10p and 1p coins. So a child purchasing 6 articles will pay with 6 tens and get 6 ones change; for 5 articles, it is 5 tens and 5 ones change, and so on. The experience should be supported by appropriate discussion with the teacher.

An easier example is to have a day when each item costs 5p. Shoppers have 5p and 10p coins and the shopkeeper gives no change.

A more difficult example is to have a day when each item costs 8p. Shoppers have only 10p coins and the shopkeeper has 10p and 2p coins. Now to purchase 4 articles the shopper tenders 4 tens and receives in change 4 twos. Again, discussion is essential for the children to learn most effectively from this experience.

Activity 5.8: board games on the hundred-square

Objective   To reinforce the procedures for addition and subtraction on the hundred-square.

Material   A hundred-square drawn on card; coloured counters; various dice.

Method   There are numerous variations of board games using a hundred-square, all of which are helpful for developing children's facility with number. Snakes and Ladders is one of the best examples. Teachers can devise their own variations to target particular number skills.

For example, to target addition and subtraction of numbers from 0 to 29, the following game might be played by two or three children. The children have two dice of different colours. One die, representing tens, has two blank faces, two labelled 1 and two labelled 2. The other, representing units, is labelled, say, 0, 2, 3, 6, 8, 9. (Alternatively, use a ten-faced die labelled from 0 to 9.) When it is their turn each child throws the two dice to generate a number from 0 to 29. For example, if the first die shows 1 and the second shows 3 their score is 13. They move their counter accordingly. On the first three turns they move forward – i.e. they add their score. But on the fourth turn they move backwards – i.e. they subtract their score. So, for example, a child having scored 13, 18, 22 on the first three turns would be on the square labelled 53. If the score on the next turn is 29, the child's counter moves back 29 to 24. The first child to reach or pass 100 is the winner. Any child who is unfortunate enough to go back beyond 1 is out – but each round does not last long and they will soon be playing again. Children should be discouraged in making their moves from simply counting in ones. So, for example, to add 18, they should move 1 ten, by moving down 1 row, and then move the 8 units, making use of ten-complements as appropriate.

SUMMARY OF KEY IDEAS IN CHAPTER 5

1. An awareness of pattern in number relationships is an important factor in developing confidence and success in manipulating numbers.
2. Many aspects of pattern in number can be understood more strongly by making connections with visual, pictorial and spatial imagery.
3. The ten-complement of a number is what you need to add to make it up to 10. Ten-complements are important for young children in developing their facility with basic addition and subtraction facts.
4. Instant recall of complements in relation to many other numbers is also very useful, especially all the numbers up to 20.
5. Being able to recall hundred-complements is important in mental manipulation of two-digit numbers.
6. Sixty-complements are significant in calculations with time.
7. Two strategies for learning basic number bonds that young children find useful are (a) reference to fives and (b) reference to doubles.
8. Tallying is a useful skill that incorporates the idea of reference to fives.
9. Instant recall of multiplication tables is an important objective for numeracy. But learning these with understanding includes recognising and using the extensive range of patterns in the tables and the relationships between various results.
10. As well as working with concrete materials, such as base-ten blocks and coins, children will benefit from extensive use of the hundred-square in the early stages of addition and subtraction calculations.
11. In the hundred-square what is significant about a number is its position in relation to other numbers: this emphasises both the ordinal aspect of number and aspects of place value.

12. Additions and subtractions on the hundred-square are experienced as spatial patterns of movements, forward and back, down and up. These experiences promote mental structures that support effective procedures for mental calculations and also emphasise addition and subtraction as inverse processes.
13. Vertical layout introduced too early, before pupils have a secure grasp of place value, can encourage a range of errors in addition and subtraction.
14. This contrasts with an approach based on the hundred-square and the number line, that develops informal, mental procedures for addition and subtraction with two-digit numbers – with an emphasis on the whole number in its ordinal aspect, rather than on the individual digits.
15. Fundamental properties of number operations include: commutativity of addition and multiplication, the principle of complements for subtraction and division, associativity of addition and multiplication, the distributive laws, properties of the additive identity (0) and the multiplicative identity (1), and inverses.

SUGGESTIONS FOR FURTHER READING

Ashlock, R. B. (3rd edition, 1982) *Error Patterns in Computation: a Semi-Programmed Approach*, Charles E. Merril Publishing, Columbus, Ohio, USA. (An enjoyable way of looking at some typical errors in children's calculations with formal, written methods.)

Bierhoff, H. (1996) *Laying the Foundations of Numeracy: a Comparison of Primary School Textbooks in Britain, Germany and Switzerland* (Discussion Paper 90), NIESR, London. (Not all the conclusions in this paper are necessarily supported by the evidence provided, but we can certainly learn from the comparisons made between the standard British approaches to written calculations in primary schools – such as the too early introduction of vertical layout – and the approaches adopted in Germany and Switzerland.)

Deboys, M. and Pitt, E. (2nd edition, 1980) *Lines of Development in Primary Mathematics*, Blackstaff Press, Belfast. (A very thorough book that many teachers and student-teachers have found helpful and that has been adopted as an Open University set text. The section on the development of number skills for infants makes good use of pattern and visual imagery.)

Haylock, D. (1995) *Mathematics Explained for Primary Teachers*, Paul Chapman Publishing, London. (Chapters 5, 7, 9 and 11 provide detailed explanations of various approaches to calculations.)

Hopkins, C., Gifford, S. and Pepperell, S. (eds) (1996) *Mathematics in the Primary School: a Sense of Progression*, David Fulton Publishers, London. (There is some useful material on teaching calculations in Section 2 of this book.)

Nunes, T., Schliemann, A.-L. and Caraher, D. (1993) *Street Mathematics and School Mathematics*, Cambridge University Press, New York. (A fascinating account of the unorthodox but dazzling skills in calculation of Brazilian street-children that makes the reader reassess the balance between teaching formal procedures and encouraging children to develop methods that make sense to them in real-life contexts.)

Ofsted (Office for Standards in Education) (1993) *The Teaching and Learning of Number in Primary Schools*, HMSO, London. (This report from Her Majesty's Inspectors of schools contains some sound advice on approaches to the teaching of arithmetic skills.)

Thompson, I. (1994) Young children's idiosyncratic written algorithms for addition, *Educational Studies in Mathematics*, 26, no. 4, pp. 323–45. (Thompson describes how children who have not been taught standard written methods use successfully a variety of idiosyncratic methods with a preference for horizontal layout.)

Walsh, A. (1991) The calculator as a tool for learning. In D. Pimm and E. Love (eds) *Teaching and Learning School Mathematics*, Hodder & Stoughton, London, in association with the Open University, pp. 61–8. (Thought-provoking reading for anyone doubting the usefulness of calculators in mathematics learning.)

Wigley, A. (1994) Teaching number: a radical re-appraisal, *Mathematics Teacher*, March, pp. 4–8. (In this article Wigley challenges readers to reappraise their teaching of number and computation strategies. He advocates the frequent use of mental transformations of known facts when doing calculations.)

6

Measurement

In earlier chapters we have frequently found ourselves discussing operations with numbers in various measuring contexts. We now turn our attention to the mathematical ideas involved in measurement itself.

WHAT DO WE MEASURE?

Some of the comments that emerged when we raised this question with teachers set the agenda for the first part of our discussion of measurement:

- Length seems to be the most straightforward form of measurement, because the children can see what they're measuring.
- It's not quite the same when you're measuring the distance from one point to another. That's much more abstract, isn't it?
- My children do a lot with volume and capacity. But we normally only deal with measuring out stuff like water and sand, and pouring it into various containers.
- I'm never sure whether we're talking about the size of the container or the amount of water in it.
- What about mass and weight?
- Aren't they the same thing? Some books say you should talk about the mass and some say weight.
- That always confuses me, so I just ignore it and talk about weight.
- We measure time as well, but children find that very difficult.
- I think that's because you can't actually see what you're measuring.

Inevitably, we tend to think of measurement as being about the things that we measure, such as length, volume, weight, time, and so on, rather than considering it in terms of the principles that underlie all measuring experiences. Of course, length, weight, and so on, are all very important concepts. But we might note that some of the basic principles of measurement can be experienced by children through invented measuring scales for such things as how much they enjoyed various television programmes or what sort of a day it's been. Their enjoyment could be measured, for example, using a system of star ratings, four stars for a great programme, three for a quite good programme, and so on. This experience, although subjective, contains the essential elements of comparison, ordering and transitivity that lie at the heart of measurement. These and other basic principles of measurement are considered later in this chapter.

But most of the time in the lower primary years, children's experiences of measuring focus on length and distance, volume and capacity, time of day and time intervals, and mass and weight. Some comments about possible confusions involved in these concepts should be made.

Length and distance

To demonstrate that understanding of the concept of length is not as straight-forward as might at first appear, consider some of the different types of situations to which, for example, the symbols '90 cm' might be connected. First, we might connect them to a straight part of some solid object, such as the edge of a table, and conclude that the table is 90 cm long, or 90 cm wide. Then we might connect '90 cm' to a straight line drawn on the floor, on the board or on a piece of paper. We sometimes connect the same symbols to an imaginary straight line running through an irregular object, such as a child – for example, when measuring the height of the child as 90 cm. We could also connect '90 cm' to an imaginary straight line passing through the air, in order to talk about the height of a table. In the last two examples, the convention is that the imaginary line must be vertical. In other circumstances, such as finding the gap between two cupboards, the convention requires a horizontal line at right angles to the edges of the cupboards.

Also we might connect the same symbols to an imaginary straight line joining two points or objects, when we say that they are 90 cm apart, or when we talk about the distance from one point to the other. To make this connection we may have to imagine a piece of string stretched between the two points. Next we might connect the symbols to other than straight lines on various objects, for example when measuring a person's waist as 90 cm. And finally we might connect '90 cm' to other than straight paths, for example, when we add up the lengths of the four sides of a rectangle to find that the perimeter is 90 cm, or when we find the length of a curved path from A to B to be 90 cm.

This analysis helps us to understand some of the confusions that arise in children's minds because – once again – we connect the same symbols to such a variety of situations. In Figure 6.1, for example, the question might be posed as

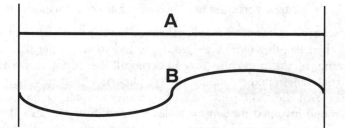

Figure 6.1   Are A and B the same length? Or is B longer?

to whether A is longer than, shorter than or the same length as B. In one sense it is true to say that A and B are the same length, if we think of B as an object and the length of it as the imaginary horizontal line passing through it. But in another sense it is true to say that B is longer than A, if we focus on the lengths of the paths.

Volume and capacity

These two words – volume and capacity – sometimes cause a little confusion. This is not just because the word 'volume' is mostly associated nowadays with a control on a television set. The volume of something is the amount of three-dimensional space it occupies. Volume is normally measured in cubic units, such as cubic centimetres (symbol: cm^3). So we might say, for example, that the volume of a cuboid 3 cm long, 2 cm wide and 4 cm high is 24 cubic centimetres (24 cm^3), meaning that it occupies the same amount of space as 24 centimetre cubes.

Only containers have capacity. The capacity of a container is simply the volume of liquid that it will hold. Although capacity and liquid volume could be measured in the same units as volume in general, there are special units, such as litres and pints, that are often used for measuring these aspects in particular.

Time

The importance of time in human experience is shown by the extensive language associated with the concept. Teachers of young children who recognise the importance of developing language in promoting understanding of mathematical and scientific ideas have a considerable agenda on their hands when they consider the everyday vocabulary that their pupils have to learn to use. The following list, while certainly not comprehensive, at least shows the extent of the teaching task:

how long, second, minute, hour, day, week, fortnight, month, quarter, year, leap year, decade, century, millennium, season, spring, summer, autumn, winter, week-end, term, life-time, long time, short time, brief, temporary, for the time being, long-lasting, interval, pause, cycle, period, extra time, non-stop, never-ending, permanent, on and on, how old, age, age-group, year-group, teenager, young, old, elderly, middle-aged, under-age, ancient, modern, up-to-date, older, elder, oldest, younger, youngest, when, daytime, night-time, dawn, sunrise, morning, tea-time, break-time, lunch-time (etc.), noon, midday, afternoon, dusk, sunset, evening, midnight, small hours, matinee, past, present, future, spell, then, now, before, after, next, previous, earlier, prior, following, later, afterwards, due, eventually, in the long run, in due course, never, always, once, once upon a time, one day, recent, soon, immediately, straightaway, in a moment, instantly, in a jiffy, while, meanwhile, till, until, up to, not yet, in the meantime, during, nowadays, sometime, sooner or later, at the last minute, often, frequent, daily, hourly, weekly, monthly, annually, occasionally, regularly, now and again, every so often, from time to time, sometimes, hardly ever, once in a blue moon, clock, watch, sundial, timer, egg-timer, meter, tick, tick-tock, dial, face, alarm, setting, hands, minute-hand, hour-hand, digital, (e.g.) three twenty-five, o'clock, a.m., p.m., half past, quarter to, quarter past, five past (etc.), twenty-five to (etc.), 24-hour clock, fourteen hours (etc.), timetable, zero hour, summer time, put clocks forward and back, overtime, half-time, slow, fast, on time, late, early, punctual, diary, calendar, date, Sunday, Monday, Tuesday, etc., yesterday, today, tomorrow, last week, January, February, etc., first, second, third, etc., nineteenth century, twentieth century, twenty-first century (etc.), nineteen-ninety-nine, the year two thousand (etc.), birthday, anniversary, mark time, beat time, keep time, rhythm, short notice, advance notice, afterthought, postpone, put off, waste time, . . .

There is one clear conclusion for the teacher: the most important activity in teaching the topic of time to young children is talking to them and with them, aiming to focus on and to develop this extensive range of vocabulary and language patterns. We will leave the reader to judge whether or not children's understanding is affected by hearing adults frequently say – but not mean – things like, 'I'll be with you in a second' and 'Just a minute'!

There are in fact two very different concepts that children will use and must learn to measure that are associated with time. First, there is 'the time' at which something occurs – what we might call *recorded time*. We use time in this sense when we consult our watch to find the time of day, or make an appointment for a particular day of the month, or recall the year in which something took place.

Then there is 'the time' that something takes to happen, or the time that passes between two events or between two moments of recorded time. This is the notion of a *time interval* – the length of time for a car journey, the time that passes from the bell signalling the start of playtime and the bell signalling its end, the time it takes to complete a train journey if the train leaves at 13:05 and arrives at 14:55, and so on. Time intervals might be measured in seconds, minutes, hours, days, weeks, months, years, decades, centuries or even millennia! Age, being the time interval from birth to the present, is one example of this rather abstract concept that children handle with surprising confidence. No doubt this is related to the fact that their age is very much part of their identity: the first two questions that people usually ask a child are 'What's your name?' and 'How old are you?'

Teachers of young children should note that 'recorded time' and 'time interval' are two very different concepts. We show later in this chapter that – because they are two different types of measuring scales – they also have quite different mathematical properties. The reader may find it a useful exercise now to go through the list of time-language given above and decide which of it is associated with each of these two aspects of time.

Mass and weight

This is a tricky one that we approach with some hesitation. There is an important distinction in scientific terms between the mass and the weight of an object. Strictly speaking, units such as grams, kilograms, pounds and ounces are units of mass, not units of weight. If teachers are puzzled by this it is not surprising, given, for example, the recent history of the National Curriculum for mathematics for England and Wales. In the first version of the curriculum pupils were required to know the most commonly used metric units for *weight*

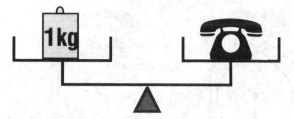

Figure 6.2   An object weighing the same as a kilogram mass

(*Mathematics in the National Curriculum*, DES and the Welsh Office, HMSO: London, 1989). The second version (1991), using inverted commas – presumably in an attempt to signal some ambiguity here – referred to units of '*weight*'. By the time the third version appeared (1995) this had metamorphosed into units of *mass*. But, of course, all three versions were referring to the same units: grams and kilograms!

We will attempt to explain. First, we will refer to those sets of plastic shapes or pieces of metal that we use for weighing things as, for example, ten-gram *masses*, kilogram *masses*, four-ounce *masses*, and so on. This language convention associates the word 'mass' correctly with the units of mass, such as grams, kilograms, ounces, and so on. If an object balances against a kilogram mass, as shown in Figure 6.2, then we deduce that it is also a kilogram mass. But what exactly is the mass of something? Well, in simple terms, the mass of an object is a measure of the amount of stuff making up the object – the quantity of matter in it – which is something to do with the number of atoms involved. Note that this is not the same thing as the volume (the amount of space it occupies), because in some objects the matter is more densely compressed together than in others.

However, when you hold an object in your hand you cannot actually experience its mass. You cannot perceive it, count it, smell it or feel it. It is the weight, not the mass, that you can feel and to which your muscles respond. This weight is the gravitational force pulling the object down towards the ground. Since weight is a force, it should be measured in the units used for measuring force. In the metric system, force – and therefore weight – is measured in newtons. Without being too technical, it may help the reader to know that a newton is about the weight of a small apple. On the earth's surface a mass of one kilogram has a weight of nearly 10 newtons. (More precisely, g newtons, where g is the acceleration due to gravity.)

Having seen film of astronauts on the moon, we are all familiar with the idea that if we were to take the object concerned to the moon, where the gravitational force would be smaller, the weight of the object would be reduced. This is true – the weight would be reduced – although the object's mass is unchanged. Our one kilogram mass would now weigh only about one and a half newtons. This is because the mass of the moon is much smaller than the mass of the earth, and therefore the gravitational pull is weaker.

This change in weight would show up if we were weighing our object on a spring-type weighing device, as shown in Figure 6.3. But it is interesting to observe that the situation in Figure 6.2 would not change if we took the

on the earth   on the moon

Figure 6.3   Change in weight indicated on spring-type weighing devices

balance to the moon. It appears therefore that the two weighing devices are measuring different things! The balance-type weighing device enables us to deduce the mass of an object, by balancing it against an equal mass. The spring-type weighing device clearly responds to weight. The former would give me the same result wherever I used it. The latter would give slightly different readings at the bottom of a coal mine or at the top of Mount Everest (due to a slight variation in the value of g as the distance from the centre of the earth changes), and a significantly different reading on the moon. In practice, of course, we will not often take our kitchen or bathroom scales to the moon. So the scales can safely be graduated in grams and kilograms, or pounds and ounces, and you can be confident that when you weigh something on the earth's surface and the arrow on the dial points to one kilogram then you do actually have a mass of about one kilogram.

Teachers may, therefore, be perplexed to be told that it is actually incorrect from a scientific point of view to say that the object *weighs* one kilogram or that the *weight* of the object is one kilogram. Strictly speaking, it is the *mass* of the object that is one kilogram. Unfortunately, nearly everyone says that the weight of the object is one kilogram, and the idea of measuring weight in newtons is too sophisticated for primary-school children. But, later on, many of these children will need in their physics lessons to distinguish between weight and mass, and the majority will find this very difficult. No doubt part of the difficulty will be unlearning the erroneous language of primary school and the market-place.

We offer some suggestions that might help with this problem. These are scientifically correct, mathematically sound and reasonably straightforward, but we accept the fact that the reader may choose to ignore them! First, be consistent in referring to those things you use to counter-balance the objects being weighed as *masses*, not weights. In the classroom cupboard you will have boxes of 1-gram masses, 10-gram masses, 100-gram masses, and so on. It seems a bit strange at first, but you soon get used to it! The word 'mass' is thus encountered when you shift from weighing with non-standard units to weighing with standard units.

Second, we suggest that young children's experience of weighing should be with balance-type weighing devices. Third, when we have weighed something we say something along the lines of: 'The book weighs the same as twenty marbles' or 'The book weighs the same as a mass of two hundred grams' or, simply, 'The book weighs the same as two hundred grams.' The key phrase is 'weighs the same as', emphasising the equivalence that has emerged. Finally, if an object weighs the same as, say, a mass of two hundred grams then we can also say that this object has a mass of two hundred grams.

MEASUREMENT IN GENERAL

In this section we will consider what might be some of the fundamental mathematical ideas involved in the process of measuring. These ideas include the notion of comparison and ordering, the principles of transitivity and conservation, and the idea of a unit. We are concerned first then with the mathematical ideas common to most aspects of measurement. However, there are actually different types of measuring scales, with different mathematical properties, and these are considered towards the end of the chapter.

Comparison

The primary purpose of making a measurement is to make comparisons between two items according to the magnitude of some attribute, such as length, weight, capacity, age, value, and so on, and thereby to put them in order. Associated with this idea is the extensive set of language of comparison given in Table 3.1 and discussed in Chapter 3: longer, shorter, heavier, lighter, younger, older, and so on.

We should note that, particularly in the early stages of measuring, comparisons of this sort can often be made directly without the use of any measuring units. So two children can stand next to each other and determine who is the taller and who is the shorter. Two objects can be put on either end of a simple see-saw balance and a deduction made about which is the heavier and which is the lighter. It is important at this stage of the child's development of understanding of the particular measuring concept that they experience objects that exaggerate the attribute in question. A large, light object can be balanced against a small, heavy object in order to focus the attention on the weight rather than the size. Water can be poured from a tall jar with a small capacity into a short, squat jar with a large capacity. Comparing by weight pairs of identical-looking sealed yoghurt cartons filled with materials of different density – sand, sawdust, ball bearings – again focuses the attention on the one way in which they are different, namely in terms of their heaviness.

We should remind ourselves of the fundamental idea that every comparison statement has an alternative equivalent form (see Table 3.1 in Chapter 3), and that children should be encouraged always to make both statements. This is such a key aspect of language and mathematical development that it cannot be overemphasised. In purely mathematical terms we are interpreting in measuring contexts this basic property of an ordering relationship: '$a > b$' is equivalent to '$b < a$' (> is the symbol for 'is greater than' and < is the symbol for 'is less than'). So, to say that a is greater than b is equivalent to saying that b is less than *a*, and vice versa. Here are some examples of pairs of such equivalent statements, demonstrating that this is a key principle that pervades all areas of measurement:

- The table is higher than the desk.
  The desk is lower than the table.
- Breakfast is earlier than dinner.
  Dinner is later than breakfast.
- The book is heavier than the pencil.
  The pencil is lighter than the book.
- John is older than Mary.
  Mary is younger than John.
- London is bigger than Norwich.
  Norwich is smaller than London.
- A motorway is wider than my street.
  My street is narrower than a motorway.
- My car is faster than your car.
  Your car is slower than my car.

In making comparisons of this sort we are attending to what is different about two objects, in other words to a transformation that occurs when we shift our attention from some attribute of one to the same attribute of the other, such as height, weight, and so on. As in the example of the identical yoghurt cartons, the two objects may in all other respects be the same.

But there is, of course, another possibility when two objects are compared for some particular attribute: we may decide that they are equal. So two objects, such as a book and a box, may be very different in a number of respects, such as their size or their shape, but be equivalent in another. For example, they may weigh the same. So we see that what have been referred to in Chapter 1 as the concepts of transformation and equivalence are here associated with the most fundamental idea of measuring. These two ideas appear to permeate all mathematical thinking. The equivalence notion, 'is the same as', will turn up frequently in measuring experiences, in such language forms as 'is the same length as', 'weighs the same as', 'happens at the same time as', and so on.

Ordering and transitivity

A second important principle common to any ordering relationship is that of *transitivity*. This principle is evident when three or more objects are being ordered according to a particular attribute, such as their lengths, their weights, their time of day, their capacity, and so on. In Figure 6.4(a) the arrow could represent any one of our comparison statements, such as 'is longer than', 'is lighter than', 'is earlier than', 'holds more than', and so on. The objects A, B and C have been ordered using such a relationship, by comparing A with B and then B with C. The principle of transitivity allows us to make the logical deduction about the relationship between A and C, shown in Figure 6.4(b), i.e. A is longer than C, or A is lighter than C, and so on. The relation is said to be

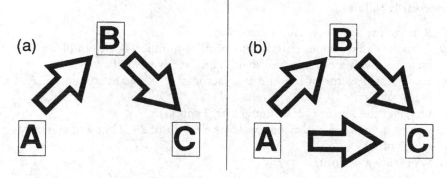

Figure 6.4   The principle of transitivity

transitive when the following is necessarily the case: if it occurs between A and B and between B and C, then it can be 'carried across' directly from A to C.

Formally, this principle is expressed in one of two ways, as follows: (a) using the symbol > to stand for any 'greater-than' relationship, 'if A > B and B > C then A > C' (if A is greater than B and B is greater than C then A is greater than C); (b) using the symbol < to stand for any 'less-than' relationship, 'if A < B and B < C then A < C' (if A is less than B and B is less than C then A is less than C). All measuring relationships satisfy these properties – putting things in order is a fundamental property of any form of measurement.

In addition to the 'greater-than' and 'less-than' transitivity properties, there is a third form of transitivity in the context of measurement. Clearly the arrows in Figure 6.4 could also represent equivalence. For example, they could stand for statements about equal length or equal weight, such as 'is the same length as', 'weighs the same as', and so on. It is not a difficult logical deduction that, if A is equal to B and B is equal to C, then A is equal to C. So, we should note therefore that equivalence also satisfies transitivity. This example of transitivity is expressed in symbols as follows: 'if A = B and B = C then A = C'. Although this might appear to be a rather obvious statement, in the context of measurement it is actually very significant, since it is this property that allows us to make repeated copies of standard measurements, such as the kilogram or the metre, without always going back to the originals! In the context of the classroom children will experience this, for example, by making their own 100-gram mass, by balancing plasticene against a standard 100-gram mass, and then using their plasticene version to generate further copies.

To understand the concept of transitivity it might be helpful for the reader to experience some non-exemplars as well as exemplars. We have seen how the arrows in Figure 6.4 might represent any relationship of the form 'is greater than', 'is less than', or 'is the same as'. But not all mathematical relationships are transitive. In fact, part of our understanding of any relationship must be an implicit awareness of whether it is or is not transitive. To demonstrate this, readers may care to assess their understanding of the concept of 'factor' by asking this question: if the arrows in Figure 6.4(a) represent the relationship 'is a factor of', where A, B and C are three natural numbers (positive whole numbers), does the relationship between A and C shown in Figure 6.4(b) necessarily follow?

S. Remind me again – what's a factor?

D. A number that divides exactly into another number. For example, four is a factor of twelve, because four divides into twelve exactly.

A. So, if A is a factor of B and B is a factor of C we want to know if A is a factor of C.

S. I haven't the foggiest idea. It might be, I suppose.

A. Four is a factor of twelve and twelve is a factor of 24. That works. Four is a factor of 24.

D. Will it always work?

Try the same exercise with other mathematical relationships, such as 'is one more than', 'is half of', 'is a multiple of'. The facility with which you make the deduction about whether or not the fact that A is related to B and B is related to C necessarily implies that A must be related to C is a good indicator of your understanding of the mathematical relationship. If you do not find it immediately obvious then you are in exactly the same situation as young children learning about measurement. Having compared A with B and B with C they will not automatically make the deduction about the relationship between A and C.

Transitivity is one of the logical principles that Piaget identified as a key indicator of a child's development in his or her understanding of measurement. Whether the difficulty for children who appear not to grasp the principle is a failure in logic or simply an inability to recall and process at the same time all the details in the situation is a matter of some debate. But, whatever the correct interpretation of children's responses to tasks assessing their grasp of this principle, it would seem to us to be self-evident that – since transitivity is such a fundamental property of measurement – children learning about measuring should simply have a considerable amount of experience of putting three (or more) objects in order according to their length, their weight, their capacity, and so on. It would appear likely that through practical experience of this kind of ordering activity – supported by well-focused questions and discussion with their teachers – they will be helped to get this mathematical structure into their thinking about measurement in general.

Conservation

Another fundamental and crucial principle that applies to many aspects of measurement is that known as *conservation*. This refers, for example, to the fact that a ball of plasticene will still weigh the same when it has been squashed into a sausage shape or broken up into a number of smaller pieces; that a piece of carpet still covers the same amount of floor when it is moved to a different part of the room or cut into two smaller pieces and rearranged; that the volume of water in a tall, thin flask does not change when it is poured into a short, squat flask; that the length of a pencil remains the same when it is displaced a little to the right. Figure 6.5 provides some examples of tasks that have sometimes been used to assess children's grasp of this principle in various measuring contexts.

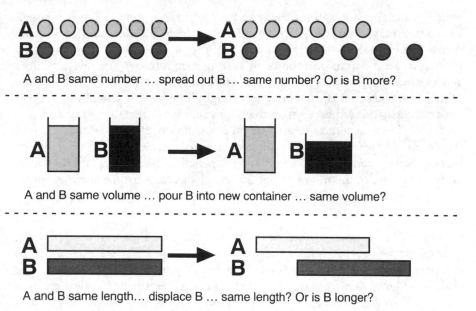

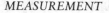

A and B same number ... spread out B ... same number? Or is B more?

- -

A and B same volume ... pour B into new container ... same volume?

- -

A and B same length... displace B ... same length? Or is B longer?

Figure 6.5   Assessing understanding of conservation

Demonstrating a grasp of this principle of conservation, first of all with number, then with length, weight, area and volume, has also been identified by Piaget as one of the key indicators of a child's intellectual development. However, many of the tasks used to assess the child's grasp of conservation, such as those in Figure 6.5, have been justifiably criticised as not being embedded in a context that has any meaning or purpose for a child. It appears to us to be the case that quite young children seem to use the principle of conservation of measurement quite happily when engaged in a purposeful task in a meaningful context. When, for example, they are cooking, they will measure out quantities of water and flour, and then they will proceed to transfer these from one container to another without any apparent concern that these activities might alter the quantities they measured out in the first place!

In spite of such reservations as these about some of the methods used to assess children's understanding of conservation, we should stress that this is nevertheless a crucial component of understanding of measurement. Children will certainly benefit from activities and discussion designed to focus their attention upon this principle. In fact, we would argue that the thinking process involved is an instance of fundamental mathematical reasoning, because the principle of conservation provides yet another experience of the concepts of transformation and equivalence that we are highlighting throughout this book. What the child has to grasp, for example, is that if you take a quantity of water in a container and apply to it certain transformations, such as pouring it into a different shaped container, the volume of water is the same. In other words, there is an *equivalence*, something the same about the two situations, in spite of the *transformation* that has occurred to, say, the height of the water level, or the shape of the water. In fact, we could say that what the child has to learn is which of the transformations that can be applied in a range of measurement contexts preserve which equivalences and which transformations destroy which equivalences. If you take a square piece of paper and transform it by moving it to a different position or by cutting it up into two triangles, the area is preserved: it will still cover the same amount of the table surface. If, on the other hand, you screw the paper up into a tight little ball, or set light to it, these are transformations that destroy this equivalence. The reader may find it a useful intellectual exercise to analyse, in terms of which equivalences are preserved or destroyed, transformations such as rearranging some building blocks, boiling some water, sharpening a pencil, rolling up a tape measure, taking an object to the moon or putting the clocks forward for summer time.

Units

Common to all aspects of measurement is the idea of a *unit*. Instead of using measurement concepts just to order two or more objects, we now move to comparing some attribute of a single object with a number of equal units. So a child would move on from making statements such as 'the book is longer than the pencil' to statements such as 'the table is about ten pencils long'. It is conventional to introduce children to the idea of a unit through the use of *non-standard* (sometimes called arbitrary) units – for example, measuring the length of a desk in pencils, or weighing objects with marbles – before moving on to standard units such as centimetres and grams. Some of the infant-teachers we talked to were very uncertain about the point of getting children to use non-standard units for measuring, especially since children will often have met the standard units from shopping. (Others commented that the automation of weighing, pricing and payment in supermarkets is making shopping a markedly less valuable educational experience for children and we cannot assume any longer that children will actually have direct experience of handling money in shopping, let alone units of weight and capacity.) We outline below a number of reasons that can be put forward for the value of incorporating experience of non-standard units.

First, by using non-standard units in the early stages, children are introduced to the concept of measuring in units through familiar objects – such as pencils, marbles, hand spans, feet, and so on – rather than going straight into these mysterious things called centimetres and grams. In this way they are not required to handle a new piece of vocabulary for the unit at the same time as meeting a new measuring experience. As far as the mathematical ideas involved are concerned, there is no difference between measuring a table in pencils and measuring it in centimetres, so if children find a familiar non-standard unit less threatening all well and good.

Second, it is suggested that the non-standard unit can be a more appropriate size of unit for the first practical measuring tasks that young children will undertake. Centimetres may be too small and therefore too numerous for your first experience of measuring the length of the desk top, or the height of a friend – and metres are clearly too large a unit for this purpose. Grams are very small units for weighing most of the objects around the classroom, such as books, scissors, shoes, and so on, and a kilogram will put the child in hospital if dropped on his or her foot. Something like a marble is likely to be a more appropriate unit to begin with, because it will result in measurements of just a handful of units, rather than hundreds of them.

Third, the experience can open children to the idea that scales can be invented for a particular measuring task when a standard scale is not available, or when the standard scale is inappropriate. For example, one group of children invented their own scale for measuring the dirtiness of water after washing clothes in it.

Fourth, we should note that adults do not always use standard units when engaged in practical measuring tasks. Whether or not they do might depend on the accuracy required by the task. For example, most of us are happy to measure out fertiliser for our lawns by the handful, and we will often use spans and paces for certain stages of practical jobs around the home.

Finally, it is argued that through using non-standard units children will become aware of the need for a standard unit – for example, when they discover that the classroom is twenty paces wide when they do the measuring, but only eleven paces wide when the teacher does it.

- When my 6-year-olds were measuring lengths in spans and feet they made me do them all as well. They seemed fascinated by the idea that my span or my feet always gave a smaller number.
- I find that a lot of useful mathematical talk takes place when a group of children are deciding what to use to measure something – like whether to use spans or cubits to measure the length of their table.
- When you talk to them about measuring with non-standard units they do seem to pick up the idea of the need for a standard unit quite quickly.

One infant-teacher, however, had serious doubts about using units like spans and paces with young children:

> I always find an element of competition creeps in when they start measuring in hand spans or paces, and the maths goes out of the window. One girl refused to admit that her span was shorter than someone else's and got quite upset. Then when they were pacing out the length of the corridor all the boys started taking enormous leaps, rather than strides, to see who could do it in the smallest number!

We take this teacher's point, and it may be that there are occasions when impersonal spoons and sticks might be preferable as units to individuals' spans and strides. But we wonder whether it is really the case that the mathematics has gone 'out of the window' in these examples. These children seem very aware of the significance of the size of the units being used and the experience has clearly provoked a competition and discussion based on mathematical criteria!

Metric and imperial units

The ability to make reasonable *estimates* of quantities in various units is an important component of our understanding of the concepts of measurement. For example, our own grasp of some of the standard units used for measurement may be indicated by how easily we answer questions like these:

- What is your approximate height in centimetres?
- If you stood on the bathroom scales, roughly how many kilograms would be indicated?
- What is the approximate temperature today in degrees celsius?
- What is a standard spoonful of medicine in millilitres?
- Roughly how far is it in kilometres from where you live to the centre of the capital city?
- About how many litres of petrol does the tank of your car take?
- How many cheese sandwiches could you make with one hundred grams of cheese?

This discussion about estimation inevitably raises questions about metric and imperial units, as shown in these comments from some of our infant-teachers:

- I can do it in feet and inches, or pounds and ounces, but I find it hard in metres or grams.
- The children grow up using metric at school – then they can't cope when they come across yards and feet.
- Or pounds and ounces. Some shops still sell some things in ounces.
- But isn't everything gradually being changed to metric?

In the United Kingdom we find ourselves today in a rather unsatisfactory position regarding the use of metric and imperial units. The situation in the United States is similar, with both systems continuing to exist side by side and only slow progress towards consistent use of metric units. These situations contrast with a number of other English-speaking countries, such as Australia, New Zealand and Canada, which have made a much more wholehearted national commitment to the conversion to metric units.

In 1965 the British government acceded to industry's request for the UK to adopt metric units, and we were soon led to believe that, under the guidance of the Metrication Board, by the late 1970s everything would have changed from the old imperial units to the universally accepted metric units. Primary-school mathematics schemes were changed to prepare the next generation of children for the new metric world in which they would grow up. Primary-school teachers were suddenly given new freedom as they were able to ditch the teaching of calculations with inches, feet, yards and miles – or with ounces, pounds, stones, hundredweights and tons – that had been one of the major preoccupations of primary mathematics. Now everything would be based on tens, hundreds and thousands, place value would be reinforced through measuring experiences, and once we all got used to the new units measurement would be so much more rational and straightforward.

Many changes took place quite quickly, such as in the pharmaceutical industry where presumably we are now all accustomed to our plastic spoonfuls of five-millilitre doses from our 200-millilitre bottles of medicine. But many areas of British life proved to be very resistant to change. Moreover, the decimalisation of money in the early 1970s had proved to be an unpopular measure, coinciding with a period of high inflation, with rising prices attributed by many people to the new money. A succession of governments with small majorities did not appear to have the will to push through further unpopular changes to the British way of life. Consequently, many imperial units survived in many areas of life, while schools were producing generations of children who had not been taught how to deal with them. Furthermore, since the Metrication Board has now been abolished, there is apparently no body with responsibility for over-seeing the completion of the task begun in 1965. More extensive use of metric units is now being forced upon the United Kingdom by the closer economic, industrial and commercial ties with Europe that have come about in recent years. For example, it is now illegal to sell pre-packaged food in imperial units. But it seems highly likely that road signs in miles, speeds in miles per hour and pints of beer, for example, will still be with us in the new millennium. There seems to be no doubt that we will have to continue to cope with the unsatisfactory mixture of units that is evident all around – as shown by the following comments that are still typical of the confusion in the world outside the classroom:

- I bought some wood the other day. Its cross-sectional dimensions were in millimetres but it was sold by the foot.
- There are still some shops that advertise the price of carpet by the square yard because it looks cheaper, but they measure it out by the metre.
- There's a sign on a road near my house that says 'Six foot six inches width restriction, 200 yards ahead.' I looked up in the manual to find out how wide my car was, and it said 1650 millimetres!
- My brother had to do an exam for a job in the railway and it was all in imperial units. He couldn't do any of it because he'd been taught metric at school.
- In my supermarket the pre-packed ham is sold in grams but at the deli-catessen counter it's sold by the quarter.

If we are preparing our children for the actual demands of the real world, it means, therefore, that we will have to incorporate in their measuring experi-ence at school – at an appropriate stage – some opportunities to measure with the imperial units actually used in the world outside. If we do not do this we will simply reinforce the idea that what goes on at school has nothing to do with life outside. Some of the units that we have noted as being still part of everyday experience and conversation are: miles, miles per hour, inches, feet and yards, ounces, pounds, quarters and halves of a pound, stones (mainly for discussing the weight of people), pints, and even fluid ounces (in older recipes). Then, of course, there are no plans to enforce the metrication of units of time. This is no doubt due to the fact that not even the European Parliament can make the earth orbit the sun in anything other than just over 365 days – and that a seven-day week is apparently ordained by God.

SI base units and other metric units

Teachers may come across references to the SI (International System) version of metric units. This is an internationally accepted convention used in trade and industry, and in technological and scientific work. The main feature of this system is that each aspect of measurement should have just one base unit.

Table 6.1 Some SI units

Measure	SI unit	Symbol
Length	metre	m
Mass	kilogram	kg
Time	second	s
Area	square metre	m^2
Volume	cubic metre	m^3
Speed	metres per second	m/s

Table 6.2 Preferred prefixes

Prefix	Meaning	Symbol	Example
mega	one million	M	I Mg = one million grams
kilo	one thousand	k	I kg = one thousand grams
milli	one thousandth	m	I mm = one thousandth of a metre
micro	one millionth	μ	I μm = one millionth of a metre

Some of these are shown in Table 6.1 for some aspects of measurement likely to concern teachers, together with the appropriate symbol. It is an accident of history that the base unit for mass is the kilogram (kg) not the gram (g).

According to the SI convention, all lengths, for example, would be measured in metres. This would mean that the width of a piece of A4 paper should be given as about 0.21 m. If other units are to be used, by the use of various prefixes, then there is a further convention that as far as possible only those representing powers of a thousand should be employed. Some of these 'preferred prefixes' are shown in Table 6.2.

The width of the piece of A4 paper could then be given as about 210 mm. However, for practical purposes other prefixes are required because the base unit or the base unit with a preferred prefix are just inappropriate sizes of unit for the task in hand. For example, for many tasks that involve measuring length the millimetre is too small and the metre too large. This is why the centimetre is used so frequently, even though 'centi' is not a preferred prefix. So, for example, we will probably find that it is more appropriate to give the width of a piece of A4 paper as about 21 cm. Some of these other prefixes are shown in Table 6.3, though of those shown here we are likely to meet only centi and deci.

There are some other metric units that are derived from SI units. The commonest of these, encountered in everyday experience, is the litre (l) and the associated millilitre (1 ml = one thousandth of a litre), centilitre (1 cl = one

Table 6.3 Some other prefixes

Prefix	Meaning	Symbol	Example
centi	one hundredth of	c	I cm = one hundredth of a metre
deci	one tenth of	d	I dm = one tenth of a metre
deca	ten	da	I dag = ten grams
hecto	one hundred	h	I hg = one hundred grams

hundredth of a litre) and decilitre (1 dl = one tenth of a litre). We have noticed that bottles of wine are variously labelled as 0.75 litre, 7.5 dl, 75 cl and 750 ml. A litre is the same volume – in the context of measuring liquid volume or capacity – as one thousand cubic centimetres solid-volume. Those who purchase solid fuel, for example, may also encounter the tonne, referred to in speech as 'the metric tonne'. This is a thousand kilograms (1000 kg) or a million grams (i.e. one megagram, 1 Mg). Landowners may come across the hectare (a contracted form of hecto-are), meaning '100 ares', where an are is an area of 100 square metres, such as a 10 m × 10 m square. So, an are is about the size of a large classroom and a hectare is about the size of an international football pitch.

We conclude this section with an assortment of facts and conventions about metric units that may be helpful.

- One litre is the same volume as 1000 cm³.
- 1 ml is the same volume as 1 cm³.
- A medicine spoon holds 5 ml.
- Base-ten materials for number work are often based on centimetres.
- If the unit is a centimetre cube then the 'ten' is a decimetre long.
- The 'hundred' is a decimetre square.
- The 'thousand' is a decimetre cube.
- A decimetre cube is 1000 cm³, i.e. the same as a litre!
- A litre of water has a mass of 1 kg.
- Hence 1 ml of water has a mass of 1g.
- And a cubic metre of water has a mass of one tonne (i.e. 1000 kg).
- The distance from the North Pole to the Equator is approximately ten thousand kilometres.
- A simple pendulum of length 1 m ticks once approximately every second.
- The symbol for litre is l, but avoid this because it is confused with 1 (i.e. one).
- Note the correct spelling of 'gram'.
- The symbol for gram is not gm but g.
- Symbols for units do not have plural forms, so do not write, for example, 5 cms, but 5 cm.
- The symbol for kilo is a lower case k, not a capital K; so we write km, not Km.
- No full stops should be used after a symbol for a unit, such as 5 cm or 10 kg, except at the end of a sentence.

Approximation and accuracy

An interesting feature of measurement is that nearly all measurement is *approximate*. Except when the measurement is simply a form of counting, such as when 'measuring' the value of the coins in my pocket, we always measure to the nearest something. It is not possible, for example, to make an exact measurement of the length of anything. All we can do is to measure the length of the table to the nearest centimetre, or nearest millimetre, and so on. Even with the most refined measuring device in the world we would still be making an approximate measurement. This is a difficult idea for us to incorporate into our thinking about measurement, because we tend to think of mathematics as an exact science.

Even in the early stages of measuring in non-standard units, young children will encounter this problem and have to find a way of expressing their observations. So they might say 'The book weighs more than 8 marbles but less than 9 marbles', or 'The book weighs a bit more than 8 marbles', or 'The book weighs between 8 and 9 marbles.' The limits of 8 marbles and 9 marbles here are examples of what are known technically as the *lower and upper bounds* of the measurement. If you have carried out a very careful measurement of the width of a piece of A4 paper to, say, the nearest millimetre, you will only be able to assert, for example, that the width of the paper lies between a lower bound of 210 mm and an upper bound of 211 mm.

We also have to learn the importance of measuring to an appropriate level of *accuracy*. In measuring age, for example, it is normally appropriate to do this to the year below or the year above. So a child might say 'I'm seven' or 'I'm eight next birthday.' It is an interesting sociological study to observe in what circumstances and in which age-brackets people tend to round their ages up or to round them down! For many purposes we measure time of day to the nearest five minutes, so that we would be amused by someone who said 'I'll meet you at about 4.23 this afternoon' – because they appear to be employing an inappropriate level of accuracy. But we would not be amused if a train timetable advertised a departure time of 16:25 and we missed the train because it had left at nearer 16:23.

Consequently, all that we have said earlier about equivalence should be understood in these terms. Phrases such as 'is the same length as' and 'weighs the same as' must be interpreted as implying that the comparison has been made to an appropriate level of accuracy. We might actually mean something like 'is the same length to the nearest millimetre' or 'weighs the same as far as we can judge using this balance'. There is no way in which we can assert that two lines are exactly the same length or that two objects have exactly the same mass.

To sum up, the notions of approximation, upper and lower bounds, and the appropriate level of accuracy are important ideas that are fundamental to most aspects of measurement. Experience and discussion of all these aspects of measurement are often insufficiently emphasised in work with children.

TYPES OF MEASURING SCALE

In the final section of this chapter we analyse three different kinds of measuring scales from a mathematical perspective.

Ratio scales

Length, mass, capacity, time interval, and so on, are examples of what is called a *ratio scale*. Mathematically this is the most sophisticated type of scale. They are called ratio scales because the ratio of two measurements has a real meaning. So, for example, we can compare a length of 90 cm with one of 30 cm not just by the difference (60 cm) but also by the ratio (3). Hence, using the ratio comparison, we would observe that a length of 90 cm is three times as long as a length of 30 cm; or that 90 cm can be made up by combining three lengths of 30 cm. Similarly, with measurements of mass, we can observe that a mass of 100 g is ten times as heavy as a mass of 10 g; or that a mass of 100 g is equivalent to ten masses of 10 g. Likewise, with measurements of time, we can assert that a time interval of 240 minutes is 6 times longer than a time interval of 40 minutes; or that a period of 240 minutes can be made up of 6 periods of 40 minutes. Notice that the two central ideas in these comparisons are ratio and scaling – two ideas that are central in division and multiplication, as explained in Chapter 4.

In fact, the basic property of ratio scales implies that these are the only kind of measurements on which it is usually legitimate to perform many aspects of arithmetic involving multiplication or division. Some of the structures of multiplication and division discussed in Chapter 4 have meaning only in those measurement contexts that are ratio scales, such as measurements of length, mass, volume and capacity, and time intervals – especially the scaling structure of multiplication and the ratio structure of division. Hence, it is legitimate and meaningful to make statements such as these, only because in each case the measurements involved are taken from a ratio scale:

- Three 25-kg sacks of potatoes have a total mass of 75 kg. (Multiplying a mass by 3: the repeated-addition structure.)
- The walk to school takes 15 minutes. There and back will be twice this, i.e. 30 minutes. (Multiplying a time interval by a scale factor of 2: the scaling structure.)
- A length of 30 m of ribbon shared between 3 people gives a length of 10 m each. (Dividing a length by 3: the equal-sharing structure.)
- From a jug of 250-ml capacity we can fill 5 containers of 50-ml capacity. (Dividing one measurement of capacity by another: the inverse-of-multiplication structure.)
- This stick of length 80 cm is 4 times the length of that stick of 20 cm. (Dividing one measurement of length by another: the ratio structure.)

We should note that 'monetary value' is also essentially a ratio scale, because we can compare two amounts of money or prices by ratio. We can, for example, make meaningful statements about how many times more expensive or less expensive is one thing than another, by what scale factor a salary might be increased or decreased, rates of inflation, percentage rises in the cost of living, and so on. These are all employing the ideas of scaling and ratio that are central to the notion of a ratio scale. The only slight difference between monetary value and the other ratio scales discussed above is that, in the context of prices and actual amounts of money, we are restricted normally to using whole numbers (if writing sums of money in pence) – or two decimal places (if using the pound notation). Theoretically no such restriction applies to measurements of length and mass, although in practice we usually impose one on ourselves when we make our measurements to the nearest something.

Interval scales

Ratio scales can be contrasted first with what are called *interval scales*. In an interval scale two measurements can be compared only by their difference, not by their ratio. The two most familiar examples of interval scales are measurements of temperature in degrees celsius (or centigrade) and the time of day.

They are called interval scales because the steps from one mark on the measurement scale to the next are equal intervals. This means that the interval between 1 and 2 is the same as that between 2 and 3, and between 3 and 4, and so on. For example, it takes the same amount of time to move from 2 p.m. to 3 p.m. as it does to move from 3 p.m. to 4 p.m. It takes the same amount of heat-energy to raise the temperature of something from 2°C to 3°C as it does to raise it from 3°C to 4°C. Of course, what is true about interval scales is also true of ratio scales. But there are more restrictions on what can be said and done meaningfully with measurements on an interval scale.

For example, to compare a temperature of 30°C with one of 10°C you can use only the difference (20°C), observing that one temperature is 20°C hotter or colder than the other. It makes no sense at all to talk about one temperature being three times hotter than the other. You cannot make up a temperature of 30°C from three temperatures of 10°C! Similarly, 6 p.m. is not in any sense three times 2 p.m. To compare 6 p.m. with 2 p.m. we can make use only of the idea of difference (i.e. it is four hours later), not the idea of ratio.

This marked contrast between the two types of measuring scale is related to the fact that in a ratio scale the 'zero' is actually 'nothing' (see the discussion of zero in Chapter 2). So, a length of 0 cm or a mass of 0 kg really is nothing. But in an interval scale the zero is arbitrary. It is quite arbitrary that in the celsius temperature scale the freezing point of water should be taken as 0°C. Similarly, it is clearly an arbitrary decision that 'zero hours' (midnight) comes when it does – otherwise we would not be able to put the clocks forward and back for summer time, or to have different time zones for various sectors of the globe. So, when the temperature falls to zero it is not the case that there is now no temperature or that the temperature has become 'nothing' – there is a very definite temperature and we can certainly feel it! And time does not disappear at midnight when your watch indicates zero hours (00:00).

The nature of interval scales means that – in contrast to ratio scales – we cannot meaningfully do any arithmetic involving many aspects of multiplication and division, particularly those related to the ideas of ratio and scaling. There are no meaningful statements in the contexts of time of day or temperatures that have the same structures as the examples of multiplication and division statements given in the previous section for ratio scales. For example, three people would not share a temperature of 30°C and have 10°C each! The three addition and subtraction structures discussed in Chapter 3 that have most application in these contexts are those of augmentation (increasing), comparison (difference), and reduction. These allow us to make statements in the contexts of measurements of temperatures and time of day such as these:

- Her temperature was 38°C yesterday, but it rose 2°C during the night and is now 40°C. (Increasing a temperature by 2°C: augmentation structure of addition.)
- The train arriving at 16:30 gets to London 2 hours later than the one arriving at 14:30. (A difference of 2 hours between two times of day: comparison structure of subtraction.)
- The temperature was 30°C at midday, but it has fallen by 10°C – it is now 20°C. (Decreasing a temperature by 10°C: the reduction structure of subtraction.)

Of course, statements with the same structures as these could also be made in the contexts of ratio scales, such as measurements of length and mass. We should also emphasise the distinction made earlier in this chapter between the two aspects of time: time intervals and recorded time (e.g. time of day). We now see that the essential difference in the way we handle these two concepts is that the first is a ratio scale and the second is an interval scale. There is a subtle point here that might be mentioned: if you have measurements on an interval scale then the intervals themselves form a ratio scale! So, for example, although time of day is an interval scale, as we have seen, measurements of time intervals (how long something takes to happen – or the difference between two times of day) are a ratio scale, allowing us to make comparisons by ratio (e.g. 'this takes twice as long as that'). The same thing applies to temperature differences: these form a ratio scale. So, it is legitimate and meaningful to make comparison by ratio of *changes* in temperature (e.g. 'the temperature last night fell twice as much as it fell the previous night').

We will mention one further legitimate and meaningful arithmetic process that can be applied to measurements on an interval (or ratio) scale. This is the process of finding an *average* (strictly called an arithmetic mean). So, for example, given three lengths of 30 cm, 20 cm and 16 cm (a ratio scale), we can legitimately add them up and divide by 3 and assert that the average length is 22 cm. Similarly, given maximum temperatures on three consecutive days of 30°C, 20°C and 16°C (an interval scale), we can add these up and divide by 3 and make the meaningful statement that the average maximum temperature was 22°C. This is permissible only because the steps between measurements on an interval scale are equal intervals. Without this property the process of finding an average (arithmetic mean) would be entirely bogus. (For further discussion of averages the reader is referred to Chapter 20 of *Mathematics Explained for Primary Teachers*.)

Ordinal scales

Finally, there is what is called an *ordinal scale*. This is a measuring scale that makes use of no more than the basic ordinal aspect of number. We show in Chapter 2 that sometimes numbers are used in just a nominal sense, to label things, and then they are used in an ordinal sense to label things but also to put them in order. It is in this way that numbers are used in ordinal scales – for labelling and putting in order. For example, we are using an ordinal scale when measuring how good a hotel is by a system of star ratings; or when determining primary-school children's achievement in the English and Welsh National Curriculum subjects using levels 1, 2, 3 and 4. Sometimes letters rather than numbers are used for an ordinal scale – for example, performance in a public examination is measured by a system of grades, such as A, B, C, D, E, F – making use of the alphabetical ordering associated with letters. These are all ordinal measuring scales because they do no more than put things in order according to specified criteria. No one could ever assert that the steps between the measurements are equal intervals, so they do not qualify as interval scales. We can assume only that a four-star hotel – according to some stated criteria – is better than a three-star (and probably more expensive!), and that a grade B result is better than a grade C, and so on.

Of course, ratio scales and intervals scales also share the same properties as ordinal scales, in that they can also be used to put things in order. But, in an ordinal scale, the measurements can be used for no more than ranking or ordering. It certainly makes no sense to use ratios for comparison of measurements of something that is only an ordinal scale, as we would with the numbers used for measurements in ratio scales. A four-star hotel is not twice as good as a two-star hotel, whereas a 4-cm rod is twice as long as a 2-cm rod. A level-4 child has not achieved twice as much as a level-2 child. It also makes no sense to talk about the intervals between various measurements, as we would with the numbers used for measurements in interval scales. The difference between an A grade and a B grade is not the same as the difference between a B grade and a C grade, whereas, as we have seen above, the difference between 1 p.m. and 2 p.m. is the same as the difference between 2 p.m. and 3 p.m. Progression from level 2 to level 3 in a National Curriculum subject is in no sense equal to progression from level 3 to level 4 – although numbers are used for these levels we should not assume that there is, say, an equal amount of learning involved! All we can deduce is that level 4 is a higher level of achievement than level 3, and so on.

The consequence of this analysis is that any attempt to do arithmetic with measurements on an ordinal scale is invalid and will lead to meaningless statements. For example, any aggregation of levels of achievement – such as calculations of averages – is invalid, simply because the intervals between different levels cannot be assumed to be equal steps. You cannot equate the achievement of three children gaining levels 1, 2 and 3 on an ordinal scale with three other children each gaining level 2, on the basis that the 'average' is the same for the two groups – because getting from level 1 to level 2 is not the same thing as getting from level 2 to level 3. This is the problem with using numbers for ordinal scales – as soon as people see numbers they start doing arithmetic with them, regardless of whether their conclusions have any mathematical validity or meaning. There is something to be said therefore for using letters for ordinal scales – although this will not stop people converting them into numbers and calculating aggregates and averages!

In conclusion, we note, therefore, that we have different types of measuring scales, characterised by different mathematical properties, with different degrees of validity for the application of various arithmetic processes. But what remains throughout, even with ordinal scales, is the ever-present transitive property. We can still conclude that if A is better than B and B is better than C, then A is better than C. For without this property we could not put things in order, and without ordering there would be no measurement.

SOME ACTIVITIES WITH CHILDREN

Clearly, children will best develop their understanding of measurement concepts through masses of practical experience of measuring. The more purposeful this is – such as solving real problems, planning events, constructing timetables, cookery, shopping, science experiments, and so on – the better. We can provide here only a few examples of other kinds of activities that might be used to focus on some of the central ideas in this chapter.

Activity 6.1: children as non-standard units

Objective To give children experience of measuring lengths and distance using non-standard units, and to explore the effects of using different-sized units.

Materials A class of children; a classroom with walls and tables; sets of any suitable identical objects – such as lolly sticks, bottle tops, rods, cubes and pennies – that can be used as non-standard units of length.

Method A group of children stand shoulder to shoulder along one of the classroom walls, from one corner to the other, and another child counts how many children there are. The children are then asked how many would be needed to fill up the opposite wall. A group of children line up shoulder to shoulder to check this. Next they estimate how many children for the length of the other two walls. This is then done and the results recorded.

This is then repeated with the children standing with arms outstretched touching fingertips, and then again standing in a queue one behind the other as close as they can get. Each time the children are invited beforehand to guess how many will be required.

This experience is then extended to estimating distances (from one point to another), as opposed to lengths of actual objects (i.e. the walls). For example, they might estimate the number of children required to stretch diagonally across the room from one corner to the other, again using the three different units (shoulder to shoulder, fingertip to fingertip, and queuing). They might then go into the hall or into the playground and try this with the distances between two chairs placed in various positions.

All this should be followed by discussion about what is discovered. Then children could undertake a similar exploration on their table tops (width, length, diagonal distance) using a variety of non-standard units, such as lolly sticks, bottle tops, and so on.

Activity 6.2: estimation challenge

Objective To familiarise children with the sizes of some standard units of measurement.

Materials A 30-cm rule; scrap paper; something to act as a small screen (e.g. a large book).

Method This is a simple but effective game for a small group of children. Players take turns to draw on a piece of scrap paper a line of any number of centimetres length they wish, using the ruler. They do this behind the screen, so that the others cannot see them doing it. The line is then shown and each of the other players estimates how long it is. One player should write down all the estimates. They then check the length of the line with the ruler. The player (or players) getting nearest wins a point. They win a bonus point if they get the length spot on.

Variations of this game can be devised using other aspects of measurement. For example, children could use a balance to weigh out quantities of sand into a yoghurt pot (using 10-g masses only), again behind a screen – the others then have to estimate the mass.

Activity 6.3: short straws

Objective To give children experience related to the concept of conservation of length.

Materials   A large supply of cheap straws or strips of thin card; scissors; a screen, as in Activity 6.2.

Method   This is a simple game for four players. In turn each player takes a set of three straws all the same length and, using the scissors, shortens one slightly. The three straws are then presented to the others in a fist in the traditional fashion, trying to disguise which one is shorter than the others. Each chooses one straw. The loser keeps the short straw, which counts as a point against him or her. This can be repeated about twenty times. At the end of the game the player with the least number of short straws is the winner. The intention is that young children will through this game experience the idea that the length of an object is not changed by its being displaced.

Activity 6.4: conservation game (volume and mass)

Objective   To give children experience related to the concept of conservation of mass and volume.

Materials   A number of different-shaped clear plastic or glass containers and measuring jars; a small cup; a supply of water; three identical non-transparent containers with lids (e.g. yoghurt pots); a supply of sand; a balance; a ball bearing.

Method   This is another game for four players, in two teams of two. Team A measures out the same quantity of water into three clear containers, and then adds one extra cupful of water to one of them. While they are doing this, team B measures out the same mass of sand into the three pots, buries the ball bearing in one of them and replaces the lids.

They then challenge each other to identify the odd one out. Team B is allowed only to look at the containers of water. Team A is allowed to pick up – but not to rattle vigorously – the pots of sand. After they have made their judgements each team can check to see if they are right, by pouring water or by balancing pots. They then swap over and repeat the experiment with team A doing mass and team B doing volume.

Activity 6.5: investigating ordering

Objective   To give children experience of transitivity and ordering.

Materials   (1) A set of cards with events of the day written or depicted on them – alarm goes off, get up, have breakfast, etc. (2) A collection of containers, such as bottles and jars. (3) A balance and a set of identical-looking sealed parcels, filled with a variety of materials, such as sand, sawdust, ball bearings. (4) A list of tasks taking various amounts of time (count to a hundred, tie up your shoe laces, do ten press-ups, etc.).

Method   These materials provide four different opportunities for children to develop a strategy for ordering three or more items (events, containers, parcels, tasks). In each case they should start with three items and order these. Then extend to four, five, six or more. The four activities are as follows.

(1) The children have to put the events of the day in order from earliest to latest. To start with, any three cards can be used. A nice touch is to have letters written on the backs of the cards, so that when the whole set is finally ordered they can be turned over to reveal a message such as '*well done*'.

(2) By pouring water from one to another the children should order three containers by capacity. Gradually extend this by adding a fourth container, a fifth, and so on.

(3) Using the balance and the parcels, the children explore the same problem with mass.

(4) Two children perform two of the tasks starting at the same time, and discover which takes the longer and which takes the shorter time. Eventually they must order the whole list from the one taking the least amount of time to the one taking the greatest.

Activity 6.6: snail race
Objective   To give children some concept of a time interval of one minute.
   Materials   A stop clock.
   Method   This is a bit of fun for a class of children learning about time. The class is taken into the hall or on to the playground, where starting and finishing lines are marked out. All watches must be removed beforehand. The children line up at the start and 'race' to the finish. The winner is the child who crosses the line nearest to exactly one minute after the start! The teacher stands on the finishing line and makes a mental note of the child crossing the line at the appropriate moment, but allows the rest to finish. All competitors must keep moving. Have several heats and then a final. Discuss after each heat whether most people were too slow or too fast.

Activity 6.7: talk about time
Objective   To develop children's understanding of the language of time.
   Materials   The list of words and phrases associated with time given earlier in this chapter.
   Method   Write on the board a small collection of words or phrases from the list of time-language. Sit the class on the carpet and hold a discussion with them incorporating the words on the board. Here are two examples of suitable collections of words and phrases: (1) day, weekend, week, life-time, long time, short time, brief, temporary, for the time being, non-stop, never-ending, permanent; (2) how old, age, age-group, year-group, teenager, young, old, elderly, middle-aged, under-age, older, elder, oldest, younger, youngest.

Activity 6.8: ordering packets
Objective   To provide more experience of ordering, and to heighten children's awareness of measurement in the world outside school.
   Materials   Children to collect as many different empty packets where the contents are marked in grams or kilograms.
   Method   Along the whole length of a wall, make a number-line frieze, marked from 0 to 2000 g. As packets are collected, children display them on the appropriate part of the number line. Write the number of grams in large numerals underneath. The children should be challenged to find packets with different numbers of grams from those already displayed.

Activity 6.9: metric or imperial?
Objective   To make explicit to children the mixture of units in use in everyday life.

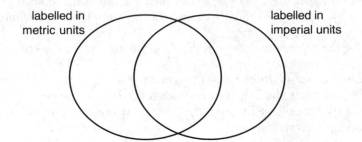

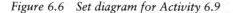

Figure 6.6   Set diagram for Activity 6.9

Materials   Whatever can be collected in the way of packets, notices, advertisements, newspaper cuttings, in which measurements of various sorts appear.

Method   The children make a display of the materials collected. They can arrange these in a set diagram, as shown in Figure 6.6, to show which ones use just metric units, which use just imperial units, and which use both.

Activity 6.10: recording with arrows

Objective   To develop understanding of the principle of transitivity in measurement.

Materials   Three objects labelled A, B and C; three cards labelled A, B and C; three arrows cut from card, labelled 'is heavier than'; three further cards labelled 'is lighter than'; a balance for weighing.

Method   The layout of arrows shown in Figure 6.4 provides a useful way for a small group of children to record their comparisons of three objects. They are given the three objects, the three cards labelled A, B and C, and the three arrows with 'is heavier than' written on them. Their task is then to compare A with B, B with C, and A with C, using the balance, to construct an arrangement of the arrows and cards as shown in Figure 6.4, and then to discuss the ordering of the three objects that emerges. The same task with the same objects should then be undertaken with the arrows labelled 'is lighter than'.

Variations on this basic activity can be devised in any measuring context, using appropriate objects and labels, with the arrows indicating various aspects of the language of comparison.

SUMMARY OF KEY IDEAS IN CHAPTER 6

1. Measurements of length and distance might refer to a wide variety of situations, such as the straight or curved parts of objects, lines drawn on paper, imaginary lines drawn through the air or through objects, straight or curved paths.
2. Volume is the amount of three-dimensional space occupied by an object.
3. Only containers have capacity. The capacity of a container is the volume of liquid it can hold. In the metric system, capacity and liquid volume are often measured in litres.
4. There are two meanings of time: the time at which an event occurs (recorded time) and the time that something takes to happen (time interval).
5. Kilograms and grams are units of mass, not weight. A key phrase for describing the results of weighing is: 'weighs the same as' (e.g. the book weighs the same as two hundred grams).

6. Fundamental ideas involved in measurement are comparison and ordering, transitivity, conservation and the idea of a unit.
7. The principle of transitivity is that if A is greater than (less than/equal to) B, and B is greater than (less than/equal to) C, then A must be greater than (less than/equal to) C.
8. Conservation of quantity involves recognising which transformations (such as pouring a quantity of water into a different-shaped container) preserve which equivalences (e.g. the volume of water stays the same).
9. There are good arguments for introducing children to measuring in units by means of experience with non-standard units.
10. It seems likely that in UK some imperial units – such as the mile and the pint – will continue to survive alongside metric units.
11. The metre, kilogram and second are examples of base units in the SI version of metric units.
12. Prefixes for deriving other units include: mega (million), kilo (thousand), hecto (hundred), deci (tenth), centi (hundredth), milli (thousandth) and micro (millionth).
13. Nearly all measurement is approximate – normally you can only ever measure 'to the nearest something'.
14. Three different kinds of measuring scales are: ratio scales, such as length and mass, in which measurement can be compared by ratio as well as by difference; interval scales, such as temperature or time of day, in which measurements can be compared by their difference, but not by their ratio; and ordinal scales, such as exam grades and levels of achievement, in which measurements can only be compared by ordering.
15. Transitivity applies in all three types of measuring scale.

SUGGESTIONS FOR FURTHER READING

Ainley, J. (1991) Is there any mathematics in measurement? In D. Pimm and E. Love (eds) *Teaching and Learning School Mathematics*, Hodder & Stoughton, London, in association with the Open University, pp. 69–76. (Ainley is surprised to discover just how much mathematics is involved in lessons on measurement.)

Blinko, J. and Slater, A. (1996) *Teaching Measures: Activities, Organisation and Management*, Hodder & Stoughton, London. (A very practical book, full of ideas for teaching measurement in the primary school.)

Dickson, L., Brown, M. and Gibson, O. (1984) *Children Learning Mathematics*, Cassell, London. (Section 2 provides a thorough and fascinating survey of what research shows us about children's understanding of measurement concepts, including consideration of Piaget's work, fundamental ideas such as conservation and transitivity, and the difference between counting and measuring. Essential reading!)

Haylock, D. (1995) *Mathematics Explained for Primary Teachers*, Paul Chapman Publishing, London. (Chapter 24 deals with measurement.)

Hopkins, C., Gifford, S. and Pepperell, S. (eds) (1996) *Mathematics in the Primary School: a Sense of Progression*, David Fulton Publishers, London. (The second half of Section 3 of this practical book provides a straightforward consideration of how to teach the measurement requirements in the National Curriculum.)

Jarvis, T. (1988) Weight and see, *Junior Education*, August, pp. 30–1. (Jarvis provides many practical examples – including children making their own balances – that helped promote her pupils' understanding of the concept of mass.)

Johnson, G. L. (1987) Using a metric unit to help pre-service teachers appreciate the value of manipulative materials, *Arithmetic Teacher*, 35, no. 2, pp. 14–20. (An article that provides useful strategies for developing a practical appreciation of the metric units used to measure length, area, volume, capacity and weight.)

Nunes, T. and Bryant, P. (1996) *Children Doing Mathematics*, Blackwell, Oxford. (Chapter 4 on young children's responses to measurement systems is well worth reading.)

Thyer, D. and Maggs, J. (3rd edition, 1991) *Teaching Mathematics to Young Children*, Cassell, London. (Chapter 4 provides a thorough coverage of approaches to teaching time to young children. The book provides plenty of practical suggestions for teaching this and other aspects of measurement.)

7

Shape and Space

Although number work and the study of shape and space appear side by side in their curriculum statements for mathematics, in commercial mathematics schemes, and in the National Curriculum for England and Wales, teachers – and the children they teach – often regard them as very different kinds of activity:

- I never think of them as being the same subject. Number work and shape are quite distinct as far as I'm concerned.
- My class do shape one session a week and number work for the rest of the time. They don't think of the shape work as real maths.
- When the parents of one of my 7-year-olds asked her what she did in maths yesterday she said, 'We didn't do maths – we did some stuff with shapes instead.'
- It's something to do with pattern, isn't it? You get patterns in number and patterns in shape.

NUMBER AND SHAPE:
TWO BRANCHES OF MATHEMATICS

It is at first sight a little surprising that two activities apparently as different as arithmetic and geometry should form the two prongs of a single subject called mathematics. We may well wonder what is the connection between two aspects of learning, one of which includes activities like place-value notation and calculations with whole numbers, fractions, decimals and percentages, and the other of which is concerned with things like putting shapes into sets, exploring symmetries and making Christmas decorations. The different natures of these two branches of mathematics are reflected in the fact that performances in these two areas are often markedly different for individual children.

One of the recurring themes in this book is that we understand mathematics by making connections. In the early chapters we talk extensively about the importance of connecting symbols with pictures, such as number lines and set diagrams. So, in fact, we are already making a link between numerical and spatial thinking. This link is made stronger in Chapter 5 where we explore the ways in which geometric patterns and images can support our understanding of number relationships. The teacher's comment above about patterns in both number and shape is pertinent to our argument here. But we would suggest that the connection is even more fundamental than that. As with our analysis of number, we show below that the two basic processes for understanding shape and spatial concepts are – yet again – equivalence and transformation.

Guess my rule

A simple game, called 'Guess my rule', that can be played with either numbers or shapes, demonstrates how the same underlying ideas are shared by these two aspects of mathematics. In this game one person challenges the other players to guess the rule they have in their mind. In the number version, the players suggest various numbers to which the challenger responds 'yes' or 'no', depending on whether or not the rule is satisfied. As they are called out the numbers are written in either the 'yes' set or the 'no' set. For example, after several suggestions something like Figure 7.1 might have been written on the board. By this stage someone may be able to articulate the rule being used, namely 'less than eleven'.

The situation we have here can be analysed using the notions of equivalence and transformation. The numbers in the 'yes' set in Figure 7.1 are different, but there is something that is the same about them, something that for the purpose of this game makes them equivalent: they are all less than eleven. You could focus on various attributes of the numbers in this set, such as noticing that six is bigger than five, or that six is twice three, and so on. But you have to ignore all such observations of how the numbers are different from one another in favour of the one thing that they have in common.

A game with exactly the same mathematical structure can be played with a set of shapes, either three-dimensional solid shapes or two-dimensional plane shapes. The set of shapes is set out on a table and once again the challenger uses a rule to sort them into a 'yes' set and a 'no' set. After a while, in a game using a set of cut-out card shapes, the situation shown in Figure 7.2 might have arisen. In identifying the rule as 'four-sided', precisely the same kind of funda-mental cognitive processing is involved here as with the number game. The

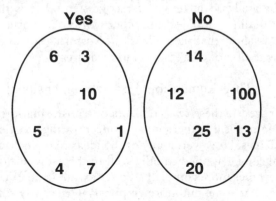

Figure 7.1 What's my rule? Numbers

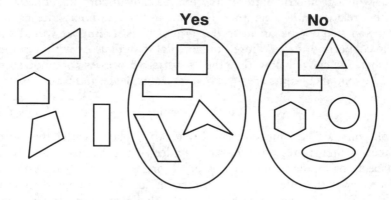

Figure 7.2   What's my rule? Shapes

shapes in the 'yes' set are all different from one another, but we are recognising them as being in some sense the same. As our eye sweeps from one shape to the other, we ignore all the transformations taking place and seek to identify the equivalence.

Equivalence and transformation again

It is our contention then that the fundamental mathematical notions of transformation and equivalence are common to understanding both number and shape, and it is this that makes these two areas into a unified subject. The two basic types of learning involved in understanding concepts of shape and space are classifying shapes and changing shapes. First, we put shapes into sets according to samenesses. Then we look at various ways of making shapes change, discussing what is different. In other words, we recognise equivalences and we apply transformations. We see right from our earliest discussions in this book that these two ideas are at the heart of mathematical thinking. In Chapter 1 we show that a statement such as '3 + 5 = 8' can be viewed both as a statement about a transformation being applied to the 3 and the 5, and to an equivalence that emerges. In Chapter 2 we show that the concept of a cardinal number can be analysed in terms of recognising what is the same about a number of sets of different objects; in other words, recognising an equivalence. In Chapter 6, we show that these ideas of transformation and equivalence are the basis of the notion of conservation in measurement.

Three-dimensional or two-dimensional

In this chapter we use these two concepts of transformation and equivalence to analyse geometrical experiences, concentrating particularly on two-dimensional shapes. However, many of the ideas that we discuss in the subsequent material can be applied equally well to three-dimensional shapes – but the analysis becomes more complex. We are aware from our discussions with infant-teachers that some put more emphasis in the early stages on activities with solid shapes:

- A lot of the schemes seem to start with three-dimensional shapes, cubes and cuboids and things like that.
- I find that the children come to school already knowing a lot of the words for flat shapes, like square and circle – but not the words for solid shapes.
- What's the argument for starting with three-dimensional? Wouldn't it be simpler to start with two-dimensional and build up?
- But they live in a three-dimensional world and are used to handling three-dimensional objects, like boxes and tins and toys. You should start with three-dimensional things you can pick up and handle, and move down to the two-dimensional shapes.
- A lot of my children call a cuboid an oblong anyway.

It seems clear to us that two-dimensional and three-dimensional experiences – flat shapes and solid shapes – need to go hand in hand. Of course, children do live in a three-dimensional world of solid shapes, but in order to describe, identify and classify these shapes, we have to focus on the shapes of their surfaces. Hence the confusion between a cuboid and an oblong. We should also bear in mind that, even before they come to school, children will have spent a lot of time looking at pictures in books and at television screens, so that much of their experience is in fact two-dimensional.

A MATHEMATICAL ANALYSIS OF SHAPE AND SPACE

In this analysis of geometric thinking we shall compare sets of two-dimensional shapes, each time asking in what sense are the shapes in the set the same, and in what ways are they different. In other words, we shall be identifying what transformations have been applied and which equivalences are preserved. The analysis is structured according to a mathematical progression, using a way of classifying geometric experiences originally proposed by a German mathematician, Felix Klein, in 1872. In our analysis we shall use one geometric shape, that shown in Figure 7.3, to generate further sets of shapes, in which the original shape is distorted more and more, until the final set of shapes considered have very little in common. But we shall see that – in spite of the extensive transformations that have taken place – they are still in some sense equivalent.

This analysis helps us to see that sometimes we as teachers expect children to focus on the ways in which things are different, and at other times to focus on the ways in which they are the same. It seems as though learning geometry is a matter of picking up clues as to what you are expected to ignore and what you are expected to take into account on any particular occasion!

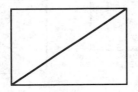

Figure 7.3   Original shape for analysis of transformation

In the course of our analysis of geometry we shall identify some of the mathematical concepts needed to discuss the samenesses and differences involved. In this way we hope teachers will see (1) how the fundamental ideas of transformation and equivalence underpin almost all geometric experiences, and (2) how the various concepts that children encounter in classifying and changing shapes fit into a coherent mathematical system. Thus, by making such connections as these we hope that teachers will feel that their own understanding of the geometric experiences they present to young children has been enhanced.

Translation

Consider the set of shapes shown in Figure 7.4. Are they the same shape?

- They look identical to me.
- But they're not actually the same, are they. They're like identical twins. They look alike in every respect but they are different people.
- They've got different names as well. This one's called A and that one's called B.
- They're drawn in different places on the page.

We had better start by noting that when we draw, for example, a 'rectangle' on a piece of paper, or on a page of a book, then we are only drawing an approximate representation of an abstract mathematical idea. This abstract idea is a four-sided figure, consisting of lines of no thickness, meeting at right angles at points of no area! So in our discussion about sameness and difference we are not concerned with the actual molecules of ink constituting the drawing on the paper, but with the abstraction that this represents. We will disregard questions such as whether the thicknesses of the lines in the various shapes are exactly the same, and questions relating to the approximate nature of all measurement. With these provisos we could then conclude that the shapes in this set are the same in every respect – except one. They are all rectangles with a diagonal drawn from the bottom left- to top right-hand corner, they have the

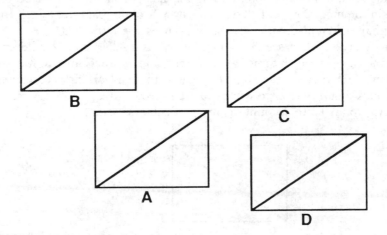

Figure 7.4   A set of shapes produced by translations

same dimensions, the angles are the same, corresponding sides point in the same direction, and so on. But they differ in that each one is drawn in a different *position*.

The transformation that changes one of these shapes into any other one in the set is called a *translation*. This is a sliding, without turning, from one position to another. To describe such translations we need concepts of *direction*, such as *up*, *down*, *left*, *right*, *forwards* and *backwards*. Young children experience a one-dimensional form of the geometry of translations and position when they move up and down the number line.

However, we do not often consider solid and plane shapes to be different if they differ only in position. When we do, we require some form of *co-ordinate* system to pinpoint position. An example would be in locating a seat in a room as, say, the fourth seat from the left in the third row.

> If we tell the children to sit at the same tables as yesterday, then we would be asking them to take position into account then, wouldn't we? The tables might be the same shape and same size, but when we say 'the same table' we mean the same position as well.

Rotation

Having discussed and identified translations, from now on in our analysis we ignore them. In other words, we do not take position into account, so that two shapes are regarded as the same if one is produced merely by translating the other. Now consider the set of shapes shown in Figure 7.5. Again we ask whether they are the same, or in what ways are they different?

- They are the same shape, but they have been turned through various angles.
- We have examples like this in our maths scheme where the children have to colour in shapes that are the same.
- Some children find it very hard to realise that a cuboid is the same if it's standing up or on its side.
- And they'll call a square a diamond if it's standing on one of its corners.

Again we see that in many contexts we would regard the shapes in Figure 7.5 as being the same shape. The difference now is that they are oriented in space

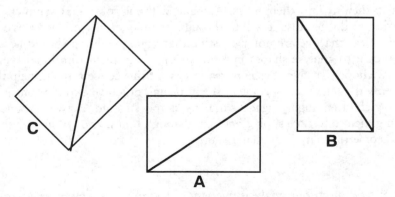

Figure 7.5   A set of shapes produced by rotations

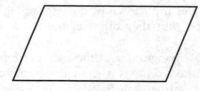

Figure 7.6   A shape with rotational symmetry

differently – corresponding lines in the shapes point in different directions. To get from one shape to another the transformation that is applied is called a *rotation*.

In order to take into account this particular transformation, the geometric concept required is that of *angle*. There are basically two ways of thinking about the concept of angle, one dynamic and the other static. Here we are using the *dynamic* aspect: an angle as a measure of the amount of turn or rotation that has occurred. For example, the transformation from A to B in Figure 7.5 is a rotation through a quarter-turn. A quarter-turn is also called a *right angle*. This is short-hand for upright angle. This is the angle that a stick turns through when you move it from flat on the ground to an upright position. To be more precise about a rotation, we might also need to specify whether it is clockwise or anticlockwise. The rotation from A to C in Figure 7.5 is half a right angle.

Sometimes a shape does not change when it is rotated through certain an-gles. For example, the diagram in Figure 7.6 can be rotated through a half-turn (two right angles) and it would look the same. To convince yourself of this just turn the book upside down. While you've got the book upside down you might decide whether some letters of the alphabet, such as **S**, **A**, **C** or **N**, have this same geometric property.

This property is called *rotational symmetry*. In their practical explorations with two-dimensional shapes, young children can experience this property by drawing a box round a shape and then seeing how many different ways the shape will fit into its box, without picking it up and turning it over. They experience the same idea when posting shapes through holes in the post-box toy – which is why this is such a popular toy with mathematically minded parents. Some shapes can be rotated into a number of different positions in which they fit into their holes. A shape without rotational symmetry is the hardest to do, because it will fit through its hole in only one way. We should make clear that we are not suggesting that young children should necessarily be taught to analyse shapes in terms of this concept of rotational symmetry. But we hope that their teachers' awareness of this concept might help them to identify the relevance of some of the informal, practical explorations in which young children might engage – moving shapes around, drawing round them, fitting them into boxes, posting them through holes, and so on – as the basis for geometric analysis at a later stage.

Reflection

From now on in our analysis, we ignore rotations as well as translations. In other words, we do not take into account changes in position or changes in

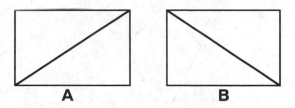

Figure 7.7   Mirror images

orientation. The result of translating or rotating a shape is regarded as the same shape. We turn our attention to the two shapes shown in Figure 7.7, and again ask in what sense are they the same shape, and in what ways are they different.

- They're different because they're mirror images of each other.
- It's like a pair of shoes. They're the same in one sense, but they're different because one's for the left foot and the other for the right foot.
- They're the same, but one's been flipped over.
- It's as though you have to learn the conventions. Sometimes in maths lessons we ask children to pick out the same shape, and expect them to regard mirror images as the same, but then we correct them when they don't distinguish between the letter d and the letter b!

Again we have a situation where for many purposes we would regard shapes as being the same, yet on other occasions we would focus on the differences. If you look in a mirror and comb your hair you are making use of the equivalence between yourself and your mirror image. When you choose a pair of shoes from the heap in the bottom of the wardrobe you look for two that are the same as each other, but then when you have to decide which shoe goes on which foot you focus on the difference between them. So both equivalence and transformation are involved in your classification and manipulation of the shapes involved.

The transformation that would change one of the shapes in Figure 7.7 into the other is called a *reflection*. Associated with each reflection is a *mirror line*. The reader can no doubt imagine where a mirror could be placed in Figure 7.7, in order that one of the shapes becomes the mirror image of the other.

To take into account the changes produced by reflections, the concepts of *left* and *right* are particularly important. Thus when you look into the mirror and raise your right arm, the person in the mirror raises their left arm. It is interesting to note that 'left and right' are different kinds of ideas from 'up and down'. Up is the same direction for all of us, all the time – at least as we move around locally on the earth's surface. But left for one person might be right for another, and what is on your left now might be on your right when you move to a new position.

Sometimes a shape does not change when it is reflected. For example, the mirror image of the diagram in Figure 7.8 would look the same as the original. To convince yourself of this, look at the diagram in a mirror, or hold the book up to the light and look through the other side of the page. While you're doing

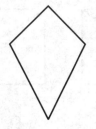

Figure 7.8   A shape with line symmetry

one of these you might investigate whether any capital letters of the alphabet, such as **S**, **A**, **C** or **N**, have this geometric property. Remember that we are disregarding changes produced by translating or rotating the book, so when you are looking at the mirror image you are allowed, for example, to turn it upside down.

This property is called *line symmetry*. In their practical explorations with two-dimensional shapes young children can experience this property in a number of different ways. They can draw a box round a shape and then investigate whether the shape will fit into its box when it is picked up and turned over. Or they can cut out a shape and discover whether it can be folded along a line so that one half matches the other half. Such a fold line is called a *line of symmetry*. The two halves are mirror images of each other, with the line of symmetry as a mirror line. They can experiment with looking at shapes in mirrors and seeing what happens when a mirror is placed along a line of symmetry. Another useful experience is to copy shapes on to tracing paper and then to compare the original with the shape that appears on the reverse side of the paper.

Similarity

If we now decide to disregard translations, rotations and reflections, when comparing shapes, then we would consider all the shapes in Figure 7.9 to be the same. Mathematicians would say that these shapes are *congruent*.

Figure 7.10 then introduces a further way in which shapes may change, while still in some senses staying the same. Now the sizes of the shapes are different, but we would still in many contexts regard them as the same shape. This is what happens when children are putting logic blocks into sets – sometimes they put the large triangles and small triangles into the same set (i.e. triangles), regarding them as the same, and sometimes into different sets (i.e. large and small), regarding them as different, depending on which attributes they are using to sort the shapes.

The transformation being applied as we move from one shape to another in Figure 7.10 is technically called a *similarity*. The shapes are said to be *similar*. This is, of course, using the word 'similar' in a precise technical sense, not in the colloquial sense where you might say that your sister or brother and yourself have similar looks. We can think of a similarity as being either a *scaling up* or a *scaling down*. We are talking about what happens, for example,

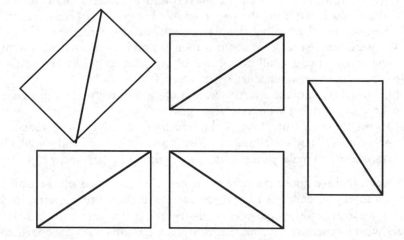

Figure 7.9   A set of congruent shapes

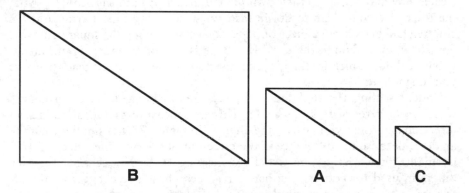

Figure 7.10   A set of shapes produced by scaling

when we use a photocopier to enlarge or reduce something. The key concept required to specify a scaling is that of *scale factor*. In Figure 7.10, for example, B is the result of scaling A by a scale factor of 2. The effect of this is to multiply the lengths of all the sides by 2. This is an instance of the scaling structure of multiplication discussed in Chapter 4. Since all the lengths are scaled by the same factor, the ratio of any two lengths in the shape remains the same. Compare the example of a percentage pay rise, given in Chapter 4, where all salaries are scaled by the same factor, in order to preserve the ratios between salaries. Here is an excellent example of the close match between numerical and spatial processes, where in both the geometric figures and the salaries we can identify a transformation (the scaling applied) and an equivalence (the ratios that are preserved).

Children experience scaling in model cars, dolls and dolls' houses, play houses, maps and plans, scale drawings, photographs, and so on, all of which provide excellent starting points for informal discussion of these ideas.

- One of my boys measured the playground to make a plan, then said he couldn't do it. He said the paper wasn't big enough, because it was only about one metre long, but the playground was thirty metres!
- We were reading a book about a monster and there was this picture of a huge foot next to a small man. None of my children got it. They didn't seem to appreciate the significance of scale at all.
- I get my class to make a larger version of a small picture, by drawing a grid over it and copying it on to a larger grid.
- I showed some of my Year 3 children how to enlarge and reduce on the photocopier. They were fascinated by it and quickly picked up which numbers you use to make things bigger or smaller, like 141 and 71.

Once again we note that there are times when we focus on the transformation, and expect children to take differences in size into account, and times when we focus on the equivalence, disregarding the difference in scale. Consider what happens when a teacher draws a large square on the board and asks the children to copy it. Without questioning the instruction, the children will all quite happily choose to ignore the size of the square and make a smaller (scaled-down) drawing on their own piece of paper. And this is probably what the teacher intends them to do. In fact, we would not think it strange if the children had been given a piece of paper too small to copy the square anyway! Somehow, even though the size of a shape is one of its most significant attributes, children pick up the idea that there are times when the teacher wants you to ignore it.

Under a scaling, the angles in a shape remain unchanged. We are using the word *angle* here in its *static* sense. This is a measure of the difference in direction between two lines. So the angle X in Figure 7.11 is smaller than the angle Y, because the difference in the direction of the two lines meeting at X is smaller than that of the two lines meeting at Y. Notice how the two diagrams used for comparison here have been chosen to exaggerate the attribute in question – see the discussion of comparison in measurement in Chapter 6.

As one of the teacher's comments above suggests, a photocopier with an enlargement facility is an effective way to explore scaling and to become explicitly aware of what remains the same under a scaling. For example, children can make a photocopy enlargement of a drawing, say, from A5 size paper to A4, as shown in Figure 7.12. They then cut out the original and the photocopy and, by placing one shape on top of the other, explore how the angles match.

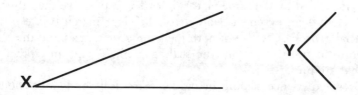

Figure 7.11   Which angle is smaller?

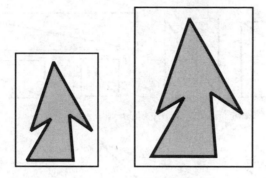

Figure 7.12   Photocopied enlargement from A5 to A4

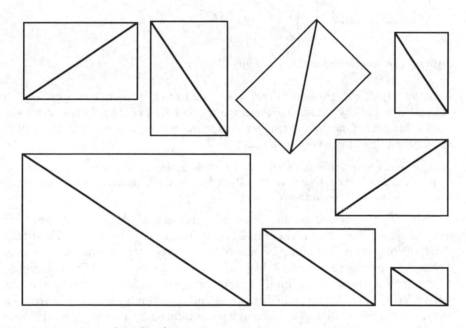

Figure 7.13   A set of similar shapes

Affinity

From now on in our analysis of geometric thinking, we regard similar shapes, such as the set shown in Figure 7.13, as equivalent. We are now disregarding differences resulting from translations, rotations, reflections, and scalings. As far as we are concerned, from this point on, all the shapes in Figure 7.13 are the same shape.

Now consider the set of shapes shown in Figure 7.14. Although our original shape has changed quite considerably, we might still recognise that there is something the same about all the shapes in this set. Even though the shapes are not geometrically similar, there is still a *family likeness*, some shared properties that lead us on some occasions to ignore the differences between the members

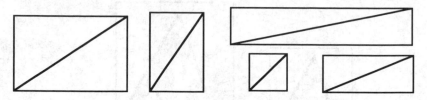

Figure 7.14   A set of shapes with a family likeness

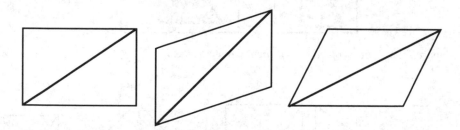

Figure 7.15   Another example of a family likeness

of the family. We might select them from a collection of shapes, recognising an equivalence and distinguishing them from other shapes that do not share the family likeness. One infant-teacher described for us an instance of a child recognising this kind of equivalence:

> My children were doing an exercise in the maths scheme where they had to colour in the cuboids on a shelf. One of them coloured in the shelf, because she said that was a cuboid as well! I thought that was very clever.

Figure 7.15 provides another example of a set of shapes, including our original shape, that share one of these family likenesses. The technical word for the transformation that changes our original shape into one of the others in either the set shown in Figure 7.14 or that shown in Figure 7.15 is an *affinity*. The precise analysis of this kind of transformation is fairly involved and not particularly helpful for a teacher of young children. But we may notice that the shapes in Figures 7.14 and 7.15 have been produced by stretching or shearing the original.

In order to recognise equivalences of this sort, we need particularly the concept of *parallel*. Two lines are parallel if they are pointing in the same direction. One condition of an affinity is that parallel lines must stay parallel.

Within the set of *polygons* (two-dimensional shapes with straight edges), we can identify families of shapes such as *triangles* (three sided), *quadrilaterals* (four sided), *pentagons* (five sided), *hexagons* (six sided), and so on. The set of quadrilaterals contains some particularly interesting examples of affinities. For example, there is the family known as *rectangles*, some of which are shown in Figure 7.16. These share the property that all four angles are right angles.

- Aren't some of those squares, not rectangles?
- Is a square a rectangle then?
- Why has the word oblong gone out of fashion?

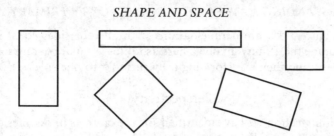

Figure 7.16   A family of rectangles

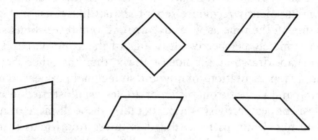

Figure 7.17   A family of parallelograms

There is a small confusion here that often arises. A square is definitely a member of the set of rectangles, since it shares the family likeness, having all four angles as right angles. It is, in fact, a special sort of rectangle, since all the sides are equal. If we want to distinguish between squares and other rectangles then we can refer to square rectangles and oblong rectangles. This confusion is reinforced if when children are sorting shapes, such as logic blocks, we refer to squares and rectangles as though they are separate sets of shapes. We can, however, sort the rectangles into those that are squares and those that are not squares.

A second important family of quadrilaterals is the set of *parallelograms*, some examples of which are shown in Figure 7.17. The family likeness here is that they all have two pairs of opposite sides that are parallel.

- So a rectangle is a parallelogram?
- And since a square is a rectangle, is it a parallelogram as well?
- What's a rhombus?

The answer to each of the first two of these questions is 'yes'. All rectangles, including squares, are parallelograms – they share the family likeness, having two pairs of opposite sides parallel. The third question leads to one last example of an affinity. The set of *rhombuses*, some examples of which are

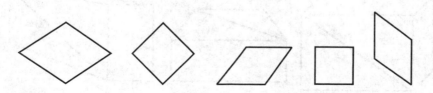

Figure 7.18   A family of rhombuses

shown in Figure 7.18, are parallelograms with all four sides equal in length. We can imagine the affinity involved here as taking a square of any size, hinged at the corners, and then transforming it by tilting it to one side or the other.

Perspectivity

In the previous section we have identified some examples of families of shapes, such as rectangles, parallelograms and rhombuses, that can be considered as equivalent because they share some particular property. But would we ever recognise the shapes shown in Figure 7.19 as being the same?

In fact, we apparently recognise sets of shapes like those in Figure 7.19 as being the same all the time as we move around our three-dimensional world, since these are merely perspective drawings of the same shape. If we imagine our original shape drawn on the side of a box, then the other shapes in Figure 7.19 are simply representations of how the shape might appear to us as we turn the box round and view it from different angles, as illustrated in Figure 7.20!

The analysis of perspectivity is a particularly difficult piece of mathematics, which should not detain us now. But it is interesting for us to observe that when we learn to recognise shapes viewed from different perspectives in our three-dimensional world, we are learning to ignore the changes in the shapes associated with perspective transformations.

One teacher asked her 4- and 5-year-olds to draw a table. Figure 7.21 provides some typical examples of their drawings. About half of the children drew a side view of the table, like those of Peter and Laura. But the other half drew what was basically a rectangle, with some legs attached somewhere, like those of Sally, Neil and Debbie. It is fascinating to note that even such young children have already learnt to recognise a rectangle, apparently ignoring the perspective changes, even when looked at from the very low angle at which they presumably view tables!

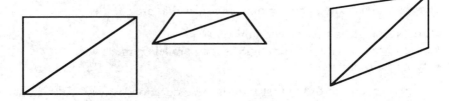

Figure 7.19   Are these all the 'same' shape?

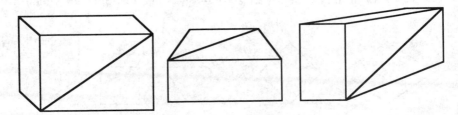

Figure 7.20   Perspective drawings of the same shape

Peter   Sally

Laura   Neil

Debbie

Figure 7.21   Four- and five-year-olds draw tables

Figure 7.22   The tables in the dining-room

This suggestion is confirmed by what happened when the children were asked to draw the tables in the dining-room. These tables were semi-hexagonal. The examples of the children's drawings in Figure 7.22 show that they realise that they are not looking at rectangles, even though most of them clearly have some difficulty in representing the actual shape.

It could be because we learn to ignore perspective transformations at such an early age, that it is actually very difficult to make ourselves consciously aware of them. So, when we look at a rectangular window as we walk past a house, even though the image on the retina of our eye must change, most of the time we are not consciously aware of the shape of the window changing. As far as we are concerned it stays a rectangle.

Topological transformation

In the course of our analysis of geometric thinking we have gradually distorted our original shape more and more, by applying various transformations to it. As we have done this we have noticed that there are still situations in which we regard the various shapes produced as being equivalent, in which we concentrate on what is the same about the shapes, rather than on what changes from one to another, even though the changes have been quite drastic. The final step in this analysis is to transform our shape to generate a set of shapes like those shown in Figure 7.23. Although in most situations we would regard these as being different shapes, we may still recognise something about them that makes them equivalent. For example, if these diagrams were representing pieces of wire constituting electrical circuits then clearly they would all be the same circuit.

To generate each of the shapes in Figure 7.23 we have applied a *topological transformation* to the original shape. In a transformation of this sort, the shape can be pulled, stretched or distorted in any way you like, provided that no lines are broken or joined in the process. Clearly none of our usual geometric properties – such as length, angle, parallelism, ratio of lengths, the number of sides, or even the straightness of sides – is preserved under such transformations. But if we think of a two-dimensional shape as no more than a network of *paths*, enclosing *regions*, meeting at *junctions*, then we can see that all the shapes in Figure 7.23 are the same. Each is a network of three paths from one junction to another, enclosing two regions.

This indicates that it is often essentially topological thinking that is involved in giving directions for a route. For example, we can describe a route like this: 'Go out of the drive, turn left, then the second on the right, just past the post box, carry on until you come to a roundabout, take the second exit, . . . ' These instructions are useful even though they contain no reference to

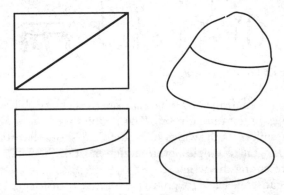

Figure 7.23 Are these in any sense the 'same' shape?

distance, scale or direction, but simply refer to a network of paths and junctions, to what is passed on a particular path, and whether you turn left or right at any particular junction. A useful topological exercise for children is to articulate their route from home to school.

Some of the most fundamental geometric ideas are those that are preserved under a topological transformation: ideas such as *between, next, meet, inside* and *outside*. So, if one junction lies *between* two other junctions in a network, it will still lie between them after a topological transformation. The *next* junction along a path will still be the next junction; two paths that *meet* will still meet; a point *inside* a region will still be inside the region, and so on. We hope that this analysis helps to make clear to infant-teachers the significance in mathematical terms of such basic spatial language as this.

We conclude this section with one final observation, which demonstrates the importance of topological thinking. An interesting phenomenon is that young children are able to recognise all the shapes in Figure 7.24 as being the same letter. In what geometric sense are they the same? They are certainly not congruent, or even similar. They are not a family of shapes, in the sense of sharing an affinity, nor are they just one shape seen from different perspectives. They are, of course, topologically equivalent. It is really quite amazing that the young human brain is capable of categorising all these shapes on the basis of what is the same about them while ignoring the many ways in which they are different.

The children's drawings of semi-hexagonal tables in Figure 7.22, like their drawings of people's faces, are also essentially topological representations of the shapes they observe. They are certainly not congruent, similar or drawn in perspective. Only in a topological sense are the drawings equivalent to the objects they represent. This suggests that this is, in fact, the most basic concept of sameness and that it forms a starting point for geometric thinking. From this basis we have to provide a range of practical experiences of shapes – picking them up and looking at them from different angles, drawing round them, cutting them out, moving them round, fitting them in boxes, matching them, comparing them, contrasting them, scaling them, looking at them in mirrors, turning them over, folding them, rotating them, fitting them together, sorting them into families, and so on, and so on – in order to equip the children with the language, skills and concepts needed to recognise the full range of equivalences outlined in this chapter. For it is this recognition of what stays the same when things change that is the basis of understanding of shape and space.

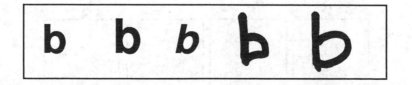

Figure 7.24   A set of topologically equivalent shapes

SOME ACTIVITIES WITH CHILDREN

The main text of this chapter contains a number of suggestions of the sorts of practical activities in which children might engage in order to experience some of the fundamental geometric ideas discussed. The shape-sorting game, 'What's my rule?' is a good starting point for any series of lessons on shape, whether with two- or three-dimensional shapes. All experiences of classification of shapes provide children with opportunities to develop the language of shape and space and to focus on equivalences. Teachers might also, for example, get children to explore rotational and line symmetry by cutting out shapes, drawing round them, looking at them in mirrors, and so on. Additionally, they might experiment with making photocopy enlargements and reductions of children's drawings and get the children to cut them out and investigate the spatial relationships. All this can be supported by discussion of what is the same and what is different. Teachers of young children will find it instructive to analyse the children's drawings of three-dimensional objects such as in the table-drawing example discussed in this chapter. We conclude with a few further suggestions for practical activities.

Activity 7.1: what are my two rules?
Objective　To give children further experience of sorting shapes according to their properties.

　Materials　A set of two- or three-dimensional shapes; a network diagram as illustrated in Figure 7.25.

　Method　This is played like 'What's my rule?', but this time the challenger has two rules. The shapes are taken along the network and sorted into four

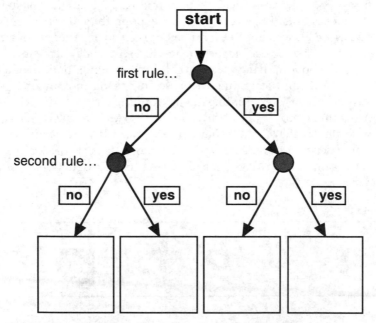

Figure 7.25　Network diagram for 'what are my rules?' (Activity 7.1)

sets, according to two rules, turning left at a junction if the shape satisfies the rule, and right if it does not. Once some shapes have been sorted the other children have to predict which way a given shape will go at each junction. Eventually the rules should be articulated and checked.

Activity 7.2: shapes in the environment
Objective To heighten children's awareness of shapes used in the world around them.
Materials A sheet for each child with drawings of shapes, as shown in Figure 7.26.
Method The children explore an area outside looking for examples of the shapes illustrated. When they find them they tick them off – or if they have

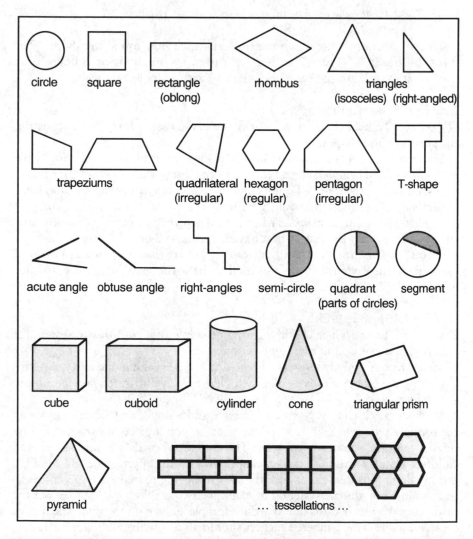

Figure 7.26 Shapes in the environment (Activity 7.2)

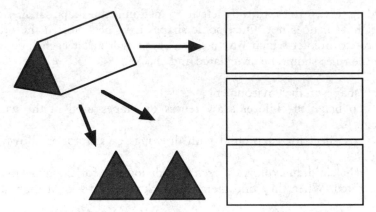

Figure 7.27   Identifying the flat surfaces in solid shapes (Activity 7.3)

watches they could write down the time at which they found the shape. (The sheet illustrated in Figure 7.26 has been used by hundreds of children on a mathematics trail around the University of East Anglia in Norwich.)

Activity 7.3: dismantling boxes
Objective   To help children to identify the plane shapes forming the constituent parts of solid shapes.

Materials   Collect two each of any interesting-shaped boxes from your shopping – pyramids, cylinders, tetrahedra (a tetrahedron is a solid with four faces), cubes, cuboids, prisms are all quite common. Children can bring in examples.

Method   The children should go round the edges of one of the boxes in each pair with a thick, black marker-pen. Then they dismantle this box, and cut out and identify the shapes that have been marked out, discarding the flaps. The other box in the pair and the cut-out shapes are then mounted in a display, to highlight the various flat surfaces used to make the solid shape, as illustrated in Figure 7.27.

Activity 7.4: picture grid
Objective   To introduce children to the principle of a co-ordinate system for referring to a position in two-dimensional space.

Materials   A grid, as shown in Figure 7.28, where along one axis are nouns and along the other adjectives, all of which are easily illustrated and familiar to the children.

Method   Each child is given an adjective and a noun, and asked to draw an appropriate picture (e.g. a spotty dog, a fat car) on a piece of card just a little smaller than the squares in the grid. The completed cards are jumbled up and children can play various games fitting them into the appropriate place on the grid. In doing this they experience the idea of having to make a two-way reference, as in a co-ordinate system. For example, two children might share out the cards, turn over their cards one at a time and place them on the grid. The first to complete a line is the winner. Teachers should discuss with children the arrangement of pictures in the rows and columns in terms of samenesses and differences.

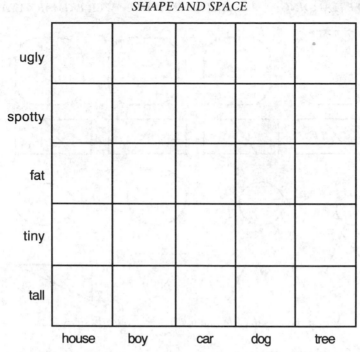

Figure 7.28   Picture grid (Activity 7.4)

Activity 7.5: symmetric designs
Objective   To give children experience of rotation and reflection in design.
   Materials   Card; scissors; thin coloured paper.
   Method   Each child draws a shape of his or her own choosing on card. This is then cut out and used as a template to reproduce eight copies of the shape in coloured paper. These copies are used to make two attractive designs, as illustrated in Figure 7.29(a) and (b). The original shape is put in the top left corner. Then in (a) the shape is rotated each time into a new position, and in (b) it is reflected each time. Children should talk with their teachers about the relationships displayed in their designs, using the language of same and different.

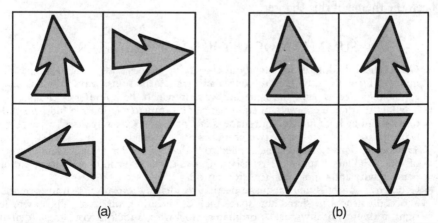

Figure 7.29   Symmetric designs produced (a) by rotation, (b) by reflection (Activity 7.5)

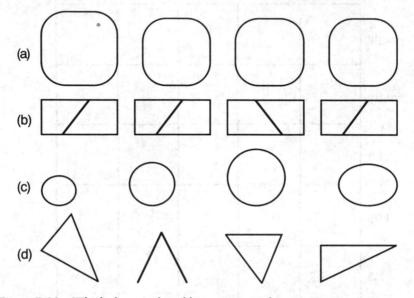

Figure 7.30   Which shape is the odd one out in each row? (Activity 7.6)

Activity 7.6: odd one out
Objective   To provide experience of transformation and equivalence in shape and space.

Materials   The teacher prepares several examples of strips of sets of shapes, as shown in Figure 7.30. Also needed are blank strips for children to use.

Method   The strips are shown to the children, who have to identify the odd one out and explain why. For example, in (b) the third drawing is the odd one out because it is a mirror image. The children can then make up their own set of drawings with three the same and a fourth as the odd one out. They challenge one another to find the odd one out. Discussion about why the three are the same and the fourth is different will bring out many of the fundamental geometric concepts associated with transformation and equivalence that have been the theme of this chapter.

SUMMARY OF KEY IDEAS IN CHAPTER 7

1. Geometrical thinking is mainly about classifying shapes and changing shapes. This involves recognising both equivalences and transformations: ways in which shapes can be regarded as being the same and ways in which shapes differ or change.
2. The fact that these concepts of equivalence and transformation are fundamental to understanding both number and shape is one of the reasons why these two aspects of learning are considered to be two branches of one subject.
3. Transformations that might be applied to a shape, in order of increasing distortion of the original shape, are: translation, rotation, reflection, similarity, affinity, perspectivity and topological transformation.
4. Geometric concepts and language needed to identify and discuss transformations and equivalences in shape and space include: position, direction, up, down, left, right, forwards, backwards, co-ordinates, clockwise, anticlockwise, angle (dynamic and static), right angle, rotational symmetry, mirror line, line symmetry, congruent,

similar, scale factor, scaling up, scaling down, family likeness, parallel, polygon, side, triangle, quadrilateral, pentagon, hexagon, square rectangles and oblong rectangles, parallelogram, rhombus, perspective drawing, path, region, junction, between, next, meet, inside, outside.

SUGGESTIONS FOR FURTHER READING

Bright, G. W. and Harvey, J. G. (1988) Learning and fun with geometry games, *Arithmetic Teacher*, 35, no. 8, pp. 22–6. (Bright and Harvey describe some geometry games that require children to visualise geometric properties, to analyse them and to make informal deductions in an interesting and challenging way.)

Dickson, L., Brown, M. and Gibson, O. (1984) *Children Learning Mathematics*, Cassell, London. (Section 1 deals with spatial thinking – fascinating and thorough, with plenty of references for further consideration.)

Haylock, D. (1995) *Mathematics Explained for Primary Teachers*, Paul Chapman Publishing, London. (Chapters 25, 26 and 27 explain the mathematics of angle, transformations, symmetry and classification of shapes.)

Hopkins, C., Gifford, S. and Pepperell, S. (eds) (1996) *Mathematics in the Primary School: a Sense of Progression*, David Fulton Publishers, London. (The first half of Section 3 of this practical book covers the National Curriculum requirements for shape and space.)

Karkoutli, C. (1996) Talking about shapes, *Mathematics Teaching*, 156, pp. 23–5. (A description of an exemplary lesson with a reception class allowing the children to explore and talk about shapes.)

Larke, P. J. (1988) Geometric extravaganza: spicing up geometry, *Arithmetic Teacher*, 36, no. 1, pp. 12–16. (A very practical article that describes how to set up a geometry fair that will generate opportunities for children to construct projects and will offer meaningful ways for them to use geometric concepts.)

Mason, J. (1991) Questions about geometry. In D. Pimm and E. Love (eds) *Teaching and Learning School Mathematics*, Hodder & Stoughton, London, in association with the Open University, pp. 77–89. (As in all his writing about mathematics teaching and learning, John Mason makes you think! This article asks and answers: What is, where do we learn, why do we learn, how can we teach geometry?)

Sicklick, F., Turkel, S. B. and Curcio, F. R. (1988) The transformation game, *Arithmetic Teacher*, 36, no. 2, pp. 37–41. (This article outlines an intriguing game for juniors that uses the notions of reflection, translation and rotation. The game is designed to sharpen children's spatial abilities and to enrich their geometric experience.)

Woodman, A. (1987) Patterns before your eyes, *Junior Education*, November, pp. 24–5. (In this article a primary-mathematics advisory-teacher describes how home-made kaleidoscopes offer an interesting way to learn about symmetry and angles.)

8

Handling Data

I put the children into groups at the beginning of the year – green apples, yellow bananas, and so on – they work in these groups for everything. Jamie never cottoned on to the fact that he was a yellow banana. He was always wandering around lost. Then when we were getting ready for the Christmas play I told all the shepherds to go to one side. Jamie didn't move. 'Go on, Jamie,' I said, 'over there – you're a shepherd.' 'No, I'm not,' he said, 'I'm a yellow banana'! (*Reception class teacher*)

Jamie has much to learn about life! He will find that he is often to be labelled and put into sets, groups, classes, categories, and so on. In the previous chapter we discuss how this process of classification is fundamental to making sense of shape – as indeed it is in all aspects of mathematics, from the first stages of counting and cardinal number onwards. In the lower primary years pupils will often engage in sorting and classifying objects (including, especially, themselves) according to various criteria. They will learn to record these experiences using a range of pictures and diagrams. From classification into various sets they will move on to considering the numbers in each set. This numerical data[1] can then be organised in frequency tables and presented in simple kinds of graphical form, such as pictograms, block graphs and bar charts. This chapter deals with some of the basic mathematical ideas involved in these early stages of classification and the processing of statistical data.

MEANINGFUL AND PURPOSEFUL

The work here has the advantage that it likely to score highly in terms of *meaningfulness* and *purposefulness*. By 'meaningfulness' we mean that the children are familiar with the context of the tasks in which they are engaged – from their own direct experience they are aware of what is significant, they recognise what is a problem and appreciate what counts as a solution. Clearly, in teaching 'handling data' there is great scope for the teacher to exploit the child's own direct experience in the questions posed and the data collected –

---

[1] We adopt the emergent usage of the word 'data' as a singular noun meaning 'a collection of information'.

and thereby to make the work meaningful. By 'purposefulness' we mean that the tasks have some purpose from the child's perspective. So much of what children do in school has very little genuine and immediate purpose other than to satisfy the demands of the teacher. With this area of mathematics – especially with the potential to link it with studies in other areas of the curriculum – the tasks can have a real purpose, such as to answer a question, to solve a problem or to gather, organise and communicate information within an area of enquiry. All our experience confirms that motivation for learning is directly proportional to the degree of purposefulness in the learning tasks. It is very appropriate, therefore, that the current (1995) English and Welsh National Curriculum should state that children should be taught to 'collect, record and interpret data arising from an area of interest . . . '.

A teacher committed to promoting meaningful learning and to motivating pupils through purposeful activities will, therefore, ensure that the data is collected and processed in order to address a specific question or to provide information on a topic of interest that is being studied by the children. The teacher will plan for the children to be involved in all the stages of handling data – not just drawing a graph, but involved in determining what data should be collected, actually collecting it and recording it, organising it, representing it and, finally, interpreting it.

For example, as part of a topic on food, one group of 7–8-year-old children were investigating some of the less familiar fruits available in the supermarket – where they came from, how they got here, what they cost, and so on. They decided to find out which of four exotic fruits were most liked by the children in their class. The children organised a tasting session and recorded in a table each child's favourite fruit from the four options. (The data, along with some other data collected by this class, is shown in Table 8.1.) Next, they produced a tally chart showing how many chose each fruit, converted this into a frequency table and then a block graph (like that shown below in Figure 8.7(c)). Finally they wrote a paragraph summarising their findings:

> The children in our class tasted 4 fruits. These were mango, papaya, star fruit and tamarillo. Most children liked the mango best. We liked the papaya and tamarillo the same. Only one boy chose the star fruit. The mango had 4 more than the tamarillo and the papaya. The star fruit had 6 less than the tamarillo and the papaya. We should tell the supermarket to sell more mangoes and if they keep the star fruit longer it might get sweeter.

PICTORIAL REPRESENTATION

Making connections

It is not difficult to recognise the significance of this kind of activity in terms of understanding mathematics, using the ideas we have developed in this book. The mathematics here starts with a real-life situation – in the example above this was the children's tasting of four exotic fruits. The observations are recorded in symbols, in a frequency table, connecting numbers with the real-life situation. This is then transformed into a graph, connecting the symbols with a picture. And the whole activity promotes mathematical language, starting with the articulation of a question to be investigated and concluding with the implications drawn from the data and the graph. The strong connections between concrete situations, symbols, pictures and language involved here imply that this is a very significant area of activity for developing children's understanding and confidence with number and number relationships. For example, the representation of the data in pictorial form makes such relationships as 'more than', 'less than', 'greatest' and 'least' transparent.

Differences between numerical and pictorial representations

What strikes you as the main differences between presenting some data in purely numerical form and presenting the same data in pictorial form, as shown in Figure 8.1? In what ways is one or other format more useful or more helpful?

The responses of some primary teachers to these questions bring out clearly the significant principles here:

- In the pictorial form the same information is more accessible visually and comparisons like 'bigger than' and 'smaller than' can be made more immediately.
- The bar chart is a more interesting way of presenting the information and it can be understood at a glance.
- You get an instant impression with the graph. It's easier to take in the important facts.
- Level 4 obviously stands out above the others – and it's immediately apparent that there are few children at levels 1 and 6.
- The pictorial representation is better where the trend over the level range is more important than the exact numbers involved.
- It might be difficult to read across if you wanted the exact numbers, so the table would be more accurate.
- The table of numbers is easier to use if you're doing calculations that need specific figures – the graph would need translating back.

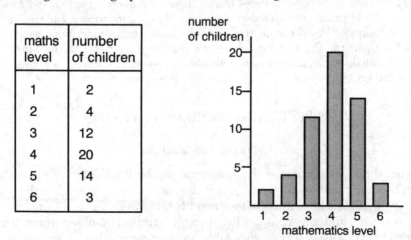

maths level	number of children
1	2
2	4
3	12
4	20
5	14
6	3

Figure 8.1 Comparing numerical and graphical presentation of data

Data in numerical form lends itself to sequential analysis, as you examine the detail of the data bit by bit. You can manipulate numbers, add them up, calculate differences and ratios, find averages and so on. By contrast, the pictorial representation provides an overall, at-a-glance picture of the situation and the relationships involved. The graph provides a global synthesis of all the data, so that you can take it all in – in one go. Some of the detail is harder to get hold of in the picture, but you get an immediate impression of the differences and ratios involved, for example, without any manipulation or calculation. Both kinds of thinking and representation are significant in doing mathematics. Often, to get started, to conceptualise a problem or a mathematical situation we need a picture that will enable us to get an overall view and some idea of what it's all about and to suggest a strategy for proceeding. Then, actually to solve the problem we usually find ourselves representing it in mathematical symbols (numbers or algebra) that are amenable to manipulation. In the course of problem-solving mathematicians will often move backwards and forwards between pictorial and numerical/algebraic representations – and will be very likely to use pictorial representations to communicate their thinking and conclusions to others. The work that young children do in school in collecting numerical data and representing it in pictorial form is, therefore, an early experience of this moving between two kinds of representation that are central to thinking and working mathematically.

Table 8.1 Some data provided by a class of 26 children

1 name	2 girl or boy	3 age in years	4 choice of exotic fruit	5 no. of letters in first name	6 no. of pages in library book	7 height in cm
A	boy	7	mango	4	63	118
B	boy	8	star fruit	8	16	115
C	girl	8	papaya	6	64	119
D	girl	7	mango	5	63	111
E	girl	8	papaya	4	87	113
F	boy	8	mango	5	83	114
G	girl	7	papaya	8	62	112
H	girl	8	mango	7	18	122
I	boy	8	papaya	3	38	118
J	boy	7	tamarillo	8	73	116
K	boy	8	tamarillo	5	73	118
L	girl	8	papaya	4	58	109
M	boy	7	mango	7	52	122
N	boy	8	tamarillo	4	38	115
O	girl	7	mango	7	68	114
P	girl	7	mango	8	42	112
Q	boy	8	mango	7	49	125
R	boy	8	tamarillo	6	53	116
S	boy	7	papaya	3	28	108
T	boy	7	tamarillo	6	25	115
U	girl	8	papaya	6	61	114
V	boy	7	mango	6	58	110
W	boy	8	mango	7	42	126
X	girl	8	mango	9	75	115
Y	girl	7	tamarillo	5	24	113
Z	boy	8	tamarillo	9	58	121

WAYS OF REPRESENTING DATA

Table 8.1 shows some examples of data provided by a class of 26 children, aged 7 and 8 years. This had been collected for various purposes at different times, but is put together here in order to illustrate the various approaches to representing different kinds of data that can be used with children in the lower primary years.

For convenience we refer to the children in column 1 by the 26 letters of the alphabet. The data in column 4 is related to the choice of exotic fruit described above. Columns 5, 6 and 7 show, respectively, the number of letters in the child's full first name, the number of pages in the book from the class library they were reading one day during 'silent reading', and their height measured to the nearest centimetre. These are typical examples of the wide range and different types of information that can be collected by children about themselves as the basis for meaningful learning in this area of mathematics. We use this data below to discuss both the different forms of representation of data and the different kinds of data that children might process in the lower primary years.

Representing classifications

The data in column 2 in Table 8.1 puts the children into two quite separate sets: boys and girls. Sets that have no members in common like these are called *discrete* sets. They can be represented simply in diagrammatic form by two enclosed regions that do not overlap, as shown in Figure 8.2(a). This kind of set-diagram is the most basic form of pictorial representation of data, showing a simple classification into two sets. The sex of the child is an example of what is called a *discrete variable* – because it is a variable (i.e. something that can vary from one member of the class to another) and it separates the class of children into discrete, non-overlapping sets. In Chapter 3 we explain how the *union* of two discrete sets (i.e. putting the two sets together to form one set) is the basis of the aggregation structure for addition (see Figure 3.1). The age of a

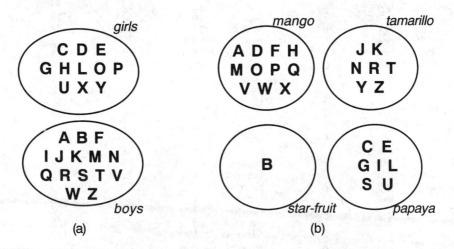

Figure 8.2 (a) Set-diagram showing boys and girls; (b) set-diagram for choice of fruit

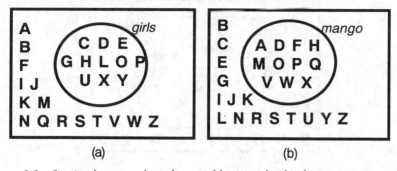

Figure 8.3 Sorting by one value of a variable: (a) girls, (b) choosing mango

child in years, as shown in column 3 in Table 8.1, is another example of a discrete variable, since it again would separate a group of children into discrete sets: 4-year-olds, 5-year-olds, 6-year-olds, 7-year-olds, and so on. It happens that, with this class of 7–8-year-old children, this variable generates just two discrete sets. Their choice of favourite fruit in column 4, however – another discrete variable – separates them into four discrete sets, as shown in Figure 8.2(b).

If we want to focus on just one particular value of the variable in question, then Figure 8.3 shows an alternative way of representing the data. In Figure 8.3(a) we have classified the children as 'girls' (inside the circle) and 'not-girls' (outside the circle), and in Figure 8.3(b) as 'mango' (inside the circle) and 'not-mango' (outside the circle). The rectangle drawn around the outside represents the *universal set* – this is a mathematical term meaning 'all the things we are considering'. In this case the universal set is all the 26 children in the class, all of whom are within the rectangle somewhere. The set of children who are 'not-girls' is called the *complement* of the set of girls. In Chapter 3 (see Figure 3.6) we discuss how the complement of a set is one example of a structure represented by subtraction. So, for example, in Figure 8.3(a) the question 'how many are not girls?' corresponds to the subtraction '26 – 11'.

Sometimes, of course, sets will overlap, because they have members in common. This is a sophisticated idea that children come to grasp gradually – as is illustrated by the anecdote at the head of the chapter where Jamie had problems with being both a yellow banana and a shepherd! However, as their experience of classification increases children will be able to engage in sorting objects (and themselves) according to two variables at a time. For example, children might be interested to show how the split between boys and girls within their class is related to the age in years. Two sets such as 'girls' and '7-year-olds' will *intersect*, because some girls may be 7-year-olds and some not. A set-diagram like that shown in Figure 8.4 provides one way of representing the classification of children by two variables such as those involved here, namely, sex and age in years. One region encloses the set of girls, the other the set of 7-year-olds. The set of children in the overlapping region (i.e. the 7-year-old girls) is called the *intersection* of the two sets. Notice that there is a place for every child. The diagram divides the set of 26 children into four subsets:

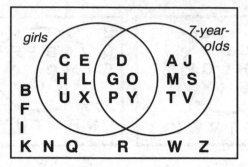

Figure 8.4   Two intersecting sets

those who are girls and 7 (the intersection), those who are 7 but not girls, those who are girls but not 7, and those who are not girls and not 7. We should also note that, because the two sets (girls and 7-year-olds) are not discrete, the union of the two sets (i.e. all those who are girls or 7 or both) does not correspond to addition: there are 11 girls and 11 seven-year-olds, but there are only 17 in the two sets put together (not 22). So, when we make the connection between addition and the union of two sets we must add the rider that the two sets are discrete, that they do not intersect.

In today's technological world all the processing of data can be done quickly and efficiently by a computer. Many examples of simple *databases* are now available in primary schools and even children in the first couple of years of schooling can have opportunities to use some of these. In the simplest versions pupils enter their answers to various questions and the computer then organises the data and displays it in an appropriate tabular or visual form. The value of this kind of activity is that the child can focus on the two stages of collecting and interpreting the data, while the computer does the more technical stages of organising it and representing it. In interpreting the data pupils can 'interrogate' the database. For example, having entered the information about sex and age, in some versions of a database children could ask to have listed 'girls *and* 7' – which would produce the intersection of the two sets. Similarly, a request for 'girls *or* 7' would produce the union of the two sets.

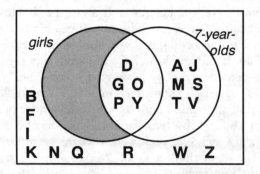

Figure 8.5   Two intersecting sets, with one subset removed

The potential in this kind of classification activity for the development of the basic language of logic is considerable – not just the vocabulary of logic (*not, all, some, none, or, and, both*) but also the characteristic language patterns of logical arguments. For example, in Figure 8.5, one of the subsets has been removed (the girls who are not 7). We can then make at least these two statements that are true about the children who are left on the diagram: (1) all the girls are 7 years old; (2) all those who are not 7 are not girls. You should now pause and convince yourself that these two statements are logically equivalent – in other words, they are two ways of saying the same thing! Similar logical challenges can be posed by removing any one of the subsets in Figure 8.4.

There are many other diagrammatic representations of these kinds of classification. Any infant classroom is likely to be full of them. In one classroom we see the names of children displayed in three columns labelled 'school dinner', 'packed lunch' and 'home'. This is a simple – but nevertheless significant – form of pictorial representation of a classification into three sets. In another classroom we see sets of words beginning with the same letter written inside spaces in the shape of that letter. Another teacher has on the wall an *arrow-diagram*, with the names of the children listed in a column down the left-hand side, with arrows matching the children to their teams.

The kind of network diagram for sorting shown in Figure 7.25 (see Activity 7.1 in Chapter 7) can be used for classification of two intersecting sets. For example, asking the two questions, 'Is the child a girl?' and 'Is the child 7 years old?', at the two stages of the sorting process, generates the same four subsets as in the set-diagram shown in Figure 8.4. Another diagrammatic representation of this kind of classification is what is called a *Carroll diagram* as shown in Figure 8.6 (named after Lewis Carroll, 1832–1898, who was not just the author of the *Alice* books, but also a mathematician and logician). This format has the advantage of making the identification of the four separate subsets clearer and the logic of the word 'not' more explicit. It also introduces the important procedure of two-way reference that is the basis of the co-ordinate system (compare Activity 7.4 in Chapter 7) – in placing an object or a name in one of the four cells in the Carroll diagram the child must refer simultaneously to both the vertical label and the horizontal label.

	girls	not girls
7-year-olds	D G O P Y	A J M S T V
not 7-year-olds	C E H L U X	B F I K N Q R W Z

Figure 8.6   Carroll diagram for two intersecting sets

Table 8.2 Frequency table for choice of fruit

choice of fruit	number of children (frequency)
mango	11
papaya	7
star fruit	1
tamarillo	7
total	26

Representing frequency

From just classifying objects and children in various sets and subsets we then move on to pictorial representations of data that show how many in each subset. For the data about choice of fruit in column 4 in Table 8.1, for example, we can count how many children chose each fruit. The number in each of these subsets is called the *frequency*. An important skill in computing the frequency, particularly with a large amount of data, is *tallying* (see Figure 5.6 in Chapter 5) – with one child calling out the values and another doing the

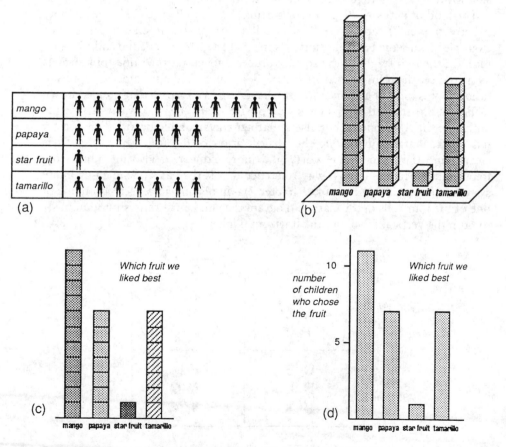

Figure 8.7 Stages in the development of pictorial representation

tallying. This can then be converted into a *frequency table*, a simple tabulation of results as shown in Table 8.2. Tabulation, because it encourages systematic processing and careful organisation of information, is an important mathematical skill that children should be encouraged to develop and use as often as possible. Now we are moving into the realms of statistical data we can refer to the universal set as the *population*.

Figure 8.7 shows four possible stages in the development of pictorial representation of data such as this. Prior to this, of course, the data can be shown using the actual objects (or children) themselves. For example, the children making the various choices of fruit can line up in the hall according to their choice, ensuring that the lines are straight and the children equally spaced in each line – like soldiers on parade. Comparisons of the numbers in each subset can be made with the children looking across the rows to answer questions such as 'How many more chose mango than chose papaya?' From using the actual objects or children themselves we move on to using a picture to represent the object or child, as shown in Figure 8.7(a). This kind of representation is called a *pictogram*. The rows of pictures can, of course, be horizontal or vertical – but what is important is that they are orderly, with the pictures equally spaced. This can be achieved by children drawing pictures on equal-sized squares of paper. Later on, with a larger population, children will learn to use one picture in a pictogram to represent, say, 10 objects – and then an appropriate part of the picture to represent less than 10.

From using a picture to represent each object children can move on to using something more abstract to represent each object, such as a cube – thus producing a three-dimensional *block graph* as shown in Figure 8.7(b). An alternative to this would be to represent the data with beads on wires or strings. Again, these arrangements could be either horizontal or vertical, although we may wish to be establishing the convention of vertical columns that is associated with block graphs and bar charts. From these three-dimensional arrangements of solid objects we can move to what is possibly a slightly more abstract representation – colouring individual squares on squared paper, as shown in Figure 8.7(c), producing a two-dimensional block graph. Each square, coloured separately, corresponds to one object or one child in the population in question. At this stage the individual contribution of each child is identifiable – and the number in each subset can be found simply by counting the number of squares. A significant step is moving from columns of individually coloured squares to the representation in Figure 8.7(d) – the conventional *bar chart*. Now the individual contributions are no longer identifiable and the frequency in each subset is represented by the *height* of the columns. In order to determine the height of the column a scale must be provided along the vertical *axis*.

- I'm never sure whether the labels on the axis should go on the lines or in the spaces.
- Sometimes you see it done one way and sometimes another. Is there any reason for this?
- Sometimes the children label the spaces and then read off the wrong value because they don't know whether it's the number above the line or below the line that they should use.

- They find it tricky learning to label the lines – especially when they're used to labelling the squares.

Note that the labels on the vertical axis in Figure 8.7(d) are correctly located on what would be the lines on the paper – if we were using squared paper – not in the spaces between these lines. This is because we are measuring the *height* of the columns, not counting the number of squares in each column. Because of this it is unnecessary and actually unhelpful to get children to draw and label a vertical axis showing the frequency when they are doing diagrams of the form shown in Figure 8.7(c). Because they are counting the squares here they would tend (rightly) to label the spaces along the axis (i.e. the spaces between the lines on their squared paper). This then becomes something they have to unlearn when they move on to representations based on the height of the column rather than the number of squares, when the labels on the axis have to line up with the tops of the columns.

Finally, in this section, we should note again that the actual organisation of the data and production of the graphs can nowadays be handed over to a computer, by using an appropriate database designed for primary schools. For example, all the data in Table 8.1 could be entered on one database. The information about each child constitutes one *record* and each column of data is called a *field*. The computer can be instructed to display the records for any given field and appropriate frequency charts and bar charts appear like magic – thus allowing the pupils to focus on the interpretation of the data rather than on the mechanics of producing the graphs.

Different kinds of variable

We explain above that, because they separate the population into discrete sets, variables such as the choice of fruit and the number of letters in the first name are called discrete variables. There is, however, a difference between these two examples of discrete variables that might be noted. In the case of the choice of fruit the order in which the data is displayed in the frequency table is arbitrary. We might decide to arrange them in alphabetical order, as shown in Figure 8.7, but this is not necessary – we could equally decide to arrange them from smallest frequency to largest frequency, once we had counted up how many in each set, or in some other order. The variable here could be called a *nominal scale*, in that it does no more than assign a label (i.e. mango, papaya, star fruit or tamarillo) to each object or child. But in the case of the number of letters in the child's name the variable is a numerical scale. Now, because of the ordinal aspect of number, it would be perverse – or at least unusual – to display the data with the subsets in anything other than their numerical order, starting with 3-letter names, then 4-letter names, and so on, as shown in Figure 8.8. So, we may sometimes classify by using an unordered, non-numerical, discrete variable, such as your favourite TV programme chosen from a list of six possibilities, your method of transport to school, or the kind of shoes you are wearing. And, at other times, we may classify using an ordered, numerical, discrete variable, such as how many children in your family, how many pets you have, or the size of the shoes you are wearing. (In a few cases of non-

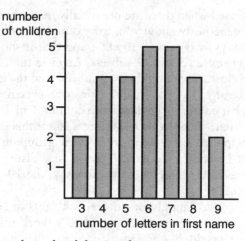

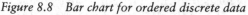

Figure 8.8   Bar chart for ordered discrete data

numerical data – such as the month of birth – there is also a specific order that would normally be used.) A case where it is significant whether the variable is non-numerical or numerical is when setting up fields for entering data on a computer database – it is usually necessary to distinguish between those fields in which the data will be 'text' and those in which it will be 'numbers'.

The data in column 6 in Table 8.1 also arises from a discrete, numerical variable. The problem here is that it separates the children into too many subsets. If we had one subset for each possible value of the variable, from the smallest number of pages in their reading books (16) to the largest (87) we would have 72 subsets (many of which would be empty)! This is an example where the data must be *grouped* in order that it be represented pictorially in a way that makes an appropriate visual impact. Normally we recommend that

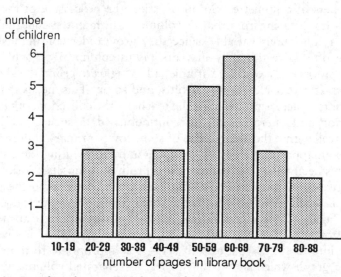

Figure 8.9   Bar chart for grouped discrete data

grouping should be used when there are potentially more than 12 values of the variable – this will generously allow you, for example, to show the months of the children's birthdays as separate subsets – and that it should aim to group the population into between 5 and 12 subsets. Any less than 5 subsets and too much information is lost. Any more than 12 subsets and the graph will contain too much detail to be any use – you might just as well present the original data. Figure 8.9 shows a bar chart for the data from column 6 in Table 8.1. We have chosen to group the data in intervals of 10 pages, since this produces 8 subsets in total. One principle to be remembered when grouping data is that the intervals used must be equal. We would give a very distorted picture of the distribution in this example if we chose to put, say, the 10–29s in one group and the 30–39s in another.

Finally, we come to the data about children's heights in column 7 of Table 8.1, which was gathered as part of the children's work on measurement of length. The height of a child, like any measurement of length, is an example of what is called a *continuous* variable. This differs from a discrete variable in that it is possible for the variable to take any value on a continuum within some range. So, for example, a person's height during their lifetime passes through every real number from their height at birth to the tallest height that they achieve. It does not jump suddenly from 125 cm to 126 cm, for example, but moves continuously through all the heights in between, including 125.1 cm, 125.367 cm, and so on. This contrasts with a discrete variable, which can only take particular, separate values and which goes from one value to another in jumps. So, for example, a child might have 7 letters in his or her name or 8 letters, but cannot have 7.456 letters! Most measurements – such as length, mass, capacity, time – are continuous variables. Now, in practice, we always make these measurements 'to the nearest something'. In the example of the children's heights we have measured to the nearest centimetre. This effectively changes the variable to a discrete variable, because now we are only allowing whole numbers of centimetres! So, in practice, the processing of the data in column 7 is no different from that in column 6. In fact, the children's age is technically a continuous variable, since they grow older continuously – but because we often give this only in years (as in column 3 of Table 8.1), it operates in practice as a discrete variable, allowing us to group the children in separate sets as 7-year-olds or 8-year-olds, and so on. This means that – with an appropriate structure provided by the teacher – the collection, organisation, representation and interpretation of 'continuous' data such as heights and masses are well within the competence of some lower primary children. Figure 8.10 shows an appropriate way of grouping and representing the data about the children's heights – in 5-cm intervals to produce 5 subsets. Notice that we have drawn the columns here touching each other, whereas in the previous graphs we have left gaps between them. This is to emphasise that the original variable in Figure 8.10 is a continuous one that moves without gaps from one value to another. When the variable is discrete – i.e. when it divides the population into distinct, separate subsets – it is appropriate to represent the data with a graph which shows the subsets as separated columns with gaps between them.

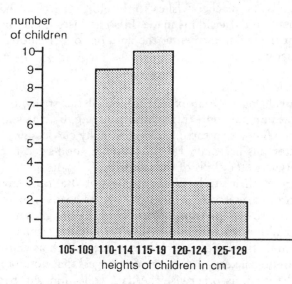

number
of children

Figure 8.10   Bar chart for data from a continuous variable

SOME ACTIVITIES WITH CHILDREN

As has been made clear in the earlier parts of this chapter, children will benefit from plenty of practical experience of posing a question, deciding what data to collect, collecting that data, organising it, representing it and interpreting it. We repeat here that the best opportunities for developing the detailed skills in handling data that have been outlined in this chapter are those where the context is meaningful and the task is purposeful. Below we give just three examples of this kind. These are chosen to make the point that the best activities for data-handling are likely to arise from non-mathematics starting points. The actual activities that a teacher might use may be similar in structure to these, but should be determined by the interests and topics being studied by their class. We also provide a few examples of activities focused on sorting and logical thinking.

Activity 8.1: voting
Objective   To provide purposeful experience of all the stages of handling discrete data in a meaningful context, by collecting data to answer a question.
   Materials   Whatever is necessary for producing a good-sized graph (pictogram, block graph, bar chart), appropriate to the skills of the children.
   Method   The teacher looks for an opportunity for the class to make a democratic decision on an issue of some concern to the children. For example: 'What shall we sing in the class assembly?' 'Where shall we go for our class outing?' The question is posed and the children discuss how it might be decided fairly. This could lead to the preparation of a simple voting sheet that is duplicated for completion by each child. One group of children can then organise and present the data in an appropriate graphical form, depending on

which particular skills the teacher wishes to develop. The class discuss and interpret the graph and the decision is made. In some cases it may be possible and appropriate for the children to enter the data on to a computer database and to process it that way.

Activity 8.2: litter survey
Objective   To provide purposeful experience of all the stages of handling discrete data in a meaningful context, including tallying, by collecting data to provide information related to a topic in the geography curriculum.

Materials   Whatever is necessary for producing a good-sized bar chart or pictogram, appropriate to the skills of the children.

Method   As part of their study of the quality of the local environment children might carry out a survey on litter in various roads near the school. Discussion might lead to the question, 'What kinds of things cause the most litter?' A group of children, escorted by an adult, could undertake a preliminary survey to determine the various categories of litter, such as cans of drink, snack packets, cigarette packets, and so on. We suggest that no more than ten categories should be used, as otherwise the data collection will become too cumbersome. The teacher may have to guide the children here. The teacher would then lead the class to design an appropriate record form for their survey and explain to them how to fill it in, using tallying. Escorted groups of children would then survey their chosen road, recording (but not collecting!) the litter observed. This can then be organised, presented in graphical form, and interpreted. In some cases this might even lead to positive action, such as the children writing politely to a local shopkeeper suggesting a litter bin outside the shop. The completed graphs could form part of a display of work related to the topic. As with the previous activity, a computer database may also be used to organise and process the data.

Activity 8.3: pulse rates
Objective   To provide experience of all the stages of data-handling in a meaningful context, by collecting and presenting grouped discrete data arising from a science investigation.

Materials   A seconds-timer; appropriate materials for production of good-sized bar charts.

Method   Much of the investigative work that young children carry out in science enquiries will generate data that can be organised, presented and interpreted purposefully. For example, in their study of the human body and the importance of exercise, a standard investigation is to measure and record pulse rates before and after exercise. This generates discrete data from a class of children that is ideal for experience of grouping into appropriately sized intervals. The 'before' and 'after' data should be processed and represented in graphs separately, in each case showing the numbers of children with pulse rates in various ranges, such as 50–59, 60–69, 70–79 . . . beats per minute. The two graphs can then be presented side by side for comparison, discussion and interpretation. Once again, a computer database might be used to process this data.

Activity 8.4: sorting the children

Objective To develop the language and visual imagery of sorting into sets according to one or more criteria.

Materials A large area, such as the playground or the school hall, with some means of marking out regions in which the children can stand.

Method Draw large regions on the playground or lay out ropes on the floor of the hall to produce large-scale versions of set-diagrams like those shown in Figures 8.2, 8.3 and 8.4. Then get the class to sort themselves according to various criteria, such as age in years, boy or girl, which village they live in, how they travel to school, whether they stay for school lunch, month of birthday, and so on. The best way to do this is to ask a question related to each set to which the answer is clearly 'yes' or 'no' for each child. For example: 'Did you walk to school today?' 'Is your birthday in a month beginning with a J?'

The most interesting classifications will be those where there are two overlapping sets (as in Figure 8.4) with some children in each of the four regions. For example, there may be some children who walked to school who have a birthday in a J-month, some who walked to school whose birthday is not in a J-month, some who did not walk to school who have a birthday in a J-month, and some who did not walk to school and whose birthday is not in a J-month. With the children sorted in this way, ask each subset in turn to describe themselves and then to sit down.

Repeat all this, sorting the children with Carroll diagrams (Figure 8.6) and also with network diagrams like that shown in Figure 7.25 in Activity 7.1.

Activity 8.5: missing block

Objective To provide the children with practice in sorting and familiarisation with the attributes of the logic block.

Materials A set of logic blocks (48 shapes comprising, for example: three different colours – red, blue and yellow; four different shapes – triangle, square, hexagon, circle; two sizes – large and small; two thicknesses – thick and thin).

Method A group of children have the set of 48 blocks jumbled up in front of them. The teacher surreptitiously removes one block. The children have to work out which block is missing and give its full description (e.g. the blue-large-thin-triangle).

A variant is for one child to choose a block, unseen by the others. The others then have to work out the full description of the missing block by asking questions to which the answer is 'yes' or 'no'.

Activity 8.6: negating

Objective To develop logical thinking and the language of logic associated with classification.

Materials A set of logic blocks.

Method A group of four children sit around a table with the logic blocks shared equally between them. Each child places one block at random in the centre of the table. The children first agree on a statement that is true about this set of four shapes of the form 'All the . . . shapes are . . . '. For example, if the set consists of the red-large-thick-triangle, the red-small-thick-hexagon, the blue-large-thin-square and the yellow-large-thin-square, they might say: 'All the red shapes are thick'. One child must then select a shape from his or her collection to add to this set to make the statement no longer true. For example, he or she could put down the red-large-thin-triangle. The children must now agree on another statement that is true about the set of five shapes – for example, 'All the square shapes are large' – and then negate this by adding a sixth shape. The activity continues in this way until they are no longer able to make a statement of the required form. The activity is not a competition between the four children. They should co-operate with one another, with the aim being to keep it going as long as possible.

SUMMARY OF KEY IDEAS IN CHAPTER 8

1. Mathematical activities are meaningful for pupils if they are familiar with the context and aware of what is significant. Activities are purposeful if they have some purpose from the child's perspective. Activities related to handling data have the potential for high levels of meaningfulness and purposefulness – particularly if the data is collected to answer a question or to provide information related to an area of interest.
2. Stages in handling data include: posing the question, determining what data should be collected, collecting it, organising it, representing it, interpreting it.
3. Mathematical problem-solving often involves moving backwards and forwards between numerical/algebraic representations and pictorial representations of the problem.
4. The purpose of pictorial representation of data is to provide an at-a-glance, overall impression of the distribution and the relationships within the data.
5. The universal set is the set of all the things being considered.
6. Discrete sets are those that have no members in common. A discrete variable is one that divides the universal set into a number of discrete subsets.
7. The union of two sets A and B consists of all those elements that are in A or B (or both). The intersection of two sets A and B consists of all those elements that are in both A and B.
8. The complement of a set A is the set of all those elements not in the set A.
9. The basic language of logic includes *not*, *all*, *some*, *none*, *or*, *and*, *both*. This is developed by discussion of various diagrams showing the classification of different elements into sets.
10. Diagrams to represent classification into two intersecting sets include: set-diagrams with two overlapping regions; network diagrams; Carroll diagrams.
11. To display pictorially the number of items in each subset (the frequency) you can use: an orderly arrangement of the objects (or children) themselves; a pictogram; a three-dimensional block graph with one cube representing each object (or child); a two-dimensional block graph, colouring in one square for each object (or child); a bar chart where the heights of the columns represent the numbers in the subsets.
12. Computer databases allow children to focus on the collection and interpretation stages in handling data. Key notions in using databases are *records* and *fields*.
13. Some discrete variables (such as choice of fruit) are non-numerical and the order in which the subsets are arranged is arbitrary. Others (such as age in years) are numerical and ordered.
14. Data arising from numerical, discrete variables with, say, more than 12 possible values should normally be grouped into equal-sized intervals, to produce between 5 and 12 groups before being represented in pictorial form.
15. A continuous variable is one such as measurement of height that can take all possible values on a continuum over an appropriate range, not just specific values

going up in jumps. Since measurements are made to the nearest something (e.g. heights to the nearest centimetre), in practice, such data can be processed like discrete data.

SUGGESTIONS FOR FURTHER READING

Haylock, D. (1995) *Mathematics Explained for Primary Teachers*, Paul Chapman Publishing, London. (Chapter 19 provides explanation of some of the ideas and techniques of data-handling and pictorial representation.)

Hopkins, C., Gifford, S. and Pepperell, S. (eds) (1996) *Mathematics in the Primary School: a Sense of Progression*, David Fulton Publishers, London. (Section 4 provides some good examples of purposeful activities for teaching data-handling in primary classrooms.)

Jared, L. and Thwaites, A. (1995) What is your favourite colour? In J. Anghileri (ed.) *Children's Mathematical Thinking in the Primary Years*, Cassell, London, pp. 110–23. (This is a thoughtful discussion of the early stages of sorting and pictorial representation.)

Thyer, D. and Maggs, J. (3rd edition, 1991) *Teaching Mathematics to Young Children*, Cassell, London. (Chapter 1 is particularly good on integrating work on pictorial representation with the development of number.)

9

Thinking Mathematically

Seven-year-old Cathy had spent almost an hour working on problem-solving and mathematical games with structural apparatus and coins when she suddenly swept everything off the table and announced, 'I'm fed up with this, I want to do some maths!' What she meant, of course, was that she wanted to sit down and complete a page of sums or some such activity where she did not have to think.

THE NATURE OF MATHEMATICS

Content and cognitive processes

Cathy's reactions and her comment raise the question, what is mathematics? We do not intend here to give a comprehensive answer to this question, but it is important that those who teach young children have clear in their minds that mathematics is more than just a collection of skills, concepts and principles. It is also a collection of ways of thinking and reasoning: ways of organising and internalising the information we receive from the external world; and ways of using and applying that information both back in the real world and also on the concepts of mathematics itself. Most people probably conceptualise mathematics in terms of its content: number, calculations, measurement, shape, equations and formulas, and so on. Of course, content of this kind is important and central to the nature of the subject. In this book we have given much of our attention to the development of understanding of such central concepts as cardinal and ordinal number, place value, addition, subtraction, multiplication, division, length, mass, time, liquid volume and capacity, and the classification of shapes. Every significant field of human knowledge has its own central concepts such as these. But, equally important, each discipline also has its own characteristic ways of making and justifying its assertions, its own distinctive ways of thinking and reasoning. This is certainly the case with mathematics. The importance in learning mathematics of the characteristic ways of thinking mathematically has been reflected, for example, in every version of the National Curriculum for England and Wales. In the current version (1995), the mathematics curriculum begins with a section entitled 'Using and Applying Mathematics'. This outlines some of the significant and characteristic cognitive processes that are involved when pupils are engaged in such tasks as solving real problems, in practical work and in undertaking mathematical investigations. These are processes present in all levels of mathematics, even in the lower primary years. In this final chapter, therefore, we explore some of the characteristic ways of thinking and reasoning mathematically. Our aims are to help teachers of young children to be more aware of what is important in mathematical work, other than just the content, and to recognise the significance of some of the kinds of reasoning that their pupils might demonstrate when they are using and applying mathematics.

So far, in the earlier chapters, we have identified a number of the most significant ways of thinking mathematically that are characteristic of learning this subject. These are the key cognitive processes that are distinctively mathematical in the way in which learners organise and internalise the information they receive from the external world. In summary, we have discussed the importance in learning mathematics of the following processes:

- recognising and applying equivalences (classification, discussing samenesses)
- recognising and applying transformations (changing, discussing differences)
- making connections – particularly between symbols, pictures, concrete situations and language
- using a symbol to represent a network of connections
- moving between symbolic representations (numerical/algebraic) and pictorial or visual representations.

In the rest of this chapter we make explicit some other fundamental aspects of thinking and reasoning that are relevant to young children using and applying their mathematics.

Two dimensions in applying mathematics

Problem-solving and investigations have been very much part of the currency of school mathematics in Britain for the past twenty years or so. Trying to make a clear distinction between those activities that count as problem-solving and those that count as investigations is not necessarily helpful. But there are some significant parameters involved here that can help us to identify different kinds of activities that are useful in promoting mathematical thinking. Figure 9.1 suggests that we can describe activities in applying mathematics by reference to two dimensions.

Along one dimension, we can consider whether the context is – at one extreme – purely abstract mathematics (i.e. just about numbers and shapes), in which the outcome is of little apparent practical significance, or – at the other extreme – whether it is a genuine, real-life situation, in which the outcome is of immediate, practical use or relevance. For example, at the 'abstract' extreme of this dimension, we might see some 6-year-old pupils engaged in finding as many ways as possible of putting numbers into a 3×3 matrix so that all the rows and columns add up to 5. At the 'real-life' extreme the same pupils might be running the tuck shop at play-time, involved in pricing drinks and biscuits, giving change, and so on.

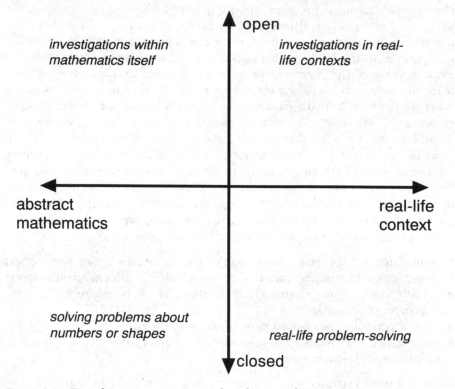

Figure 9.1   Two dimensions in using and applying mathematics

Along the other dimension, we can consider the extent to which the nature of the task is either closed or open. By a closed task, we mean one in which the goal is clearly prescribed. There is just one goal that is provided for the pupil and the activity is complete when that goal is achieved. In an open task, however, there may be several possible goals, the pupil may have the opportunity to participate in determining the goal, and when one goal is achieved there may be further goals that come to light. For example, some 4-year-olds might be given the task of fitting a set of shapes into a box. This is a closed activity with one prescribed goal – when the shapes are in the box the task is completed. On another occasion, they may be given the set of shapes and allowed to experiment with them, to explore different ways of fitting them together, to find out what other shapes they can make, and so on. This is an open activity, without a clearly prescribed goal, giving the children some opportunity to determine their own goals. The word 'problem' is best used, therefore, to refer to an activity towards the 'closed' end of the open–closed dimension, involving the application of mathematics to a situation where there is a clearly defined goal. The word 'investigation' is appropriately used to refer to an activity involving the application of mathematics that is towards the 'open' end of this dimension, where the goal or goals is or are not too tightly prescribed. Both problems and investigations (closed or open applications of mathematics) can be in the context of more abstract mathematics or in a real-life situation.

Here are four examples of mathematical tasks, each with problem-solving or investigative aspects, that illustrate the range of activities indicated by Figure 9.1:

1. A closed task in an abstract context. Find how many squares there are on a 3 × 3-square grid. (*The answer is more than 9!*)
2. A closed task in a real-life context. Arrange 16 A4 pages for photocopying back-to-back on A3 paper to produce a 16-page booklet, with the pages in the right order.
3. An open task in an abstract context. What patterns can you discover in the multiplication tables (written out in a 10 × 10 array)?
4. An open task in a real-life context. As part of our transport project, what can you find out about the journeys to school of the children in our class?

In planning opportunities for children to use and apply mathematics, teachers should aim to cover the whole range of these two dimensions, for two reasons: first, because the whole range represents the true nature of mathematics from 'pure' to 'applied' and from problem-solving to open-ended investigating; second, because different pupils will be most motivated by different categories of activity. For some children it is often a matter of searching for just the right kind of activity that will stimulate them to engage with mathematics. One teacher had given three of her 6–7-year-olds a set of tangram shapes, demonstrated how they could be used to make a boat and then suggested that the children might like to see what pictures they could make. This open-ended task with a set of mathematical shapes was just the thing that caught one child's attention:

> Emma and Rachel lost interest after about ten minutes and asked to do something else. Cassandra – who in most mathematical tasks is noted for her limited concentration span – concentrated for over half an hour on this task and produced 20 pictures. Next to her work she wrote: 'I did these all by myself and no one helped me'!

SOLVING A REAL-LIFE PROBLEM

A real-life problem about transport

The following is a genuine, real-life problem – towards the 'closed' end of the open–closed dimension – that faced one of our local first schools recently:

> How many coaches do we need to book for the school outing to the North Norfolk coast?

Below we work slowly through the stages of solving this problem, imagining it to be a real problem that we are tackling. We do this to make explicit some of the key strategies and processes of mathematical problem-solving. This example is a teacher's problem – although it could be tackled by some 7–8-year-olds – but the same principles and strategies of problem-solving would apply equally to the real-life problems that would be within the range of younger children. We should mention here that some mathematics educators – with some justification – argue that we should talk about 'challenges' rather than 'problems', since the first word promotes a more positive image of mathematical activity. We would encourage teachers to take this idea on board in the

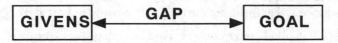

Figure 9.2   The three Gs of problem-solving

language they use to present activities to pupils, although we do not do this ourselves in the discussion below – simply because 'problem-solving' is such an established area for study and research in the field of mathematics education. 'Challenge-meeting', unfortunately, generates very few references in a search through the literature of mathematics education.

Givens, goal and gap

The *givens*, the *goal* and the *gap* are what we call the three Gs of problem-solving. Using these components a problem can be represented by the diagram in Figure 9.2.

A problem starts with a given situation and a specified goal. In the example we have here, the goal is fairly clear: to secure enough coaches to transport the whole school to the Norfolk coast. The givens are: the fact that it has already been decided that we are taking the whole school on this outing; that we are going by coach; plus various information that we have available or can obtain about the size of the school and the number of seats in the coaches. Now this constitutes a *problem* for us if there is a *gap* between the givens and the goal – in other words, if we do not have immediately available a procedure, a formula or an algorithm that takes us straight from the givens to the goal. The problem will be solved when we have closed the gap, when we have found a route from the givens to the goal.

The first steps in problem-solving of this kind are often to clarify the givens and to clarify the goal. 'What do you know about this?' 'What else do you need to know to get started?' 'What are you trying to find out?' 'What do you need to be able to say at the end of this?' These are the kinds of question that teachers will ask to help pupils to clarify the givens and the goal. In our example, clearly we will need to know that there is a total of 299 children and 18 adults going on the trip. The coach company informs us that the coaches available are 57-seaters without seat-belts or 49-seaters with seat-belts. This leads us to clarify the goal: do we require a coach with seat-belts? It is decided that we do, so we now know that we are booking coaches with 49 seats.

Mathematical modelling

Figure 9.3 is a diagrammatic representation of the way in which mathematics is often used in solving real-life problems. The process here is called 'mathematical modelling'. This refers to the way in which mathematical symbols can provide a model of a problem in the real world and the way in which manipulation of those symbols then leads to a solution. Step 1 of the modelling process in Figure 9.3 is to represent the real-world problem using mathematical symbols. In the example we are considering, the problem is modelled by

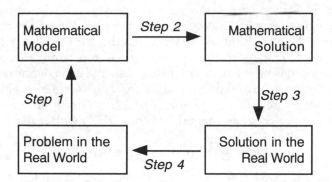

Figure 9.3   The process of mathematical modelling

'317 ÷ 49'. This is the calculation that has to be entered on a calculator to solve this problem.

This first step in the modelling process – deciding what mathematics is needed – is clearly crucial. This is why we pay so much attention in Chapters 3 and 4 to analysing the structures that correspond to addition, subtraction, multiplication and division. To use mathematics to solve real problems, pupils must learn to recognise what calculation must be done in situations with all the different structures that we identify in those chapters. This is why asking the question, 'What do you have to enter on a calculator to work this out?' is so helpful in developing mathematical thinking. It focuses the child's attention not on the demands of doing the calculation but on identifying the mathematical structure – the first step of the modelling process. In the problem we are considering here we have an example of what we call the inverse-of-multiplication structure, modelled by division.

The mathematical solution

Step 2 in Figure 9.3 takes us from the mathematical model (317 ÷ 49) to the mathematical solution. To do this calculation we have a choice. We can: (1) use a standard written method, like 'long division' – if we are lucky enough to be able to remember how to do it; (2) use a combination of mental methods and informal written jottings; (3) use a calculator. We prefer choice 2 or 3. Choice 2 relies more on understanding than choice 1 – and less on what might frequently be a poorly remembered obstacle course. So, tackling this calculation informally by an *ad hoc* method, we might reason along these lines: '6 × 50' is 300, so '6 × 49' will be 6 less than that, which is 294; that's 23 short of 317, so '317 ÷ 49' must be '6 remainder 23'. Given that the numbers involved here are quite large, choice 3 would also be justified – using a calculator we get 6.4693877. So the mathematical solution, depending on the method of calculation employed, is either '6 remainder 23' or '6.4693877'.

In terms of using and applying mathematics, it is important to stress that this step of the modelling process – obtaining the mathematical solution – is only one of four steps. All four steps are important and all involve genuine mathematical thinking. Deciding what calculation to do (step 1) is just as important as doing the calculation (step 2). Step 2 is the only part of the whole process that can be handed over to an inexpensive piece of accessible technology. When the calculation is difficult and the numbers involved are large, as, perhaps, in the example above, there would seem to be a strong case for letting the calculator do this one step, in order that the child can concentrate on the mathematical thinking involved in the other three. It would be a pity to deny children the opportunity to engage in real problem-solving just because they cannot handle the calculations that arise from working with realistic data.

Interpreting the mathematical solution

The third step in the modelling process, shown in Figure 9.3, is interpreting the mathematical solution back in the real world. Teachers should be aware of how significant is this aspect of thinking mathematically. Getting an answer to a calculation is of little use if we do not know how to interpret it. This is illustrated vividly in our example, where the two different forms of answer obtained on the calculator (6.4693877) and that obtained by non-calculator methods (6 remainder 23) require different interpretations. Clearly, the 6 in each case represents 6 coaches, but what do we make of the 'remainder 23' and the '.4693877'?

- The remainder 23 means 23 people left over if you have 6 coaches.
- And the '.4693877' represents a fraction of a coach! So, it's saying you need 6 coaches and a bit of a coach.
- So the remainder and the bit after the decimal point don't refer to the same thing. One is a number of people and the other is a bit of a coach!

So, after step 3 we have two possible solutions in the real world: 6 coaches with 23 people left over, or 6 coaches and a bit of a coach.

Taking into account the constraints of the real world

Step 4 is to compare this interpretation with the constraints of the original problem. Obviously, neither of the two solutions above will work! We cannot leave 23 people behind and we cannot order a bit of a coach. (We might be able to order a smaller coach, although in this case it happens that we cannot.) So step 4 leads us to the conclusion that we must book 7 coaches. Notice that it is the actual context of the problem that determines that we round the answer up to 7 coaches, rather than to round it down to 6 coaches. In practice, whether we round up or round down when a division does not work out as a whole-number answer (or when there is a remainder) is normally determined by the context, not by some rule about whether the figure after the decimal point is bigger or smaller than 5. Step 4 in solving real problems is always to consider the actual context and realities of the problem. Consider, for instance, that the problem was: 'How many coaches costing £49 can we hire with £317?' In this case the mathematical model and mathematical solution are the same ($317 \div 49 = 6.4693877$), but the context would determine that we round down the real-world solution of '6 coaches and a bit of a coach' to 6 coaches.

Step 4, then, is also an important stage of solving real problems – to discuss the constraints and realities of the actual situation in which the problem arises. Too often the kinds of 'problem-solving' tasks children do in mathematics are sanitised, so that they do not have to face such constraints. The numbers are carefully chosen, division problems have nice answers, things work out neatly – and it all looks nothing like reality and perpetuates the perception that mathematics has little to do with the real world. Again, this is the advantage of selective use of calculators – to enable pupils to engage in all the steps of the modelling process by handling realistic data that does not always work out nicely. Teachers should avoid the temptation to focus most of their discussion with children on step 2 of the modelling process, i.e. on doing the calculations, as though this is the 'real' mathematics. Steps 1 and 3 are also crucial – children need time to talk about what calculation to do and how to interpret the answers. But also, to complete the modelling process, to think mathematically, they need step 4 – the opportunity and freedom to discuss the constraints and realities of the actual problem. It is interesting to consider who is 'thinking mathematically' in the quotation below – the teacher or the children?

> Some children in my class were working out how many boxes were needed to hold 73 calculators, if each box could hold 12 calculators. Because this gave 6 remainder 1, I wanted them to decide that the answer was 7 boxes. But they were insistent that 6 boxes would be enough – because you could always squeeze the extra calculator into one of the boxes, or keep it in the drawer!

Finding a route

We do not want to give the impression that problem-solving in mathematics is a routine process, involving a number of clearly defined steps that are followed one by one until the solution is obtained. It is rarely like that. The models in Figures 9.2 and 9.3 are provided simply to make explicit, in terms of mathematical thinking, the significance of all the components of problem-solving. The substance of the following conversation may have already occurred to the reader:

A. At what stage of the process did the 299 children and 18 adults become 317 people?

D. At some stage we must have decided that to get to the final goal we needed first to get to this sub-goal – knowing the total number of people going.

B. That would have needed a simple mathematical model as well, wouldn't it?

A. And if we had said, 'What do we enter on the calculator to work that out . . . ?'

B. It's just addition, . . . the aggregation structure, . . . '299 + 18'.

This conversation raises an important point. Often, in getting from the givens to the goal we find that we have to specify and reach sub-goals. In this case, we must have realised quickly that in order to determine the appropriate number of coaches we needed to know the total number of people, not just the separate numbers of adults and children. The reasoning involved is something like planning a journey. One of the authors, living in Norwich, is planning a visit to an orphanage in a village in Tamil Nadu in South India. He knows that he can get to the village if he can first get to Trivandrum. Now the problem is to find a way of getting to Trivandrum. Eventually a flight from Gatwick to Trivandrum is tracked down. Now the problem is reduced to finding a way of getting from Norwich to Gatwick. He knows how to do that, so the problem is solved. This kind of reasoning is typical of mathematical problem-solving. It is rarely a matter of proceeding directly from the givens to the goal, with one journey step by step round the modelling cycle. Sometimes you start at the givens and work forward; sometimes you start at the goal and work backwards, identifying sub-goals; and sometimes you work backwards and forwards between the two until the two directions of reasoning meet in the middle. But in the end you have to link together the various bits of the solution into the appropriate, logical sequence. Often, the constraints of the actual problem will be taken into account at an early stage of the process, not just at the end. Some children were working out how best to organise the class library on the bookshelves. They had decided on putting the books into various sets and determined that a sub-goal was to find out how much shelf-space would be needed for each set. Trying to do this practically, using the actual books, led them to take into account a constraint of the actual situation in which the problem was posed – that books over a certain size would fit only on the bottom shelf.

When the problem is solved the challenge is then to communicate the solution to other people. This too is an important part of thinking mathematically. Solving a problem may be a somewhat chaotic, backwards and forwards, roundabout, hit-and-miss, trial-and-error process. But presenting the solution requires the problem-solver to organise his or her ideas into a careful, logical sequence. So communicating your mathematical thinking is an important aspect of using and applying mathematics. Children need the opportunity to do this as part of their experience of solving real-life problems and help from the teacher in organising their ideas and conclusions. The children who had sorted out the class library, for example, would then explain to the other children how they had classified the books, how they had worked out how much space was needed for each group, what they had done about the taller books, and so on – with the teacher (and the other children) prompting them with appropriate questions.

Round the modelling cycle again

The problem about the school outing is not yet finished. Having decided that we need seven coaches, we now have to determine how to distribute the 317 people between them. At this stage, the realities of the actual situation might lead us to redefine the goal. For example, we might determine that, rather than having six of the coaches filled and the seventh more than half-empty, it would be sensible to distribute the passengers equally between the coaches. It now appears that the problem was not quite as 'closed' as we imagined at first. We find ourselves going round the modelling cycle again. On this journey, a sub-goal might be to find a way of distributing the 299 children equally between the 7 coaches (worrying about the adults later). How do the four steps of the modelling process help us to achieve this sub-goal?

Step 1 This is an equal-sharing structure – a set of 299 children shared equally between seven coaches. The mathematical model is '299 ÷ 7'.

Step 2 Doing the calculation, you get 42 remainder 5. If you do it on a calculator you get 42.714285. These are two forms of the mathematical solution.

Step 3 So, that means we put 42 children in each coach, with 5 children left over – or we put 42 children and a bit of a child in each coach!

Step 4 Considering the constraints of reality, what we will actually do is to put 42 children in two coaches and 43 in the other five. Checking: that's '2 × 42' plus '5 × 43', i.e. '84 + 215', which is 299, as required.

This then is another characteristic of mathematical thinking in solving real problems. Often, we will be not quite satisfied with our first solution and we will want to refine it or improve it in some way. As in the above example, this may involve going around the modelling cycle again. Teachers aiming to develop in their pupils the characteristics of thinking mathematically will, therefore, as a matter of course, encourage them to question whether their solution is the best answer, whether it can be improved, whether there are further refinements that they might make, whether there are other factors to be taken into consideration, and so on.

MAKING GENERALISATIONS

An investigation with newspapers

Below, we work step by step through some of the mathematics that might come out of an investigation with newspapers that we have used with numerous groups of children from about 7 years of age upwards. As with the transport problem above, we do this to make explicit some important aspects of mathematical thinking. Even in the first years of schooling, teachers can begin to develop in their pupils the same aspects of thinking mathematically that emerge in this discussion.

In this investigation a group of children have been given a newspaper and invited to find out what they can about the way the page numbers are arranged on the separate sheets of paper. The teacher ensures that they understand the way in which the words 'page' and 'sheet' are being used. This newspaper happens to have 40 pages and 10 sheets. After dismantling the paper and writing down some things they have noticed – with a little nudging from the teacher to find a way of recording their observations – the children decide to tabulate the page numbers, as shown in Table 9.1. After considerable prompting from the teacher, they have found a way of referring to the four pages on each sheet – as the front, inside left, inside right and back – and put these as headings for the columns of page numbers. If the children have experience of investigations that generate sequences of numbers, *tabulation* is likely to be a familiar process that they may turn to fairly readily.

Table 9.1   The page numbers on the 10 sheets of a 40-page newspaper

front	inside left	inside right	back
1	2	39	40
3	4	37	38
5	6	35	36
7	8	33	34
9	10	31	32
11	12	29	30
13	14	27	28
15	16	25	26
17	18	23	24
19	20	21	22

Table 9.2   Observations about the patterns in Table 9.1

1. There are 4 pages on each sheet.
2. As you go down the columns the inside page numbers get closer to each other.
3. All the fronts are odd numbers and all the inside lefts are even numbers.
4. The backs are all even numbers and the inside rights are all odd numbers.
5. The fronts and inside lefts go up by 2 each time.
6. The backs and inside rights go down by 2 every time.
7. The inside left is always 1 more than the front page.
8. The back page is always 1 more than the inside right.
9. The two inside pages always add up to 41 and the front and back always add up to 41 as well.
10. The two odd-numbered pages always add up to 40, which is the number of pages in the newspaper.

Articulating patterns

There are a number of observations about the patterns in these page numbers that are often made by children – with varying degrees of prompting by the teacher. Some of these are shown in Table 9.2.

It is likely that most of us would recognise observations like those in Table 9.2 as genuine mathematical thinking. But what specifically is it about these kinds of observations that make them represent the kind of thinking that we should be encouraging in investigations of this kind?

The language of generalisations

The ten observations about the patterns in the page numbers given in Table 9.2 are all examples of *generalisations*. In each statement there is a reference to something that is *always* the case. They are not observations about a specific case (such as 'pages 1, 2, 39 and 40 are on the same sheet'). In articulating a pattern, the children are making one statement that is true about a number of specific cases. Even an observation as simple as the first one ('there are 4 pages on each sheet') demonstrates this fundamental mathematical cognitive process of making a generalisation. As soon as children begin to put words such as 'each', 'every', 'all' and 'always' into their observations they are making gener-alisations – and, therefore, thinking mathematically. This level of observations and these uses of language are what teachers should aim to encourage in investigational mathematics, with questions such as: 'What is the pattern you can see here?' 'Is that always true?' 'Does that happen every time?' 'Does that work for all of them?' The statements of fundamental properties of number-operations – commutativity, the principles of complements, associativity and the distributive laws – in Chapter 5 of this book are some examples of particularly important generalisations.

Sequential generalisations and conjectures

Often, in articulating a pattern, the child will focus on what changes each time in a sequence of numbers (or shapes). Statements 2, 5 and 6 in Table 9.2 are of this kind. The child is focusing on what is different from one number to the next. These are called *sequential* generalisations. We might note that this is essentially another instance of recognising and articulating a *transformation* in mathematics. The statement tells us how to get from one item in the sequence to the next. If the sequence were to continue, this generalisation is a pattern that would enable you to predict the next item, and the next, and so on. So, for example, when recording these results, it is possible that some children might stop using the actual sheets of newspaper after having recorded the first five or six lines in Table 9.1. They would fill in the rest by using the sequential generalisations, i.e. by adding or subtracting 2 to or from the numbers in each column to determine the next numbers.

Using a generalisation in this way to *predict* an outcome is sometimes referred to as making a *conjecture*. In making a conjecture we may be fairly confident that what we are asserting is correct, but we do not have sufficient grounds to be absolutely certain. With specific conjectures like this one, arising from a sequential generalisation, we can *check* the conjecture fairly easily – in this case by producing the actual sheets of newspaper and confirming the page numbers predicted. Making conjectures and checking them are two more important aspects of thinking mathematically – to be encouraged by teachers and prompted by appropriate questions, such as: 'What do you think will come next?' 'Are you sure?' 'How can you check that?'

Global generalisations

Instead of focusing on what changes from one row to the next in Table 9.1, many of the statements given in Table 9.2 are about what is the same each time. These are called *global* generalisations. For example, the observation that all the front pages are odd numbers is a global generalisation, since it is referring to something that is the same about each number in that column. The numbers change as you go down the column, but we notice that this property does not change: the numbers are always odd. The global generalisations in the list in Table 9.2 (numbers 1, 3, 4, 7, 8, 9 and 10) range from what we might recognise as fairly obvious statements, such as 'there are 4 pages on each sheet', to the very sophisticated 'the two odd-numbered pages always add up to 40'. Statements such as these are further instances of recognising and articulating *equivalences* in mathematics – because each of them is an observation

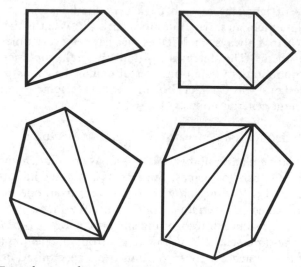

Figure 9.4   Triangles-in-polygons investigation

about something that is the same, something that does not change. So, it is interesting to note that in making sequential and global generalisations we see yet another instance of the two fundamental mathematical concepts of transformation and equivalence.

Comparing sequential and global generalisations

Often, when articulating patterns arising from the tabulation of results, the sequential generalisation is much easier to make and to use for predicting further results than the global generalisation. For example, children may be looking at how many triangles are produced by joining up one corner (vertex) of a polygon to the other corners (vertices), as shown in Figure 9.4.

They find that, starting with a four-sided polygon, two triangles are produced, with a five-sided polygon, three triangles, and so on. The results for the four polygons in Figure 9.4 are tabulated as shown in Table 9.3.

The children would quickly spot the sequential generalisation here – that the number of triangles increases by one each time. And they could easily continue this to predict how many triangles for an eight-sided polygon, a nine-sided polygon, and so on – and then check these conjectures by drawing the shapes. This is good mathematical thinking. But could they predict how many triangles would be produced in a polygon with 100 sides? To do this, without first

Table 9.3   Tabulation of results for Figure 9.4

A number of sides	B number of triangles
4	2
5	3
6	4
7	5

finding out all the ones in between, they need to formulate the global gener-alisation: that the number of triangles is always 2 less than the number of sides. This is much more difficult to articulate. Teachers can often help children towards this kind of global generalisation by reciting the results in an almost musical way with an exaggerated rhythm that emphasises the pattern of the results: 'With *four* sides, we get *two* triangles; with *five* sides, we get *three* triangles; with *six* sides, we get *four* triangles; with *seven* sides, we get *five* triangles, . . . so what's the rule for getting from the number of sides to the number of triangles?' Once the global generalisation has been made we have a much more powerful rule than the sequential generalisation, which we can use to predict the number of triangles for any polygon.

For mathematicians, the real significance of this kind of global generalisa-tion is that it is the foundation of algebraic thinking. This is because the letters used in algebra represent 'any number', not a particular number. It is not a huge step from saying 'the number in column B is always 2 less than the number in column A' to making the algebraic statement 'B = A − 2'.

Counterexamples and special cases

Another important aspect of mathematical thinking to be mentioned here is the use of a *counterexample* to challenge or to modify a generalisation. For instance, in Table 9.3, having discovered that a four-sided polygon produces 2 triangles in Figure 9.4, a child may leap to the generalisation that the number of sides is double the number of triangles – especially since the pattern of doubles is very prominent in children's thinking about numbers, as we discuss in Chapter 5. (Generalising from a sample of one is *not* good mathematics or sound reasoning, although we frequently spot instances of this tendency in the pronouncements of many people – from politicians to school inspectors – who should know better!) However, as soon as the child who has made the above generalisation checks it with the case of a five-sided polygon, it becomes clear that it is wrong. The case of the five-sided polygon thus provides a *counter-example* to disprove the assertion that had been made.

On other occasions a counterexample may lead us to refine or to modify the generalisation. For example, someone might produce the seven-sided polygon shown in Figure 9.5 and point out that joining the point A to the other corners produces only 4 triangles, not 5 as we would expect from our earlier gener-alisation (see Table 9.3). This counterexample would probably prompt us to respond that this is not the kind of polygon we meant! So the counterexample

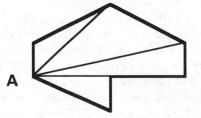

A

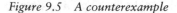

Figure 9.5   A counterexample

leads to a refined generalisation making clear that, for example, it refers to *convex* polygons (i.e. those with no internal angles greater than 180°).

One further instance of important mathematical thinking arises from the activity in Figure 9.4 and Table 9.2. This is the notion of a *special case*. What happens if the polygon has 3 sides, i.e. if it is itself a triangle? Does this special case still fit the sequential and global generalisations? In this example, we think the answer is 'yes' – because, with a 3-sided figure, each corner is already joined to the other two, so you just have the 1 triangle that is there anyway – but readers may care to think this through for themselves.

Sometimes special cases do fit with the generalisations; sometimes they do not. For example, in Figure 9.6, children might be looking for a pattern in the number of matches you need to make a chain of squares.

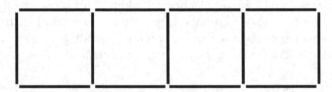

Figure 9.6   A chain of 4 squares needs 13 matches

Table 9.4   Tabulation of results for Figure 9.6

number of squares	number of matches
1	4
2	7
3	10
4	13

The tabulation of results in Table 9.4 records their findings – to make 1 square you need 4 matches, for 2 squares you need 7 matches, for 3 squares you need 10, and so on, with the number of matches increasing by 3 each time.

Continuing this sequential generalisation upwards from the top would suggest that for 0 squares you need 1 match – which is clearly incorrect, since you do not need any matches to make no squares. So, this is an example where the special case does not fit the pattern.

Hypotheses and higher-order generalisations

A generalisation for which we do not have enough evidence to be absolutely certain that it is true in all cases is properly called a *hypothesis*. For example, the child's assertion that the number of sides was double the number of triangles (in Figure 9.4) was a hypothesis. In this case it was quickly shown to be a false hypothesis by the generation of one counterexample.

One powerful aspect of mathematical thinking is that we can often move from one order of generalisations to a higher one, usually by formulating a hypothesis that can then be investigated. For example, in the newspaper investigation (see Tables 9.1 and 9.2), statement 10 about the 40-page newspaper might lead to the interesting hypothesis that the sum of the two odd-numbered pages on any sheet of any newspaper (not just our 40-paged one) always gives the total number of pages in the newspaper! (We are assuming here that the newspaper has 4 pages on each sheet. Sometimes this is not the case, of course.) Now we are talking not just about the 10-sheet, 40-page newspaper, but newspapers with any number of sheets and pages. This is, therefore, a higher order of generalisation. Similarly, we might generalise further statement 9 in Table 9.2, changing the '41' to 'one more than the total number of pages'. In fact, we could generalise further all the other eight statements as well, so as to make them apply to a newspaper with any number of pages, not just to this particular one. To investigate these hypotheses we would obviously want to start by taking apart lots of different-sized newspapers and seeing if any of them provided counterexamples. The longer our investigation goes on with no counterexamples discovered the greater becomes our conviction that the hypothesis in question is true.

Explaining and proving

After we had checked a thousand examples of newspapers and found no counterexamples to our hypothesis someone might justifiably point out that even a thousand specialisations are not enough to prove a generalisation. Of course, we would not do a thousand. Five or six would probably be enough to convince most people that the generalisation would always work. But mathematicians are fussy people sometimes. They would say, 'But how can you be sure that it will always work? Can you *prove* it?' The final stage in thinking mathematically would be to produce a proof – a logical argument that is valid in all the cases being considered and that convinces a sceptic that the generalisation really must be true in all cases. A discussion of the nature of mathematical proof and the different kinds of proof that can be employed is well beyond the scope of this book. Pupils in lower primary years are not expected to *prove* their hypotheses. (Although, we should note that this is not the same thing as *checking a conjecture* – young children can certainly experience this.) But they can begin to experience this stage of mathematical thinking by formulating simple *explanations*. They can be prompted to begin to think in these terms by looking for counterexamples and by questions such as: 'Does it work for . . . ?' 'Are you sure?' 'What if . . . ?' 'Can you explain?' 'Why does that happen?'

For example, children may have formulated the hypothesis that the number of pages in a newspaper is always four times the number of sheets. With appropriate prompting they could begin to explain why this must be the case – and to link the generalisation with the 4-times table. They may have hypothesised that it is always the case that the numbers on the inside pages get closer to each other as you work through the paper from the beginning, and then to go on to say why this might happen – because the left pages are counting forwards and the right pages are counting backwards until they meet in the middle.

So, here ends our discussion of understanding mathematics and thinking mathematically. As we indicated at the start of the book, we hope that this will have helped the reader to be more aware of the significance of the mathematical ideas and experiences that are appropriate for the first few years of schooling and increased their own confidence in teaching them. If not, at least, after reading this chapter, you now have the option of dismantling this book and investigating the way the page numbers are arranged.

SOME ACTIVITIES WITH CHILDREN

Throughout this chapter we have indicated the kinds of activities that infant-teachers might use or adapt for their classes to promote genuine mathematical thinking. We conclude with a few further examples of problem-solving and investigative activities that might be used with children in the lower primary years.

Activity 9.1: sheep in a field
Objective   To provide experience of an investigation with potential for making and checking conjectures, formulating a generalisation, considering special cases, and modifying the generalisation accordingly.

Materials   A set of coloured rods representing the numbers from 1 to 10, with a good supply of 1s.

Method   The children are given three 'kits' of rods, each kit consisting of two rods of one length and two rods that are 2 units longer. For example, they might be given three kits consisting of two 5-rods and two 7-rods. The story given to the children is that a farmer is to use these as fences around a field to keep the sheep in. The children have to arrange their kits of fences in the three different ways shown in Figure 9.7. Now find out how many sheep they can get in each field – the sheep are, of course, the 1-rods! It is to be hoped that they will discover that the three fields, although made with the same fences, can hold different numbers of sheep (21, 24, 25). Discussion of this might lead them to notice that the square field holds the most sheep.

They can then be given three kits of, say, 4-rods and 6-rods. They may conjecture that once again the square will hold the largest number of sheep – and then investigate whether this is the case. When they find that it is, they might now hypothesise the generalisation that the square will always hold the most sheep – and check this with other kits, such as 3-rods and 5-rods, 6-rods and 8-rods, and so on.

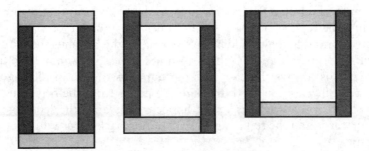

Figure 9.7   Three 'fields' made with the same 'fences' (Activity 9.1)

A special case arises with kits comprising 2-rods and 4-rods, since one of the arrangements will not hold any sheep at all! But does the generalisation still hold? (An even more special case arises with kits of 1-rods and 3-rods, but we will probably disallow these since the 1-rods are actually sheep!)

So far the kits have always had one size of rod 2 units longer than the other. What happens if we drop this restriction? For example, what happens with a kit of two 4-rods and two 7-rods? The children may find that they can still make the three different fields, but none of them is a square. How must the generalisation be modified now? With appropriate discussion, the children might be able to see that it is the shape that is *closest* to a square that holds the largest number of sheep.

If the teacher and the children want to take this further they can then investigate how many pigs (2-rods) can be put into the various fields. And then how many cows (3-rods).

Activity 9.2: odd and even generalisations
Objective   To give children the opportunity to formulate generalisations about adding odd and even numbers, to check this and to begin to articulate a simple explanation in terms of pattern.

Materials   A supply of plastic cubes that can be linked together to form towers, in two colours (say, red and white).

Method   A small group of children should use the coloured linking-cubes to construct two towers for each number from 1 to 10. Each tower should be made from alternating red and white cubes. For the odd numbers one of the two towers should have red cubes at both ends and the other should have white cubes at both ends. The children should sort the towers into two sets: odd and even.

They then investigate what happens when you combine an odd number with an odd number to form one tower. They must do this in a way that preserves the pattern of alternating red and white cubes (which is why they have the two different versions of each odd tower). Which set does the new tower go in? Does this always happen? Discussion should lead to the formulation of a generalisation: an odd number added to an odd number always gives an even number. The pattern of alternating colours may even enable the children to articulate some form of explanation as to why this is. They can then check their generalisation by using a calculator to add pairs of large, odd numbers.

The same procedure can then be followed for an even number added to an even number, and then for an odd number added to an even number.

As an extension, children can investigate subtraction with odds and evens, starting with a collection of towers from 1 to 20 and then removing various numbers to discover whether the result is odd or even.

Activity 9.3: polygon chains
Objective   To provide opportunity for tabulation of numerical results derived from geometric patterns, and for formulation of sequential and – possibly – global generalisations.

Materials A supply of dead matches – or something similar – for constructing polygons.

Method The investigation with chains of squares shown in Figure 9.6 can be posed in terms of triangles. How many matches are needed to make 1 triangle, a chain of 2 triangles, 3 triangles, 4 triangles, and so on, arranged as shown in Figure 9.8? This can lead to tabulation of the results for the triangles, similar to that shown in Table 9.4 for the squares. Children can be led, through discussion, to formulate the sequential generalisation – the number of matches increases by 2 each time – and possibly to explain this with reference to how the next triangle in the chain is made by adding two further matches. The global generalisation is more tricky – the number of matches is 2 for each triangle, plus 1 – but some children may be able to articulate something along these lines.

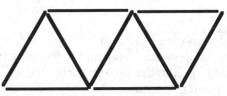

Figure 9.8   A chain of 4 triangles needs 9 matches (Activity 9.3)

The corresponding generalisations in the case of the squares were: (1) the number of matches needed increases by 3 each time; (2) the total number of matches used is 3 for each square, plus 1. Some children might then go on to look at chains of pentagons and chains of hexagons. (There is even the potential here for a higher level of generalisation. For example, the sequential generalisation might be generalised further as: the number of matches needed each time increases by one less than the number of sides in the polygon. But this will be well beyond most children in the lower primary years.)

Activity 9.4: bridge-building
Objective To involve children in practical problem-solving.

Materials A supply of assorted building blocks; two toy cars.

Method There are many construction challenges that involve children in problem-solving in the context of play and that provide practical experience of handling three-dimensional shapes. Bridge-building is a good example. Working individually or in pairs, children have to use the building blocks to construct a bridge so that one toy car can pass underneath. It must be secure enough to hold the other toy car on the top. This fits well with the problem-solving model in Figure 9.2. The child has a clear goal (to make the bridge with one car underneath and the other on top) and a clear set of givens (the building materials and the cars). But the child does not know immediately how to get from the givens to the goal. This will be a process of exploration, trial and error, trial and improvement, while using and learning about the properties of the various shapes and the relationships between them on the way.

In some cases teachers may judge it appropriate to challenge some children to find a 'better' solution than their first one (refining the goal) or they might disallow the use of certain blocks that make the task too easy (modifying the givens).

Activity 9.5: planning the drinks
Objective   To provide practical experience of the modelling process through using and applying mathematics in a real-life problem.
   Materials   Orange squash; beakers; measuring jugs; or whatever else the children require.
   Method   Many opportunities arise in the normal course of school life for children to use their mathematics to solve real problems. We would encourage teachers to look for regular opportunities of this kind where mathematics can be used in a way that has immediate and genuine relevance to the children. Here is just one example. A group of children might be given the task of planning how much squash should be bought for the class Christmas party and finding out how much it will cost. This will involve them in all the stages of the modelling process – deciding what calculations are needed, doing the calculations, interpreting the answers, taking into account the constraints of the real world – with much practical mathematics involved, such as the measurement of liquid volume. With this kind of task mathematics really can be seen to be something that can be used and applied in a meaningful context with a genuine purpose.

SUMMARY OF KEY IDEAS IN CHAPTER 9

1. Learning mathematics includes not just a collection of skills, concepts and principles, but also the development of characteristic ways of thinking.
2. Key cognitive processes, discussed in earlier chapters, for organising and internalising mathematical information are: recognising equivalences and transformations; making connections, particularly between symbols, pictures, concrete situations and language; using a symbol to represent a network of connections; moving between symbolic and pictorial or visual representations.
3. Two dimensions for identifying activities in using and applying mathematics are: (1) the context, ranging from purely abstract mathematics (numbers or shapes) to practical, real-life situations; (2) the nature of the task, ranging from closed problem-solving to an open investigation, determined by how tightly prescribed is the goal.
4. Problem-solving can be discussed in terms of the givens, the goal and the gap between them. The first step in problem-solving is to clarify the givens and the goal.
5. Mathematical modelling of a real-life problem can be described in four stages: (1) setting up the mathematical model – deciding what mathematics should be used; (2) obtaining the mathematical solution – e.g. by doing some calculations; (3) interpreting the mathematical solution back in the real world; (4) taking into account the constraints of the actual situation in which the problem arose.
6. Problem-solving is rarely as straightforward as this. Often it involves specifying sub-goals, working backwards as well as forwards, modifying or refining the goal, and going round the modelling cycle more than once.
7. Formulating generalisations is a characteristic of thinking mathematically. A generalisation is a statement that is true about a number of specific cases and involves the use of language such as 'each', 'every', 'all', 'always'.
8. A sequential generalisation is a statement about the way in which the items in a sequence change each time, from one item to the next – for example, in a set of results that have been tabulated in order. This is focusing on the transformation, i.e. how specific cases are different.

9. A global generalisation is a statement that describes what it is that stays the same for the items in a sequence, what is true about all of them. This focuses on the equivalence. Global generalisation is the basis of algebraic thinking.
10. Making a conjecture and checking it is an important aspect of mathematical thinking. A conjecture is a prediction of an outcome where there is insufficient evidence to be certain that it will occur.
11. A counterexample is a specific instance that shows that a generalisation is false or that it needs to be modified or qualified in some way.
12. Consideration of whether special cases do or do not fit a generalisation is sometimes an important part of a mathematical investigation.
13. A hypothesis is a generalisation for which there is insufficient evidence to be certain that it is true in all cases.
14. To be convinced of the truth of a hypothesis, a mathematician would demand a proof – that is, a valid logical argument. Mathematical proof is not something to be introduced in the lower primary years, but pupils can discuss whether they are sure about various assertions and, in some cases, begin to explain why certain results occur.

SUGGESTIONS FOR FURTHER READING

Atkinson, S. (ed.) (1992) *Mathematics With Reason: the Emergent Approach to Primary Mathematics*, Hodder & Stoughton, London. (A very practical and thoughtful book produced by teachers and academics involved in mathematics education. It acknowledges that many practitioners find themselves working with commercial schemes and suggests some realistic alternatives.)

Brissenden, T. (1988) *Talking About Mathematics: Mathematical Discussions in Primary Classrooms*, Blackwell, Oxford. (This is an excellent account of the way in which discussion in primary classrooms can promote genuine mathematical thinking, with plenty of practical suggestions for activities.)

Burton, L. (1994) *Children Learning Mathematics: Patterns and Relationships*, Simon and Schuster, Hemel Hempstead. (Burton places her emphasis in this book on the use of patterns and relationships in constructing meaning in mathematics through problems and investigations.)

Clarke, S. and Atkinson, S. (1996) *Tracking Significant Achievement in Primary Mathematics*, Hodder & Stoughton, London. (This book provides an original approach that includes examples of investigational mathematics with young children revealing significant progress in mathematical learning.)

Davies, J. (1988) From foxes to Ferraris, *Junior Education*, March, pp. 20–1. (In this short article, Davies describes a highly successful investigational project involving a new by-pass, some enthusiastic juniors, multiplication, division and much calculator practice!)

Department for Education and Science (1989) *Mathematics in the National Curriculum: Non-Statutory Guidance*, National Curriculum Council, York. (Although written to accompany an earlier version of the National Curriculum for England and Wales, section 5 of this non-statutory guidance is an excellent statement of what constitutes an appropriate range of experiences for children learning mathematics.)

Gardner, J. H. (1991) How fast does the wind travel: history in the primary mathematics classroom. In D. Pimm and E. Love (eds) *Teaching and Learning School Mathematics*, Hodder & Stoughton, London, in association with the Open University, pp. 16–25. (A stimulating account of some cross-curricular mathematics.)

Giles, G. (1994) Practical tasks in the classroom: arithmetic in real-life problems, *Mathematics Teaching*, 146, pp. 15–17, 21. (This article proposes that to learn arithmetic effectively children need to see the point of it in terms of real-life problems.)

Haylock, D. (1991) *Teaching Mathematics to Low Attainers, 8–12*, Paul Chapman Publishing, London. (This book shows in particular how low-attaining pupils in mathematics can be helped through an emphasis on purposeful activities in meaningful contexts. See especially Chapter 9, on using mathematics to make things happen.

Although aimed at an older age range, the principles would apply equally to teaching mathematics in any phase.)

Hiebert, J. *et al.* (1996) Problem solving as a basis for reform in the curriculum and instruction: the case of mathematics, *Educational Researcher*, May, pp. 12–21. (This is a provocative article written by eight mathematicians. They argue for a curriculum based on 'reflective enquiry' – rather than a more traditional approach – which incorporates problem-solving into the mix of ongoing classroom activities.)

Hopkins, C., Gifford, S. and Pepperell, S. (eds) (1996) *Mathematics in the Primary School: a Sense of Progression*, David Fulton Publishers, London. (Section 1 on using and applying mathematics covers the National Curriculum requirements for this area.)

Kamii, C. (1985, 1989, 1994) *Young Children (continue to) Reinvent Arithmetic*, Teachers' College Press, New York. (In these three books Kamii describes some fascinating work with first, second and third graders who learn mathematics through a diet of games, problem-solving and daily activities.)

Lewis, A. (1996) *Discovering Mathematics with 4- to 7-Year-Olds*, Hodder & Stoughton, London. (This is a lively book with plenty of practical suggestions for using and applying mathematics with younger children.)

Schwartz, S. L. (1995) Authentic mathematics in the classroom, *Teaching Children Mathematics*, 1, no. 9, pp. 580–4. (We approve of the title of this article! Schwartz presents strategies that teachers have developed to provide authentic use of mathematics through everyday activities in school, such as recording attendance and organising school lunches.)

Smith, J. (1996) Mathematical modelling, *Mathematics in School*, September, pp. 14–17. (This piece gives examples of the modelling process in mathematics and places it in the context of the National Curriculum.)

Thyer, D. (1993) *Mathematical Enrichment Exercises*, Cassell, London. (Thyer provides a range of challenging problems designed for 7–13-year-olds that may be adapted to suit more able younger children.)

Books for Further Reading

Burton, L. (1994) *Children Learning Mathematics: Patterns and Relationships*, Simon and Schuster, Hemel Hempstead. (A detailed and informed discussion of the conditions appropriate for effective mathematics education.)

Buxton, L. (1981) *Do You Panic About Maths?* Heinemann, London. (The title says it all! This book is reassuring and readable, being especially appropriate for those with little confidence in their mathematical abilities.)

Clemson, D. and Clemson, W. (1994) *Mathematics in the Early Years*, Routledge, London. (In this book the authors consider the contexts in which young children learn mathematics and the implications for classroom practice.)

Department for Education and the Welsh Office (1995) *Mathematics in the National Curriculum (England and Wales)*, HMSO, London. (Essential reference for those teaching in primary schools in England and Wales!)

Desforges, C. and Cockburn, A. D. (1987) *Understanding the Mathematics Teacher: a Study of Practice in the First School*, Falmer Press, Lewes. (This book is useful in that it gives valuable insight into mathematics education and provides teachers with an understanding of the constraints within which they work.)

Dickson, L., Brown, M. and Gibson, O. (1984) *Children Learning Mathematics*, Cassell, London. (To our knowledge, no book has replaced this detailed review of highly relevant research in the teaching and learning of mathematics.)

Harling, P. (1990) *100s of Ideas for Primary Maths: a Cross-Curricular Approach*, Hodder & Stoughton, London. (A popular book with students that explains how to introduce mathematics in a cross-curricular manner.)

Haylock, D. (1995) *Mathematics Explained for Primary Teachers*, Paul Chapman Publishing, London. (This book explains in a straightforward, practical and comprehensive way the concepts and processes of the mathematics taught in primary schools.)

Hopkins, C., Gifford, S. and Pepperell, S. (eds) (1996) *Mathematics in the Primary School: a Sense of Progression*, David Fulton Publishers, London. (This practical book, written by experienced teacher-trainers, draws effectively on case studies of classroom practice in teaching mathematics in primary schools. It is strongly based on the National Curriculum.)

Hughes, M. (1986) *Children and Number: Difficulties in Learning Mathematics*, Blackwell, Oxford. (A highly relevant book in which Martin Hughes considers pre-schoolers' substantial knowledge of number and the difficulties they encounter when presented with formal, written symbolism.)

Nunes, T. and Bryant, P. (1996) *Children Doing Mathematics*, Blackwell, Oxford. (This is a very readable, thought-provoking book that provides a review of the substantial research into children's understanding of mathematics and presents some important new work on understanding of number, measurement and arithmetic, both in and out of school.)

Thyer, D. and Maggs, J. (3rd edition, 1991) *Teaching Mathematics to Young Children*, Cassell, London. (This book offers practical guidelines for those teaching, or intending to teach, mathematics to 5–8-year-old children.)

Williams, E. and Shuard, H. (4th edition, 1994) *Primary Mathematics Today*, Longman, Harlow, Essex. (The various editions of Williams and Shuard's work have seen many generations of trainee teachers through their courses in primary mathematics and still have considerable relevance in this latest edition.)

Index

Activities